## Prentice Hall

# *LITERATURE*

# All-in-One
# Workbook

*Grade Six*

## PEARSON

Upper Saddle River, New Jersey
Boston, Massachusetts
Chandler, Arizona
Glenview, Illinois

**BQ Tunes Credits**
Keith London, Defined Mind, Inc., Executive Producer
Mike Pandolfo, Wonderful, Producer
All songs mixed and mastered by Mike Pandolfo, Wonderful
Vlad Gutkovich, Wonderful, Assistant Engineer
Recorded November 2007 – February 2008 in SoHo, New York City, at Wonderful, 594 Broadway

ISBN-13: 978-0-13-366811-7
ISBN-10:  0-13-366811-8

9 10   V039   13 12

# CONTENTS

## "Aaron's Gift" by Myron Levoy

## "The King of Mazy May" and "Aaron's Gift"

## "The Fun They Had" by Isaac Asimov
## "Feathered Friend" by Arthur C. Clarke

## UNIT 3    Types of Nonfiction

## "Zlata's Diary" by Zlata Filipovic

## "Water" by Helen Keller

## "Hard as Nails" by Russell Baker

All-in-one-Workbook
xii

**"The Three Wishes" and "The Stone"**

**"Lob's Girl" by Joan Aiken**

**"Jeremiah's Song" by Walter Dean Myers**

**Reading Fluency Practice and Assessment**

**Standardized Test Practice**

**Answer Sheets**

 **BQ Tunes**

## Get My Point Across, performed by Hydra

If I win that means that's your loss /
I guess that makes me the new boss /
and I don't even have to go and use brute force / Nah,
I just have to get my point across

Have to get my point across
I just have to get my point across
Have to get my point across

This is not an act this is **fact** / a true non fiction description /
no need to interact you can sit back and listen /
too many rappers rap but that's all contradiction /
they act one way in their rap but that's not how they're living /
if all that were true they would all be in prison / instead we fall victim to
the **fiction** they've written / they made it up, yup, imaginary ideas / is it a **fantasy** or
should we believe what we hear? /
So we're here to question them yea, **investigate** them /
see if they can **prove** or give **evidence** of what they're saying / just a verbal
discussion with words in a song / I think they're lying let's see if they can prove me
wrong /
Let's get it on . . .

If I win that means that's your loss /
I guess that makes me the new boss /
and I don't even have to go and use brute force / Nah,
I just have to get my point across
Have to get my point across
I just have to get my point across
Have to get my point across

Now its my **opinion,** my personal view / you shouldn't even want to do
The things they say they do / I mean most of it is criminal (criminal), and if your song
was a police interview well that would be the end of you / come on now who you
kidding? You? /
you, never do that stuff you say you do, its all too **unbelievable** /
It's not conceivable to put into my mind /

*Continued*

that anything you say is true so why don't you stop lying /

why don't you stop trying to be a gangster just end it /

write about your actual life man keep it **realistic** /

it's one thing to create a character to be artistic /

but they act like that's really them so the point, they missed it /

so that's why I dissed it, after putting it to the **test** /

I tried to see if it was genuine but found out it was less /

So I'm not going to rest until I can decide who's real /

And **determine** who's just acting for the money and the deal but either way...

If I win that means that's your loss /

I guess that makes me the new boss /

and I don't even have to go and use brute force / Nah,

I just have to get my point across

Have to get my point across

I just have to get my point across

Have to get my point across

See I studied you dudes' moves I research your ways /
you only say what you say cuz you think that it pays /

sometimes it does but at least show what's next /

and doing negative eventually has negative effects /

Use better judgment making **decisions** on what you say in songs /

Or I will pull your card if what you're saying is wrong /

And I will never lose, I've got the title I earned it /

You know what I'm saying's **true** listen the hook **confirms** it.

If I win that means that's your loss /

I guess that makes me the new boss /

and I don't even have to go and use brute force / Nah,

I just have to get my point across

Have to get my point across

I just have to get my point across

Have to get my point across

---

Song Title: **Get My Point Across**
Artist: Performed by Hydra
Vocals: Rodney "Blitz" Willie
Lyrics by Rodney "Blitz" Willie
Music composed by Keith "Wild Child" Middleton
Produced by Keith "Wild Child" Middleton
Technical Production: Mike Pandolfo, Wonderful
Executive Producer: Keith London, Defined Mind

All-in-One Workbook
**2**

Name _____  Date _____

# Unit 1: Fiction and Nonfiction
# Big Question Vocabulary—1

**The Big Question: How do we decide what is true?**

In your textbook, you learned words that will help you talk about what is true and what may not be true. These words can be useful in classroom discussions and when talking to friends in everyday conversation.

**fantasy:** an idea or a belief that is not based on facts

**fiction:** a story or book that is about imaginary people and events

**realistic:** based on what is actually possible rather than on how a person might like things to be

**true:** based on facts

**unbelievable:** hard to believe because it does not seem probable

Lacy told the following story to Bill, Stuart, and Kim: "I was at home, minding my own business, when the doorbell rang. My mom opened the door to a woman that I never saw before. She was wearing lots of shiny jewelry and a long silver gown. She had a magic wand. She said, 'Lacy, there you are! Come here my child, and I will grant you three wishes!' I wished for three things. The next thing I knew all three wishes came true!"

Each of Lacy's friends had a different reaction to the story.

**DIRECTIONS:** *Use the word(s) given in parentheses to write what each friend said to Lacy.*

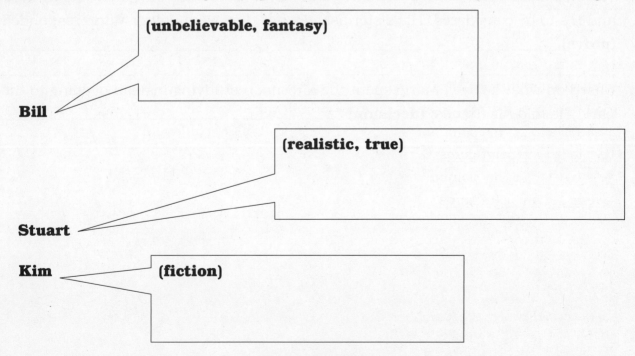

(unbelievable, fantasy)

Bill

(realistic, true)

Stuart

Kim     (fiction)

# Unit 1: Fiction and Nonfiction
# Big Question Vocabulary—2

### The Big Question: How do we decide what is true?

People must learn facts in order to make decisions. The following words can help you talk about how to separate facts from opinions.

**decision:** a choice or judgment that a person makes after discussion or thought

**determine:** to find out the facts about something

**fact:** a piece of information known to be true

**opinion:** a person's belief about something

**prove:** to show that something is true by using facts and information

**DIRECTIONS:** *Fill in the dialogue using the word(s) in parentheses.*

"I think that you should study hard and get good grades so you can go to a good college," Mario's father told him.

1. Mario did not believe that he needed better grades to go to a good college. He said to his father: **(opinion)** "_____

   _____"

2. His father wanted to do some research to see if he was correct. He said: **(determine, fact)** "_____

   _____"

3. They looked at some college Web sites and Mario discovered that he would need A's and B's to be considered. His sister asked what they were doing. Mario responded: **(prove)** _____

   _____"

4. Based on what he saw, Mario spent the afternoon studying instead of going to the park. He told his friends: **(decision)** "_____

   _____"

# Unit 1: Fiction and Nonfiction
# Big Question Vocabulary—3

**The Big Question: How do we decide what is true?**

Sometimes it takes work to find out the truth. The following words will help you talk about how people work to get at the truth.

**confirm:** show that something is definitely true by getting more proof

**evidence:** a fact, an object, or a sign that makes you believe something is true

**investigate:** to try to find out the truth about something

**study:** to find out more about a subject

**test:** to examine something in order to get information

**DIRECTIONS:** *Read the passage. Then, fill in the dialogue using the words in parentheses.*

"Aha! said Dr. Trooper. "My experiment will prove that I am correct. Carrots improve eyesight!"

"How do you know that?" asked Mia.

"My dear, it has been my life's work," said Dr. Trooper. "Come to my laboratory. Let me show you."

Mia followed Dr. Trooper into his laboratory. In the laboratory, they found Doug, Dr. Trooper's assistant. He was eating carrots and reading very fine print on a sheet of paper.

Mia asked, "What are you doing?"

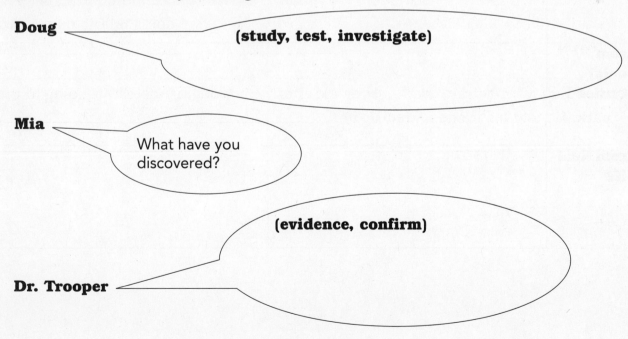

**Doug**        (study, test, investigate)

**Mia**      What have you discovered?

                (evidence, confirm)

**Dr. Trooper**

All-in-One Workbook
5

Name _____ Date _____

# Unit 1: Fiction and Nonfiction
# Applying the Big Question

### How do we decide what is true?

**DIRECTIONS:** *Complete the chart below to apply what you have learned about how to decide what is true. One row has been completed for you.*

| Example | Information, situation, or event | True/untrue | How I decided | What I learned |
|---|---|---|---|---|
| **From Literature** | In "Greyling," a seal becomes a child. | Untrue | I know that an animal cannot change into a human. | I can sometimes use my own knowledge to decide what is true. |
| **From Literature** | | | | |
| **From Science** | | | | |
| **From Social Studies** | | | | |
| **From Real Life** | | | | |

**Jane Yolen**
# Listening and Viewing

## Segment 1: Meet Jane Yolen
• According to Jane Yolen, writers have a love-hate relationship with movies. Why does she think that it is important to read a book even if there is a movie version of it? Which do you usually prefer, the book or the movie? Why?

_____

_____

_____

## Segment 2: Fiction and Nonfiction
• Jane Yolen says writers often take something old and make it new again. How does she accomplish this with the story of the selchie? How is this story a combination of fiction and nonfiction?

_____

_____

_____

## Segment 3: The Writing Process
• How does Jane Yolen gather ideas for stories? Where do you get your ideas for stories?

_____

_____

_____

## Segment 4: The Rewards of Writing
• According to Jane Yolen, what is the real reward of writing?

_____

_____

_____

# Learning About Fiction and Nonfiction

Literature may be either **fiction** or **nonfiction.** The following chart compares and contrasts these two types of literature.

| Characteristics | Fiction | Nonfiction |
| --- | --- | --- |
| Features | Fiction tells about *imaginary* people or animals called **characters**. They experience a series of made-up events called the **plot**. The plot contains a problem, or **conflict**, that the characters must solve. | Nonfiction tells about *real* people, animals, places, things, experiences, and ideas. Nonfiction contains only facts and ideas. |
| Sample Forms | short stories, novels | articles, essays, biographies, autobiographies |
| Author's Purpose | to entertain | to explain, inform, persuade, to entertain |

**A. DIRECTIONS:** *Read each item. Decide whether it is an element of* fiction *or* nonfiction, *and then write* fiction *or* nonfiction *on the line provided.*

_____ 1. a story about a talking horse

_____ 2. a newspaper article that describes farming in France

_____ 3. a magazine article that explains how to make a kite

_____ 4. a novel in which a boy turns into a bird

**B. DIRECTIONS:** *This paragraph begins a piece of literature. Read it carefully. Then, decide whether it is fiction or nonfiction. Circle your choice. Then, on the lines below, explain what information led you to make your choice.*

Jerry was eager to perform with Harry in the school talent show. He had practiced with Harry for three days. Jerry was sure that Harry would be able to solve the math problem. After all, Harry was a hard worker. He was also a very smart dog.

Circle your choice:   FICTION   NONFICTION

Explain your choice:

_____

_____

_____

Name _____ Date _____

**"Greyling"** by Jane Yolen
# Model Selection: Fiction

**Fiction** is writing that tells about imaginary people or animals called **characters.** They experience a series of made-up events called the **plot.** The plot contains a problem, or **conflict,** that characters solve. The action takes place at a certain time and location, called the **setting**.

The plot is told by a speaker called the **narrator.** If the narrator is a character, he or she tells the story in **first-person point of view.** If the narrator stands outside the story, he or she tells it in **third-person point of view.**

**DIRECTIONS:** *"Greyling" is a piece of fiction. Use this chart to provide details about its characters, plot, setting, and narrator.*

| Element of Fiction | Details |
|---|---|
| Characters | _____<br>_____<br>_____ |
| Plot | What conflict, or problem, do the characters face?<br>_____<br>_____ |
| Narrator | Is the narrator inside or outside the story? _____<br>Does the narrator use the first-person or the third-person point of view? _____<br>What hints in the story led to your answers? _____<br>_____<br>_____<br>_____ |
| Setting | _____ |

**All-in-One Workbook**
© Pearson Education, Inc. All rights reserved.
**9**

Name _____ Date _____

### "My Heart Is in the Highlands" by Jane Yolen
# Learning About Nonfiction

**Nonfiction** is writing that tells about real people, animals, places, things, experiences, and ideas. Examples include biographies, autobiographies, letters, articles, essays, journals, speeches, and diaries.

Unlike fiction, which contains made-up details and characters, nonfiction presents facts and discusses ideas. Nonfiction is told from the **author's perspective,** or point of view. The author has a definite **purpose for writing.** That purpose might be:

- to explain ("How To Make a Mask")
- to entertain ("My Funny Experience")
- to share thoughts and experiences ("My Trip to Spain")
- to persuade ("Support Our Soccer Team!")
- to inform ("The Products of India")

**A. DIRECTIONS:** *Answer the following questions about "My Heart Is in the Highlands."*

1. What real people does it mention? _____

2. In what real location does it take place? _____

3. Summarize the real experience that the author shares. _____

   _____

   _____

4. List three facts that the author presents. _____

   _____

   _____

5. Summarize the author's point of view about her fiction writing. _____

   _____

   _____

**B. DIRECTIONS:** *Authors often have more than one purpose in mind when they write a piece of nonfiction. Jane Yolen had two purposes in mind when she wrote "My Heart Is in the Highlands." Look at the list of purposes at the top of this page. Tell which two purposes she had for writing. Support your answer with examples.*

_____

_____

_____

_____

_____

_____

**"Stray"** by Cynthia Rylant
# Writing About the Big Question

### How do we decide what is true?

## Big Question Vocabulary

| | | | | |
|---|---|---|---|---|
| confirm | decision | determine | evidence | fact |
| fantasy | fiction | investigate | opinion | prove |
| realistic | study | test | true | unbelievable |

**A.** *Use one or more words from the list above to complete each sentence.*

1. Some scientists decided to _____ the effects on people of having pets.

2. They found scientific _____ that people with pets are happier.

3. The _____ also showed that people with pets live longer.

4. The results _____ that having a pet can be good for you.

**B.** *Respond to each item with a complete sentence.*

1. Describe a pet that you have had or would like to have.

   _____

   _____

2. Explain how the pet you described helped or would help you. Use at least two Big Question vocabulary words.

   _____

   _____

**C.** *In "Stray," Doris is upset because her parents tell her they cannot afford to keep the stray dog she found. Is it true that keeping a dog as a pet can be expensive? Complete the sentence below. Then, write a short paragraph connecting this situation to the Big Question.*

   Dog owners spend money on _____

   _____

   _____

   _____

   _____

   _____

Name _____ Date _____

"**Stray**" by Cynthia Rylant
# Reading: Use Prior Knowledge to Make Predictions

A **prediction** is a logical guess about what will happen next in a story. You can **use your prior knowledge** to help you make predictions. To do this, relate what you already know to the details in a story. For example, you have prior knowledge about stray animals. If you haven't seen one, you have read about them. You know how they look. You know how they make you feel. Then, as you read details about the abandoned puppy in "Stray," you are ready to make a **prediction,** a logical guess, about what might happen next.

What if your prediction turns out to be wrong? No problem. Part of the fun of reading is adjusting your predictions as you get more details. As you read, use story clues and your own knowledge to make predictions along the way.

**DIRECTIONS:** *You have prior knowledge about dogs. You know a lot about how children relate to adults in a family. You have prior knowledge about families that have little money. Start with your prior knowledge. Combine it with a detail from the story. Then, make a prediction on the chart that follows. One entry has been modeled for you.*

| Prior Knowledge About Strays | | Detail From Story | | Prediction |
|---|---|---|---|---|
| They're hungry. | + | This one shivers with cold. | = | Doris will bring it in and feed it. |
| 1. About dogs _____ _____ | + | _____ _____ | = | _____ _____ |
| 2. About children and adults in a family _____ | + | _____ _____ | = | _____ _____ |
| 3. About families with little money _____ | + | _____ _____ | = | _____ _____ |

Name _____ Date _____

"The Homecoming" by Laurence Yep
# Writing About the Big Question

## How do we decide what is true?

## Big Question Vocabulary

| | | | | |
|---|---|---|---|---|
| confirm | decision | determine | evidence | fact |
| fantasy | fiction | investigate | opinion | prove |
| realistic | study | test | true | unbelievable |

**A.** *Use one or more words from the list above to complete each sentence.*

1. Some _____ stories describe events that could really happen.

2. Their characters and settings are _____, just like life.

3. Other stories, like folk tales and fairy tales, are set in a _____ world.

4. Things happen that are strange and _____.

**B.** *Respond to each item with a complete sentence.*

1. Describe a realistic story you have read. Tell how it is like real life.

   _____

   _____

2. Describe a fantasy story you have read. Explain how it is different from real life.

   _____

   _____

**C.** *In "The Homecoming," the main character, a woodcutter, is a busybody. He is so distracted with everybody else's business that he has no time to cut wood. Is he really a woodcutter? Complete the sentence below. Then, write a short paragraph connecting this situation to the Big Question.*

   If a woodcutter never cuts wood, he is _____

   _____

   _____

   _____

   _____

   _____

   _____

Name _____ Date _____

# Reading: Use Prior Knowledge to Make Predictions

A **prediction** is a logical guess about what will happen next in a story. You can **use your prior knowledge** to help you make predictions. To do this, relate what you already know to details in a story. For example, you have prior knowledge about board games like chess. If you haven't played chess, you have read about it. You may have played a similar game like checkers or Monopoly. You know how a board game looks. You know how the players concentrate on the game. Then, as you read details about the chess game in "The Homecoming," you are ready to make a **prediction,** a logical guess, about what might happen next.

What if your prediction turns out to be wrong? No problem. Part of the fun of reading is adjusting your predictions as you get more details. As you read, use story clues and your own knowledge to make predictions along the way.

**DIRECTIONS:** *You have prior knowledge about people who give unwanted advice. You have prior knowledge about characters in stories and movies who look strange. You know what happens when someone gets very hungry. Start with your prior knowledge. Combine it with a detail from the story. Then, make a prediction on the following chart. One entry has been modeled for you.*

| Prior Knowledge About Board Games | Detail From Story | Prediction |
|---|---|---|
| They take hours to play. + | The men play for seven days. = | There is something magical about this game. |
| **1. About people who give unwanted advice** + | | = |
| **2. About characters who look strange or magical** + | | = |
| **3. About someone who is hungry** + | | = |

Name _____ Date _____

# Literary Analysis: Plot

The **plot** of "The Homecoming" is the arrangement of events in the story. The elements of plot include:

- **Exposition:** introduction of the setting, characters, and basic situation
- **Conflict:** the story's central problem
- **Rising action:** events that increase the tension
- **Climax:** high point of the story when the story's outcome becomes clear
- **Falling action:** events that follow the climax
- **Resolution:** the final outcome

All the events in a plot follow one after another in a logical way. Like most stories, "The Homecoming" centers on a conflict or struggle. You keep reading because you want to find out who will win the conflict or how the problem will be solved. At the climax of the story, you know who or what will win. The problem is solved. The story ends.

**A. DIRECTIONS:** *The following questions focus on the exposition, the rising action, and the falling action in "The Homecoming." Answer each question in the space provided.*

1. The exposition introduces the setting, characters, and basic situation. Here is one exposition detail:

   **Exposition detail:** The woodcutter will be an important character.

   On the lines, write another exposition detail.

   **Exposition detail:** _____

   _____

2. The events in the rising action come before the climax. There are many events in the rising action of "The Homecoming." Here is one event in the rising action:

   **Rising action event:** The woodcutter leaves the village.

   On the following lines, write two additional events that happen in the rising action.

   **Rising action events:**

   a. _____

   _____

   b. _____

   _____

3. In "The Homecoming," there are many events in the falling action. Here is one:

   **Falling action event:** The woodcutter goes home.

   What is another event that happens in the falling action?

   **Falling action event:** _____

   _____

Name _____ Date _____

"The Homecoming" by Laurence Yep
# Vocabulary Builder

**Word List**

charitable    distracted    escorting    fascinating    murmured    recognize

**A. DIRECTIONS:** *In each question below, think about the meaning of the underlined word from the Word List. Then answer the questions.*

1. Listening to music <u>distracted</u> you from studying for a spelling test. Is your teacher likely to accept that as a good reason for your getting a poor grade? Why or why not?

   **Answer:** _____

   **Explanation:** _____

2. You see your friend standing across the street, so you wave to him. He doesn't <u>recognize</u> you. What could be the explanation?

   **Explanation:** _____

3. Six small boats are <u>escorting</u> a ship. Why might the small boats be doing this?

   **Answer:** _____

   **Explanation:** _____

4. Would you be ashamed if you acted in a <u>charitable</u> way toward a friend? Why?

   **Answer:** _____

   **Explanation:** _____

5. The speaker <u>murmured</u> when he spoke. Was he easy to hear? Why or why not?

   **Answer:** _____

   **Explanation:** _____

6. There is a <u>fascinating</u> show on television. Would you like to watch it? Why or why not?

   **Answer:** _____

   **Explanation:** _____

**B. WORD STUDY:** *The Latin suffix -able means "having qualities of." Think about the meaning of each underlined word that ends with -able. Then, answer the questions.*

1. What qualities might make a person <u>likeable</u>?

   _____

2. If you eat a <u>sizeable</u> meal, how might you feel?

   _____

3. If someone's mood is very <u>reasonable</u>, how might he behave?

   _____

**"Stray"** by Cynthia Rylant
**"The Homecoming"** by Laurence Yep
## Integrated Language Skills: Grammar

### Common and Proper Nouns; Possessives

Nouns may be either common or proper. Some nouns are made up of more than one word.

- A **common noun** names any one of a group of people, places, things, or ideas.
  **Examples:** girl, city, dogs, chairs, freedom, computer room, teacher, ice cream

- A **proper noun** names a particular person, place, or thing. A proper noun always begins with a capital letter. *Do not confuse a proper noun with a common noun that is capitalized because it is the first word of a sentence.*
  **Examples:** Doris, Mr. Amos Lacey, North Carolina, "The Homecoming," Asian American Museum, United States of America

The **possessive** of a noun shows ownership or possession. An **apostrophe,** which looks like a comma that has jumped up into the space above the line, is used to form the possessive.

- To form the possessive of a singular noun (naming one person, place, thing, or idea), add an apostrophe and an **s.**
  **Examples:** Doris's dog, West Virginia's farmland, the computer room's radiator

- To form the possessive of a plural noun that ends in **s,** add only the apostrophe.
  **Examples:** five minutes' time, the Beckmans' address, the girls' team

- To form the possessive of a plural noun that does *not* end in **s,** add an apostrophe and an **s.**
  **Examples:** children's stories, mice's cheese, the women's meeting

**Never** use an apostrophe to form the plural of a noun. Remember: An apostrophe, when used with a noun, shows ownership.

Incorrect: The birds' left their eggs behind in the nest.

Correct: The birds' eggs were left behind in their nest.

**A. DIRECTIONS:** *Underline each noun in the sentences below. Above each noun, write* C *if it is a common noun and* P *if it is a proper noun. Add another line under the possessive nouns.*

1. Cynthia Rylant discovered that her life's story interested children.

2. Rylant spent part of her childhood in West Virginia's hills.

3. Like the main character in "Stray," Rylant loves animals.

4. Laurence Yep was born and raised in San Francisco, California.

5. Yep began writing stories in high school.

Name _____ Date _____

**"Stray"** by Cynthia Rylant
**"The Homecoming"** by Laurence Yep

# Integrated Language Skills: Support for Writing a News Report

You are going to write a news report. Use the chart below to take notes for your news report. Describe the character, tell the story, and explain what happened.

| |
|---|
| **Headline (Title)**_____ |
| **Lead sentence (Capture attention!)** _____ <br> _____ |
| **Who?**_____ <br> _____ |
| **What?** _____ <br> _____ |
| **When?** _____ <br> _____ |
| **Where?** _____ <br> _____ |
| **Why?** _____ <br> _____ |
| **How?** _____ <br> _____ |

Use your notes to write a news report that sums up the basic facts. Include facts and quotes. Remember to focus on what happened.

**"The Drive-In Movies"** by Gary Soto
# Writing About the Big Question

### How do we decide what is true?

## Big Question Vocabulary

| | | | | |
|---|---|---|---|---|
| confirm | decision | determine | evidence | fact |
| fantasy | fiction | investigate | opinion | prove |
| realistic | study | test | true | unbelievable |

**A.** *Use one or more words from the list above to complete the following sentences.*

1. If someone is nice to you only when he or she has something to gain, you may _____ that that person is not really nice.

2. If someone's words do not match his or her actions, those words are _____.

3. We can use evidence to _____ what is fact and what is _____.

4. Sometimes it is possible to _____ your opinions to see whether or not they are true.

**B.** *Respond to each item. Use at least two Big Question vocabulary words in each answer.*

1. Describe a time when somebody you thought was a good person did something that was not nice.

   _____

   _____

2. After the issue was resolved, did you determine that the person was a good person or not? Explain.

   _____

   _____

**C.** *Complete the sentence below. Then, write a short paragraph connecting this situation to the Big Question.*

   A truly "extra good" person is _____

   Is it true that somebody can be "extra good"? Or does everyone have a good side and a bad side? How do you know?

   _____

   _____

   _____

All-in-One Workbook
**21**

Name _____ Date _____

# Reading: Read Ahead to Verify Predictions

**Predictions** are reasonable guesses about what is most likely to happen next. Your predictions should be based on details in the literature and your own experience. After you have made a prediction, **read ahead to check your prediction.** Making and checking predictions improves your understanding by helping you notice and think about important details.

For example, at the beginning of "The Drive-In Movies," you might wonder if Gary's mom is going to take her children to the movies. You read the story clue that Mom might be tired from working all week. You know that when parents are tired they might want to get to bed early. You might predict that the children won't get to the movies. You keep reading and you find out at the end of the story if your prediction is right or wrong.

**DIRECTIONS:** *As you read "The Drive-In Movies," use the chart below to help you predict events in the story. First, read the question in column 1. Fill in column 2 with a story clue. In column 3, note information from your own experience. Then make a prediction in column 4. Finally, read to see if your prediction is correct. If your prediction is correct, write the letter C in the narrow column. If it is wrong, write the letter W.*

| 1. Question | 2. Story Clue | 3. What You Know from Experience | 4. Prediction | C or W |
|---|---|---|---|---|
| Will Rick help? | | | | |
| Will a good job be done on the car? | | | | |
| How will Mom react to the way the car looks? | | | | |
| Will Gary enjoy the movies? | | | | |

**"The Drive-In Movies"** by Gary Soto
# Literary Analysis: Narrator and Point of View

The **narrator** is the voice that tells a true or imagined story. **Point of view** is the perspective from which the story is told. These two points of view are the most commonly used:

- **First-person point of view:** The narrator participates in the action of the story and refers to himself or herself as "I." Readers know only what the narrator sees, thinks, and feels.

  One Saturday I decided to be extra good.

- **Third-person point of view:** The narrator does not participate in the action of the story. A third-person narrator can tell things that the characters do not know.

  Rick, Gary, and Debra wanted their mother to love each of them best.

Most true stories about a person's life are told in first-person point of view.

**A. DIRECTIONS:** *If the sentence is spoken by a first-person narrator, write* FP *on the line. If the sentence is spoken by a third-person narrator, write* TP *on the line.*

____ 1. My knees hurt from kneeling, and my brain was dull from making the trowel go up and down, dribbling crumbs of earth.

____ 2. His knees hurt from kneeling, and his brain was dull from making the trowel go up and down, dribbling crumbs of earth.

____ 3. His brother joined him with an old gym sock, and their sister, happy not to join them, watched while sucking on a cherry Kool-Aid ice cube.

____ 4. My brother joined me with an old gym sock, and our sister watched us while sucking on a cherry Kool-Aid ice cube.

**B. DIRECTIONS:** *In the space provided below, rewrite the following paragraph with Mom as the first-person narrator. The first sentence is done for you.*

Mom came out and looked at the car. She saw that the waxed side was foggy white. The other side hadn't even been done. She said, "You boys worked so hard." She turned on the garden hose and washed off the soap her sons had not been able to get off. Even though she was tired from working all week, she took her children to the drive-in that night. She knew that Gary had worked most of Saturday. He had been extra good and he especially deserved a treat.

I went out to look at my car.

_____

_____

_____

Name _____ Date _____

"The Drive-In Movies" by Gary Soto
# Vocabulary Builder

## Word List

evident    migrated    prelude    pulsating    vigorously    winced

**A. DIRECTIONS:** *In each item below, think about the meaning of the underlined word. Look for clues in the rest of the sentence. Then, answer the question.*

1. When the band plays the <u>prelude</u> to your favorite march, is the musical piece ending? Why or why not?

    _____

2. If wild geese have <u>migrated</u> to your town for the winter, are they likely to stay all year? Why or why not?

    _____

3. My dad <u>winced</u> when he buttoned his shirt collar. Was the collar too loose? Why or why not?

    _____

4. If the identity of the thief is <u>evident</u> to everyone, will the police know who robbed the bank? Why or why not?

    _____

5. Which part of the human body is always <u>pulsating</u>, the kidneys or the heart? Explain your answer, using a synonym for *pulsating*.

    _____

6. John wanted to get someplace quickly. Would he walk <u>vigorously</u>? Why or why not?

    _____

**B. WORD STUDY:** The Latin prefix *pre-* means "before." Read each sentence. Decide whether it makes sense. If it does, write *Correct*. If it doesn't make sense, revise it so that it does.

1.  After I wore my new jeans, I washed them to *preshrink* the fabric.

    _____

2. The United States Constitution ends with a *preamble*.

    _____

3. Early in the day, you can *precook* the main course and then reheat it in the microwave just before dinner is served.

    _____

**"The Market Square Dog"** by James Herriot
# Writing About the Big Question

### How do we decide what is true?

## Big Question Vocabulary

| | | | | |
|---|---|---|---|---|
| confirm | decision | determine | evidence | fact |
| fantasy | fiction | investigate | opinion | prove |
| realistic | study | test | true | unbelievable |

**A.** *Use one or more words from the list above to complete the following sentences.*

1. To _____ that information is true, we can _____ the facts.

2. When making a _____, it is important to have _____ information.

3. Sometimes people's beliefs about what is _____ cannot be _____.

4. People may have _____ that are not _____.

**B.** *Respond to each item. Use at least one Big Question vocabulary word in each answer.*

1. Describe a situation in which you determined that something everyone thought was true was really fiction.

_____

_____

2. How did the evidence change what you did?

_____

_____

**C.** *Complete the sentence below. Then, write a short paragraph connecting this situation to the Big Question.*

In order to be a truly great pet, a dog needs to be _____

_____

_____

_____

_____

_____

Name _____ Date _____

# Reading: Read Ahead to Verify Predictions

**Predictions** are reasonable guesses about what is most likely to happen next. Your predictions should be based on details in the literature and your own experience. After you have made a prediction, **read ahead to check your prediction.** Making and checking predictions improves your understanding by helping you to notice and think about important details.

For example, at the beginning of "The Market Square Dog," you might wonder what will become of the little dog. You read the story clue that the dog runs away whenever someone gets near him. You know that a dog that fears people will have trouble finding a home. You might predict that this dog is in danger of being injured by a vehicle. You keep reading, and you find out if your prediction is right or wrong.

**DIRECTIONS:** *As you read "The Market Square Dog," use the following chart to help you predict events in the story. First, read the question in column 1. Fill in column 2 with a story clue. In column 3, note information from your own experience. Then make a prediction in column 4. Finally, read to see if your prediction is correct. If your prediction is correct, write the letter* C *in the narrow column. If it is wrong, write the letter* W.

| 1. Question | 2. Story Clue | 3. What You Know from Experience | 4. Prediction | C or W |
|---|---|---|---|---|
| Will the dog be caught? | | | | |
| Will the dog survive the accident? | | | | |
| Will the dog's owners claim him at the kennels? | | | | |
| Will the dog find a good home? | | | | |

Name _____    Date _____

**"The Market Square Dog"** by James Herriot
# Literary Analysis: Narrator and Point of View

The **narrator** is the voice that tells a true or imagined story. **Point of view** is the perspective from which the story is told. These two points of view are the most commonly used:

- **First-person point of view:** The narrator participates in the action of the story and refers to himself or herself as "I." Readers know only what the narrator sees, thinks, and feels.

  I knew he would make a perfect pet for anyone.

- **Third-person point of view:** The narrator does not participate in the action of the story. A third-person narrator can tell things that the characters do not know.

  He worried about what had become of the dog. He wondered if it had been hit by a car.

Most true stories about a person's life are told in the first person.

**A. DIRECTIONS:** *If the sentence is spoken by a first person narrator, write* FP *on the line. If the sentence is spoken by a third-person narrator, write* TP *on the line.*

____ 1. I always think a dog looks very appealing sitting up like that.

____ 2. He always thought a dog looked very appealing when it sat up like that.

____ 3. I visited the kennels often, and each time the shaggy little creature jumped up to greet me, laughing into my face, with his mouth open, his eyes shining.

____ 4. "Well, you certainly took me in," he said, not minding in the least that Funny Phelps had played a joke on him.

____ 5. "Well, you certainly took me in," I said.

**B. DIRECTIONS:** *In the space provided below, rewrite the following paragraph with the policeman as the first-person narrator. The first sentence is done for you.*

The policeman told the vet he had arrested the dog. The vet was surprised. He asked if he could see the dog. The policeman said that he would take the vet to the dog. They walked to a pretty cottage and saw the dog curled up in a big new doggy bed. Two small girls were sitting by him, stroking his coat. The policeman laughed and told the vet that this was his house and that he had taken the dog as a pet for his two daughters. He said they had wanted a dog and he thought this one would be just right for them.

It was hard for me not to laugh when I told the vet I'd arrested the dog he had operated on. _____

_____

_____

_____

_____

**All-in-One Workbook**

**27**

**"The Market Square Dog"** by James Herriot
# Vocabulary Builder

**Word List**

anxiously    bewildered    classified    custody    devoured    trotted

**A. DIRECTIONS:** *In each item below, think about the meaning of the underlined word. Look for clues in the other sentences. Then, answer the question.*

1. When the children at the party saw the girl go by on her skateboard, they <u>trotted</u> after her. Do you think they will catch up with her? Why or why not?

   _____

   _____

2. Your family <u>anxiously</u> watches television for news of the hurricane. Are they worried about where it will strike? Why or why not?

   _____

   _____

3. We hear that the person suspected of breaking into our car was taken into <u>custody</u> yesterday. Will we feel that the car is safer tonight? Why or why not?

   _____

   _____

4. The horse <u>devoured</u> the bucket of oats. Did the horse seem hungry or annoyed before he did that? Explain.

   _____

   _____

5. The children seemed <u>bewildered</u> by the puzzle. Will they be able to solve it quickly? Why or why not?

   _____

   _____

6. Ms. Snow, the librarian, <u>classified</u> the book as nonfiction. Did that action suggest that she thought it was a good book? Why or why not?

   _____

   _____

**B. WORD STUDY:** The Old English prefix *be-* often means "to make." Read each sentence. Decide whether it makes sense. If it does, write *Correct.* If it doesn't make sense, revise it so that it does.

1. Please clean the floor so that it is *besmeared* with mud.

   _____

2. For the drama, Harry was *bewigged* with gray hair so he'd resemble an old wise man.

   _____

3. On that beautiful, clear day, the island was totally *befogged.*

   _____

Name _____ Date _____

**"The Drive-In Movies"** by Gary Soto
**"The Market Square Dog"** by James Herriot
# Integrated Language Skills: Grammar

## Singular and Plural Nouns

A **singular noun** names one person, place, or thing.
   **Plural nouns** name more than one person, place, or thing.

- To form the plural of most nouns, add **s** to the singular form of the noun.

| cake | Add s | cakes |
|------|-------|-------|
| market | Add s | markets |
| shark | Add s | sharks |

- When nouns end in **-y** after a vowel, add **s**.

| day | Add s | days |
|------|-------|-------|
| toy | Add s | toys |
| turkey | Add s | turkeys |

- When nouns end in **-s, -ss, -x, -sh,** or **-ch**, add **es**.

| bus | Add es | buses |
|------|--------|--------|
| dress | Add es | dresses |
| box | Add es | boxes |
| wish | Add es | wishes |
| lunch | Add es | lunches |

**A. DIRECTIONS:** *Write the plural form of each singular noun on the line provided. Use a dictionary to help you spell the word correctly.*

1. fox _____

2. dish _____

3. cross _____

4. mark _____

5. key _____

6. lake _____

7. couch _____

8. Saturday _____

9. pet _____

10. stray _____

11. hippopotamus _____

12. sandwich _____

13. class _____

14. wax _____

All-in-One Workbook
© Pearson Education, Inc. All rights reserved.
**29**

Name _____  Date _____

# Integrated Language Skills: Support for Writing

For your autobiographical narrative, begin by making a timeline. Use the graphic organizer below to list chronologically a few important events in your life. On the diagonal lines, write a few words about big events or periods of time that you remember well. For example, you might write "moved to new school."

**Timeline**

**Birth**                                                                                              **Now**

Choose an event from the timeline for your autobiographical narrative and write the event on the Event line below. Then list details about the event on the Details lines. Number the details in the order they occurred. Use your numbered list to help you write your autobiographical narrative.

**Event** _____
**Details** _____

_____

_____

_____

_____

_____

_____

_____

_____

_____

_____

Name _____ Date _____

*"My Papa, Mark Twain"* by Susy Clemens
# Writing About the Big Question

**How do we decide what is true?**

## Big Question Vocabulary

| | | | | |
|---|---|---|---|---|
| confirm | decision | determine | evidence | fact |
| fantasy | fiction | investigate | opinion | prove |
| realistic | study | test | true | unbelievable |

**A.** *Use one or more words from the list above to complete the following sentences.*

1. Often people form an _____ about another person that is not
   _____ .

2. It is not _____ to think you know somebody with whom you have
   very little personal contact.

3. To make a _____ about a person, you must get to know him or her.

4. Impressions that we have about public figures may be wrong because they are not
   based on _____ .

**B.** *Answer the questions. Use at least one Big Question vocabulary word in each answer.*

1. What opinion might somebody form about you when he or she first met you?

   _____

   _____

   _____

2. What part of that opinion would be realistic? What would be false?

   _____

   _____

   _____

**C.** *Complete the sentence below. Then, write a short paragraph connecting this situation to the Big Question.*

   To find out what a person is really like, you must _____

   _____

   _____

   _____

   _____

   _____

*"My Papa, Mark Twain"* by Susy Clemens
# Reading: Recognize Clues That Indicate Fact or Opinion

Nonfiction works often include an author's opinion as well as facts. A **fact** is information that can be proved. An **opinion** is a person's judgment or belief. **Recognizing clues that indicate an opinion** will help you evaluate a work of nonfiction. To do this:

- Look for phrases that indicate an opinion, such as *I believe* or *in my opinion*.
- Look for words that indicate a personal judgment, such as *wonderful* or *terrible*.
- Be aware of words such as *always, nobody, worst,* and *all* that might indicate a personal judgment or viewpoint.

**Fact:**  Susy Clemens wrote a biography of her father when she was thirteen.

**Opinion:**  It is obvious from her biography that Susy loved her father all her life.

**DIRECTIONS:** *Read the following passages from Susy Clemens's description of* The Prince and the Pauper *in "My Papa, Mark Twain." Underline details that indicate an opinion, personal judgment, or viewpoint. On the lines below each passage, rewrite the passage to include only facts. The first one has been done for you.*

1. Papa's appearance has been described many times, but <u>very incorrectly</u>.

   **Fact:** Papa's appearance has been described many times.

2. One of papa's latest books is "The Prince and the Pauper" and it is unquestionably the best book he has ever written, . . .

   **Fact:** _____

   _____

3. I have wanted papa to write a book that would reveal something of his kind sympathetic nature, and "The Prince and the Pauper" partly does it.

   **Fact:** _____

   _____

4. The book is full of lovely charming ideas, and oh the language! It is perfect.

   **Fact:** _____

   _____

5. I never saw a man with so much variety of feeling as papa has; now "The Prince and the Pauper" is full of touching places, but there is always a streak of humor in them somewhere.

   **Fact:** _____

   _____

Name _____   Date _____

*"My Papa, Mark Twain"* by Susy Clemens
# Literary Analysis: Author's Perspective

An **author's perspective** is the viewpoint from which he or she writes. This perspective is based on the writer's beliefs and background. The author's perspective reveals his or her own feelings or personal interest in a subject.

Many authors have written a biography of Mark Twain. Most of them include details that reveal their perspective, feelings, or personal interest. For instance, a biographer who dislikes Twain might include details that reveal these feelings. Twain's daughter Susy adored her father. She includes the kind of details that reveal her love for him.

**A. DIRECTIONS:** *Read the following passage from "My Papa, Mark Twain." Then, answer the questions.*

> We know papa played "Hookey" all the time. And how readily would papa pretend to be dying so as not to have to go to school! Grandma wouldn't make papa go to school, so she let him go into a printing office to learn the trade. He did so, and gradually picked up enough education to enable him to do about as well as those who were more studious in early life.

1. What situation or event does the author describe?

   _____

   _____

2. How does the author feel about her father's dislike of school?

   _____

   _____

3. Underline the parts of the passage that reveal the author's perspective on the results of her father's education.

**B. DIRECTIONS:** *Write a brief letter that Grandma (Mark Twain's mother) might write to a relative. In the letter, show Grandma's perspective on her son's reluctance to attend school.*

   _____

   _____

   _____

   _____

   _____

   _____

   _____

   _____

   _____

Name _____ Date _____

"My Papa, Mark Twain" by Susy Clemens
# Vocabulary Builder

## Word List

absent-minded     consequently     impatient     incessantly     peculiar     striking

**A. DIRECTIONS:** *For each item below, follow the instructions and write a sentence. Be sure that you use the Word List words correctly and that your sentence expresses the meaning of each word.*

1. Use *absent-minded* and *consequently* in a sentence about homework.

_____

_____

_____

2. Use *striking* and *incessantly* in a sentence about a fireworks display.

_____

_____

_____

3. Use *impatient* in a sentence about standing in a long line of customers at a store.

_____

_____

4. Use *peculiar* in a sentence about a strange costume.

_____

_____

**B. WORD STUDY:** The Latin root -*sequ*- or -*sec*- means "to follow." Use context clues and what you know about this root to answer each question.

1. What is the correct *sequential* order of these months: May, February, March, September?

_____

2. Which student would be most likely to attend a *secondary* school, a 5-year-old or a 16-year-old? Explain.

_____

3. Would a *sequacious* person tend to be a leader or a follower? Explain.

_____

Name _____ Date _____

**"Stage Fright"** by Mark Twain
# Writing About the Big Question

### How do we decide what is true?

## Big Question Vocabulary

| | | | | |
|---|---|---|---|---|
| confirm | decision | determine | evidence | fact |
| fantasy | fiction | investigate | opinion | prove |
| realistic | study | test | true | unbelievable |

**A.** *Use one or more words from the list above to complete the following sentences.*

1. Sometimes what somebody shows on the outside is not a _____ reflection of how they are feeling.

2. To get a _____ idea of how someone is feeling, you should ask him or her.

3. If you think it is _____ for an actor to be calm in front of a large audience, you may be right. He may be acting.

4. An actor in a play is creating a _____ for the audience.

**B.** *Respond to each item. Use at least two Big Question vocabulary words in each answer.*

1. How could you confirm that a friend is feeling okay when you think she might be feeling bad but hiding it?

   _____

   _____

   _____

2. In what circumstance might you make the decision to hide your true feelings?

   _____

   _____

   _____

**C.** *Complete the sentence below. Then, write a short paragraph connecting this situation to the Big Question.*

   If a friend needed help hiding his or her true feelings, _____

   _____

   _____

   _____

*"Stage Fright"* by Mark Twain

# Reading: Recognize Clues That Indicate Fact or Opinion

Nonfiction works often include an author's opinion as well as facts. A **fact** is information that can be proved. An **opinion** is a person's judgment or belief. **Recognizing clues that indicate an opinion** will help you evaluate a work of nonfiction. To do this:

- Look for phrases that indicate an opinion, such as *I believe* or *in my opinion.*
- Look for words that indicate a personal judgment, such as *wonderful* or *terrible.*
- Be aware of words such as *always, nobody, worst,* and *all* that might indicate a personal judgment or viewpoint.

**Fact:** "Stage Fright" is a speech that Mark Twain gave after his daughter's first singing recital.

**Opinion:** "Stage Fright" is a funny description of Mark Twain's first stage appearance.

**DIRECTIONS:** *Read the following passages from Mark Twain's "Stage Fright." Underline details that indicate an opinion, personal judgment, or viewpoint. On the lines below each passage, rewrite the passage to include only facts. The first one has been done for you.*

1. If there is an <u>awful, horrible</u> malady in the world, it is stage fright—and seasickness.

   **Fact:** Stage fright and seasickness are illnesses.

2. It was dark and lonely behind the scenes in that theater, . . .

   **Fact:** _____

   _____

3. Right in the middle of the speech I had placed a gem.

   **Fact:** _____

   _____

4. I had put in a moving, pathetic part which was to get at the hearts and souls of my hearers.

   **Fact:** _____

   _____

5. Well, after the first agonizing five minutes, my stage fright left me, never to return.

   **Fact:** _____

   _____

Name _____ Date _____

## "Stage Fright" by Mark Twain
# Literary Analysis: Author's Perspective

An **author's perspective** is the viewpoint from which he or she writes. This perspective is based on the writer's beliefs and background. The author's perspective reveals his or her own feelings or personal interest in a subject.

"Stage Fright" is a speech that Mark Twain gave after his daughter sang in public. In his speech, Twain gives an account of the first time he gave a lecture in front of an audience. "Stage Fright" reveals his perspective or feelings about his first appearance on the stage.

**A. DIRECTIONS:** *Read the following passage from "Stage Fright." Then, answer the questions.*

> Right in the middle of the speech I had placed a gem. I had put in a moving, pathetic part which was to get at the hearts and souls of my hearers. When I delivered it, they did just what I hoped and expected. They sat silent and awed. I had touched them.

1. What situation or event does Mark Twain describe?

_____

_____

2. When he gave the lecture, how did Twain feel about the middle part of his speech?

_____

_____

3. How do you think Twain felt later about that part of his speech?

_____

_____

4. Twain says that the audience "sat silent and awed." How do you think the audience really felt?

_____

_____

5. Underline the part of the passage that reveals the author's perspective on his first appearance as a lecturer.

**B. DIRECTIONS:** *Imagine that you were in Mark Twain's audience the first time he spoke in public. Write a brief letter to a friend telling about the event from your perspective.*

_____

_____

_____

_____

_____

"**Stage Fright**" by Mark Twain
# Vocabulary Builder

**Word List**

agonizing     awed     compulsion     hereditary     intently     sympathy

**A. DIRECTIONS:** *For each item below, follow the instructions and write a sentence. Be sure that you use the italicized Word List words correctly and that your sentence expresses the meaning of each word.*

1. Use *compulsion* in a sentence about people who participate in a dangerous sport.
_____
_____

2. Use *intently* in a sentence about how a cat hunts a mouse.
_____
_____

3. Use *sympathy* in a sentence about a bike accident.
_____
_____

4. Use *awed* in a sentence about a tornado.
_____
_____

5. Use *agonizing* in a sentence about a difficult event.
_____
_____

6. Use *hereditary* in a sentence about the color of a person's eyes.
_____
_____

**B. WORD STUDY:** The Latin root *-pel-* or *-pul-* means "to drive." Words containing this root include *repulse* ("to drive people away due to poor behavior") and *propel* ("to push forward"). Consider the meanings of these two words as you revise the following sentences so that they make sense.

1. A child might *repulse* neighbors with kindness and courtesy.
_____

2. The strong wind hit us in the face and *propelled* us onward.
_____

**"Stage Fright"** by Mark Twain
**"My Papa, Mark Twain"** by Susy Clemens
## Integrated Language Skills: Grammar

**Possessive Personal Pronouns**

A pronoun takes the place of a noun. **Possessive personal pronouns** show ownership. They can modify nouns or be used by themselves. Notice that a possessive pronoun never uses an apostrophe (').

| Possessive Pronouns Used Before Nouns | Possessive Pronouns Used By Themselves |
|---|---|
| my | mine |
| your | yours |
| our | ours |
| their | theirs |
| her | hers |
| his | his |
| its | its |

**A. DIRECTIONS:** *Underline the possessive personal pronoun in each sentence.*

1. This is a photo of our family.
2. His gray hair is not too thick or any too long, but just right.
3. Mother liked to carry her little kitten on her shoulder.
4. It troubles me that so few people really know my Papa.

**B. DIRECTIONS:** *Rewrite each sentence to replace the noun with a possessive personal pronoun. Then, rewrite the sentence again to use a possessive personal pronoun by itself. The first one has been done for you.*

1. This backpack belongs to you.   This is your backpack.   The backpack is yours.
2. Kathy's home is on Grant Street.

_____

_____

3. The speech that I will make will be brief.

_____

_____

4. The cheers you heard came from us.

_____

_____

"**My Papa, Mark Twain**" by Susy Clemens
"**Stage Fright**" by Mark Twain

# Integrated Language Skills: Support for Writing a Dramatic Scene

Before you write your script for a dramatic scene, decide which passage from the selection you will use. Choose a passage that mentions a situation with at least two characters. Imagine what might happen before, during, and after that situation. You may invent words and actions that build on what Mark Twain said in his speech or on what Susy Clemens wrote about her father.

What happens in the passage you have chosen?

_____

_____

List the characters in your scene.

_____

_____

Use the chart below to make notes on the dialogue and actions in your scene.

| Character and Characters' Dialogue | Actions |
|---|---|
|  |  |
|  |  |
|  |  |

When you write your scene, place each character's name at the left. Follow the name with a colon. Stage directions are words that tell about the actions. Put your stage directions in brackets before or after the lines of dialogue. Here is an example of the format.

**Governor's wife:** How can I help you, Mr. Twain? I want you to give a wonderful speech in this magnificent theater.

[Governor's wife gestures grandly toward the theater seats.]

**Twain:** [in a nervous, shaky voice] I'm afraid no one is going to laugh at my jokes.

Use your notes to write your dramatic scene based on the passage you chose.

Name _____ Date _____

"Names/Nombres" by Julia Alvarez
# Writing About the Big Question

**How do we decide what is true?**

## Big Question Vocabulary

| | | | | |
|---|---|---|---|---|
| confirm | decision | determine | evidence | fact |
| fantasy | fiction | investigate | opinion | prove |
| realistic | study | test | true | unbelievable |

**A.** *Use one or more words from the list above to complete the following sentences.*

1. If a friend is being unfriendly, I find it _____ if that friend denies that he is angry at me.

2. If someone thinks I did something wrong when I didn't, I will make an effort to _____ that I am innocent.

3. In a friendship, people should make a _____ to be honest and open about their feelings.

**B.** *Respond to each item. Use at least one Big Question vocabulary word in each answer.*

1. Describe how you might confirm that a friend is not angry with you.

   _____

   _____

   _____

2. When you find something that someone tells you is unbelievable, what do you do to get at the truth?

   _____

   _____

   _____

**C.** *Complete the sentence below. Then, write a short paragraph connecting this situation to the Big Question.*

Sometimes it takes courage to show your true feelings because _____

   _____

   _____

   _____

   _____

Name _____ Date _____

**"Names/Nombres"** by Julia Alvarez
# Reading: Understand the Difference Between Fact and Opinion; Use Resources to Check Facts

In order to evaluate a work of nonfiction, you must understand the difference between fact and opinion. A **fact,** unlike an opinion, can be proved. An **opinion** expresses a judgment that can be supported but not proved. For example, the statement "The Dominican Republic is in the Caribbean Sea" is a fact that can be proved by observation. All you need to do is look at a map. The statement "The climate in the Dominican Republic is perfect" is a judgment based on the weather.

You can **check facts by using resources** such as

- dictionaries
- encyclopedias
- reliable Web sites on the Internet
- maps

**A. DIRECTIONS:** *Identify the following passages from or about "Names/Nombres" as fact or opinion. Write* F *if the statement is a fact and* O *if it is an opinion.*

____ 1. "We had been born in New York City when our parents had first tried immigration."

____ 2. The Dominican Republic is south of Bermuda.

____ 3. "It was the ugliest name she had ever heard."

____ 4. "Tía Josefina . . . was not really an aunt but a much older cousin."

____ 5. "Our goodbyes went on too long."

**B. DIRECTIONS:** *Each statement below contains an error. Name the resource you would consult to check the statement. (If you would consult a Web site, write the name of the site.) Then, look up the statement in that resource, and rewrite it correctly.*

1. Julia Alvarez moved to the United States for good in 1962.

   **Fact-checking resource:** _____ **Correction:** _____

   _____

2. Julia Alvarez wrote a book called *How the Alvarez Girls Lost Their Accents.*

   **Fact-checking resource:** _____ **Correction:** _____

   _____

3. The Dominican Republic is on the same island as Cuba.

   **Fact-checking resource:** _____ **Correction:** _____

   _____

4. Bermuda is an island in the Caribbean Sea.

   **Fact-checking resource:** _____ **Correction:** _____

   _____

Name _____ Date _____

### "Names/Nombres" by Julia Alvarez
# Literary Analysis: Tone

The **tone** of a literary work is the writer's attitude toward his or her audience and subject. The tone can often be described in one word, such as *playful, serious,* or *humorous.* Factors that contribute to the tone are word choice, sentence structure, and sentence length. Notice how the writer's word choice creates a friendly, informal tone:

By the time I was in high school, I was a popular kid, and it showed in my name.

Sometimes, as in "Names/Nombres," humorous ideas, exaggeration, and dialogue help create a casual, informal tone. Alvarez's use of contractions, such as *wouldn't* and *didn't,* also adds to the informal tone.

**A. DIRECTIONS:** *As you read "Names/Nombres," look for details that add to the essay's informal, humorous tone. On the spider diagram, write one example of each contributing factor.*

**Informal word:** _____

**Mispronunciation of Spanish:** _____

**Untranslated Spanish word:** _____

**Exaggeration:** _____

**Humorous idea:** _____

**Sentence fragment:** _____

**Another informal word:** _____

**Contraction:** _____

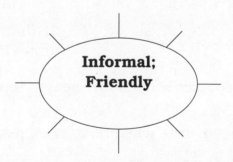

**B. DIRECTIONS:** *Read the following passage from "Names/Nombres." Underline three phrases or sentences that contribute to a relaxed, informal feeling. Then, rewrite the passage using a formal tone.*

At the hotel my mother was *Missus Alburest,* and I was little girl, as in, "Hey, *little girl,* stop riding the elevator up and down. It's *not* a toy."

**Passage written in formal tone:** _____

_____

_____

_____

Name _____ Date _____

"Names/Nombres" by Julia Alvarez
# Vocabulary Builder

## Word List

chaotic    inevitably    inscribed    mistook    pursue    transport

**A. DIRECTIONS:** *Write the letter of the word or phrase whose meaning is most nearly* the same as *the meaning of the Word List word.*

___ 1. inevitably
   A. finally
   B. unavoidably
   C. never
   D. invisibly

___ 2. chaotic
   A. confused
   B. noiseless
   C. tiny
   D. orderly

___ 3. transport
   A. bring in
   B. carry across
   C. send out
   D. extend

___ 4. inscribed
   A. remembered
   B. sewn
   C. scratched
   D. written on

___ 5. mistook
   A. became lost or stolen
   B. made a mistake
   C. provided help
   D. bragged

___ 6. pursue
   A. follow or go after
   B. forget
   C. dream or imagine
   D. wish or hope for

**B. WORD STUDY:** The Latin root *-scrib-* or *-scrip-* means "to write." Answer each question.

1. What message does a doctor write when he or she *prescribes* something?

_____

2. A *scriptorium* is a special room in a monastery. What activity do the monks do in this room?

_____

3. What *inscription* would you probably find on a birthday card?

_____

**"The Lady and the Spider"** by Robert Fulghum
# Writing About the Big Question
### How do we decide what is true?

## Big Question Vocabulary

| | | | | |
|---|---|---|---|---|
| confirm | decision | determine | evidence | fact |
| fantasy | fiction | investigate | opinion | prove |
| realistic | study | test | true | unbelievable |

**A.** *Use one or more words from the list above to complete the following sentences.*

1. Sometimes people think that their _____ are facts.

2. If someone is an expert on a subject, he or she has probably worked hard to _____ the facts.

3. To become an expert on something, you must _____ hard.

4. If you are a scientist with a new theory, you will have to _____ the theory in order to _____ it.

**B.** *Respond to each item. Use at least one Big Question vocabulary word in each answer.*

1. Tell how you distinguish between fact and fiction when you are reading something.

   _____

   _____

   _____

2. What words are a clue that you are reading or listening to an opinion as opposed to a fact?

   _____

   _____

   _____

**C.** *Complete the sentence below. Then, write a short paragraph connecting this situation to the Big Question.*

   An important truth about spiders is _____

   _____

   _____

   _____

   _____

   _____

Name _____ Date _____

**"The Lady and the Spider"** by Robert Fulghum
# Reading: Understand the Difference Between Fact and Opinion; Use Resources to Check Facts

To evaluate a work of nonfiction, you must understand the difference between fact and opinion. A **fact,** unlike an opinion, can be proved. An **opinion** expresses a judgment that can be supported but not proved. For example, the statement "Spiders have eight legs" is a fact that can be proved by observation. All you need to do is look at a spider. The statement "Spiders are scary" is a judgment based on emotions.

You can **check facts by using resources** such as

- dictionaries
- encyclopedias
- reliable Web sites on the Internet
- maps

**A. DIRECTIONS:** *Identify the following passages from "The Lady and the Spider" as fact or opinion. Write F if the statement is a fact and O if it is an opinion.*

_____ 1. This is my neighbor.

_____ 2. Nice lady.

_____ 3. Tries opening the front door without unlocking it.

_____ 4. Spiders. Amazing creatures.

_____ 5. Been around maybe 350 million years.

**B. DIRECTIONS:** *Each statement below contains an error. Name the resource you would consult to check the statement. (If you would consult a Web site, write the name of the site.) Then, look up the statement in that resource, and rewrite it correctly.*

1. A spider has six legs.

    **Fact-checking resource:** _____ **Correction:** _____

    _____

2. Spiders eat only gnats.

    **Fact-checking resource:** _____ **Correction:** _____

    _____

3. The scientific word describing the class that includes spiders is spelled *aracknid*.

    **Fact-checking resource:** _____ **Correction:** _____

    _____

4. In temperate climates, 20 species of spiders are dangerous to human beings.

    **Fact-checking resource:** _____ **Correction:** _____

    _____

Name _____ Date _____

### "The Lady and the Spider" by Robert Fulghum
## Literary Analysis: Tone

The **tone** of a literary work is the writer's attitude toward his or her audience and subject. The tone can often be described in one word, such as *playful, serious,* or *humorous.* Factors that contribute to the tone are word choice, sentence structure, and sentence length. Notice how the writer's sentence structure creates a playful tone:

> Spiders. Amazing creatures. Been around maybe 350 million years, so they can cope with about anything.

Sometimes, as in "The Lady and the Spider," exaggeration and surprising comparisons help create a casual, informal tone. Fulghum's use of contractions, such as *that's* and *what's,* also adds to the informal tone.

**DIRECTIONS:** *As you read "The Lady and the Spider," look for details that add to the essay's informal, playful tone. On the spider diagram, write one example of each contributing factor.*

1. **Informal word:** _____
2. **Sentence fragment:** _____
3. **Short sentence:** _____
4. **Exaggeration:** _____
5. **Surprising idea:** _____
6. **Humorous idea:** _____
7. **Joke word:** _____
8. **Contraction:** _____

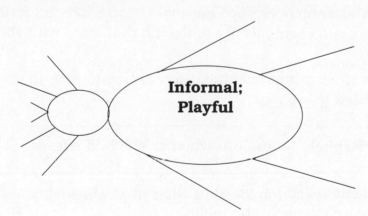

Informal;
Playful

**"The Lady and the Spider"** by Robert Fulghum
# Vocabulary Builder

## Word List

catastrophe    dimensions    equipped    frenzied    inhabited    mode

**A. DIRECTIONS:** *Write the letter of the word or phrase whose meaning is most nearly* the same as *the meaning of the Word List word.*

____ 1. inhabited
   A. dressed up    B. disowned    C. empty    D. lived in

____ 2. frenzied
   A. frantic    B. calm    C. angry    D. unhappy

____ 3. mode
   A. model    B. up-to-date    C. manner    D. dessert

____ 4. equipped
   A. provided with    B. missing or lacking    C. classified    D. joked

____ 5. dimensions
   A. problems    B. rewards    C. measurements    D. activities

____ 6. catastrophe
   A. celebration    B. disaster    C. illness    D. stage or phase

**B. WORD STUDY:** The Latin root *-met-* or *-mens-* means "to measure." Words containing this root include *thermometer* ("an instrument for measuring temperature"), *parking meter* ("a device for measuring the amount of time a car is parked in a given location") and *barometer* ("an instrument for measuring atmospheric pressure"). Each of the following sentences does not make sense. The underlined word is used incorrectly. Correct each sentence by replacing that word with *thermometer, parking meter,* or *barometer.*

1. When stormy weather is approaching, there is a reduction in air pressure. You can measure this with a <u>television</u>.

   _____

2. Brenda used a <u>flashlight</u> to find out whether she had a fever.

   _____

3. Mom's appointment lasted longer than she expected, so she had to dash out to the street and put more money in the <u>mailbox</u>.

   _____

**"The Lady and the Spider"** by Robert Fulghum
**"Names/Nombres"** by Julia Alvarez
## Integrated Language Skills: Grammar

### Interrogative and Indefinite Pronouns

A **pronoun** is a word that takes the place of a noun or another pronoun.

- **Interrogative pronouns** are used in questions. Interrogative pronouns include *who, whom, whose, what,* and *which.*

- **Indefinite pronouns** can be singular or plural, depending on how they are used. Indefinite pronouns include *some, one, other,* and *none.*

**A. DIRECTIONS:** *In each of these sentences, underline the interrogative and indefinite pronouns. Above the interrogative pronouns, write* Inter, *and above the indefinite pronouns, write* Indef.

1. Who can remember some of the names Julia Alvarez gave herself?

2. From whose point of view do the spider and the lady see each other?

3. None of Julia's classmates seemed able to pronounce her name correctly.

4. Which essay do you prefer: the one by Alvarez or the one by Fulghum?

5. What do you think of some of the lady's and spider's reactions to each other?

6. What sort of name is Judy Alcatraz?

**B. WRITING APPLICATION:** *Write a brief paragraph about "The Lady and the Spider" or "Names/Nombres." Write at least four sentences, and use at least one interrogative pronoun and two indefinite pronouns. Then, underline those pronouns.*

_____

_____

_____

_____

_____

Name _____ Date _____

"**Names/Nombres**" by Julia Alvarez
"**The Lady and the Spider**" by Robert Fulghum

# Integrated Language Skills: Support for Writing a Personal Anecdote

To prepare to write your anecdote, use this graphic organizer. First, name the experience you plan to write about. Then, in the left-hand column, write down the events that made up the experience. Write them in the order in which they happened. Finally, in the right-hand column, write your thoughts about each event.

**The time when** _____

| Events | Thoughts About the Events |
|---|---|
| Key event in the beginning: _____ _____ _____ _____ | _____ _____ _____ _____ |
| Key event in the middle: _____ _____ _____ _____ | _____ _____ _____ _____ |
| Key event at most exciting moment: _____ _____ _____ _____ | _____ _____ _____ _____ |
| Key event at end: _____ _____ _____ _____ | _____ _____ _____ _____ |

Now, use your notes to write your personal anecdote. Be sure to describe your thoughts about the experience.

**"The Sound of Summer Running"** by Ray Bradbury
**"Eleven"** by Sandra Cisneros
# Writing About the Big Question
**How do we decide what is true?**

## Big Question Vocabulary

| | | | | |
|---|---|---|---|---|
| confirm | decision | determine | evidence | fact |
| fantasy | fiction | investigate | opinion | prove |
| realistic | study | test | true | unbelievable |

**A.** *Use one or more words from the list above to complete the following sentences.*

1. To _____ the true meaning of a symbol, I would have to ask some-one who understood its meaning.

2. The fact that a symbol stands for something it is not makes it a _____ that is accepted by a lot of people.

3. To _____ whether a symbol was widely known by a lot of people, I would have to talk to many people to see if they knew what it meant.

**B.** *Respond to each item. Use at least one Biq Question vocabulary word in each answer.*

1. How do authors use symbols in works of fiction?

_____

_____

_____

2. In your opinion, are symbols always clearly understood in works of fiction?

_____

_____

_____

**C.** *Complete the sentence below. Then, write a short paragraph connecting this situation to the Big Question.*

If people relate happy or sad feelings or experiences to an object, it may become a symbol because _____

_____

_____

_____

_____

_____

**"The Sound of Summer Running"** by Ray Bradbury
**"Eleven"** by Sandra Cisneros
# Literary Analysis: Symbol

A **symbol** is a person, place, or thing that, in addition to its literal meaning, has other layers of meaning. In literature, symbols often stand for abstract ideas, such as love or hope. Writers often use symbols to reinforce the theme or message of a literary work. They might also use symbols to help express how a character feels. For example, a commonly recognized symbol is a flag that stands for a nation or a state.

**DIRECTIONS:** *Read the passages and answer the questions that follow.*

**from "The Sound of Summer Running"**

"Don't you see?" said Douglas. "I just *can't* use last year's pair."

For last year's pair were dead inside. They had been fine when he started them out, last year. But by the end of summer, every year, you always found out, you always knew, you couldn't really jump over rivers and trees and houses in them, and they were dead. But this was a new year, and he felt that this time, with this new pair of shoes, he could do anything, anything at all.

1. What time of year do last year's shoes symbolize for Douglas?

    _____

2. What feeling do last year's shoes symbolize for Douglas?

    _____

3. Underline the phrase that tells you how Douglas feels about new shoes. What feeling do the new shoes symbolize for Douglas?

    _____

**from "Eleven"**

"Rachel," Mrs. Price says. She says it like she's getting mad. "You put that sweater on right now and no more nonsense."

"But it's not . . ."

"Now!" Mrs. Price says.

This is when I wish I wasn't eleven, because all the years inside of me—ten, nine, eight, seven, six, five, four, three, two, and one—are all pushing at the back of my eyes when I put one arm through one sleeve of the sweater that smells like cottage cheese, and then the other arm through the other and stand there with my arms apart as if the sweater hurts me and it does, all itchy and full of germs that aren't even mine.

4. What object symbolizes Rachel's feelings about her birthday?

    _____

5. Underline two phrases that tell you how Rachel feels about the sweater. What feelings does the sweater symbolize?

    _____

**"The Sound of Summer Running"** by Ray Bradbury
**"Eleven"** by Sandra Cisneros
## Vocabulary Builder

**Word List**

alley    invisible    raggedy    revelation    seized    suspended

**A. DIRECTIONS:** *In each sentence, a word from the Word List is used incorrectly. Revise each sentence to use the underlined vocabulary word correctly. The first one is done for you as an example.*

1. He rolled the trash bin to the <u>alley</u> above his house.

   *He rolled the trash bin to the <u>alley</u> behind his house.*

2. She <u>seized</u> the dog's leash as he sat quietly at her side.

   _____

3. The tennis match was <u>suspended</u> due to beautiful weather.

   _____

4. After a sudden <u>revelation</u>, the math problem confused Charles.

   _____

5. Words such as *dog* and *horse* name concepts that are <u>invisible</u>.

   _____

6. Because my coat was <u>raggedy</u>, it was thick and warm.

   _____

**B. DIRECTIONS:** *Use the Word List words in a sentence according to the instructions given.*

1. Use *seized* in a sentence about someone learning to skate.

   _____

2. Use *suspended* in a sentence about a track meet.

   _____

3. Use *revelation* in a sentence about a detective.

   _____

4. Use *alley* in a sentence about a traffic jam.

   _____

5. Use *raggedy* in a sentence that describes an old banner or flag.

   _____

6. Use *invisible* in a sentence that describes a hidden treasure.

   _____

Name _____ Date _____

# Integrate Language Skills: Support for Writing a Paragraph

Before you draft your paragraph explaining how the symbols in these selections express feelings, complete the graphic organizers below. For each selection, write the main symbol the author uses, the feelings expressed by the symbol, and details from the story that help show those feelings.

| The Sound of Summer Running |
|---|
| **Main symbol:** |
| **Feelings expressed by symbol:**<br><br><br><br>Is the author expressing positive or negative feelings? _____ |
| **Details from the story that show these feelings:** |

| Eleven |
|---|
| **Main symbol:** |
| **Feelings expressed by symbol:**<br><br><br><br>Is the author expressing positive or negative feelings? _____ |
| **Details from the story that show these feelings:** |

Now use your notes to write a paragraph explaining how the authors of these selections use symbols to express positive or negative feelings.

BQ Tunes

## Into the Light, performed by DogDay

We **challenge** and engage the contest

The **battle** to be fought

The storm gathers at the horizon

Life's not a **game** played at any cost

There's no glory in test of wills

We **compete**, but the race is lost

I **defend** against your abuses

In roiling seas, the ship is tossed

In roiling seas, the ship is tossed

In the end I reach the conclusion

I'm not **convinced** the fight's worth the price

Resist, refuse to accept it

Bring a new way into the light, into the light, into the light

We **argue**, force our points of view

But the **issue** isn't what's at stake

The problem is who's in control

Your pound of flesh is mine to take

**Win**, success is how you see it

Does it pay to **negotiate**?

To share some common ground

Peace lies far before heaven's gate

Peace lies far before heaven's gate

In the end I reach the conclusion

I'm not convinced the fight's worth the price

**Resist**, refuse to accept it

Bring a new way into the light, into the light, into the light

We can gamble with our survival

But to live is to win

Once we **lose**, all is lost

A failure paid with life and limb
**Resolve** that peace is the answer
Decide that's where to begin
It's the key to all our questions
All tears are shed in vain
All tears are shed in vain

In the end I reach the conclusion
I'm not convinced the fight's worth the price
Resist, refuse to accept it
Bring a new way into the light, into the light, into the light

---

Song Title: **Into the Light**
Artist / Performed by DogDay
Vocals & Guitar: Joe Pascarell
Lyrics by Keith London
Music composed by Keith London, Joe Pascarell & Mike Pandolfo
Produced by Mike Pandolfo, Wonderful
Executive Producer: Keith London, Defined Mind

Name _____ Date _____

# Unit 2: Short Stories
# Big Question Vocabulary—1

**The Big Question: Is conflict always bad?**

It is impossible to have relationships with people without some conflict arising. One kind of conflict is an argument between friends. The following words are used to talk about arguments.

**argue:** to disagree with someone in words, often in an angry way

**conclude:** to bring something to an end

**convince:** to get another person to think the same way as you

**issue:** a problem or subject that people discuss

**resolve:** to find an acceptable way to deal with a problem or difficulty

**DIRECTIONS:** *Write about a disagreement that you have had with a friend or family member, using the words in parentheses.*

1. **Description of the disagreement:**

   | (argue, issue) |
   | --- |
   | |

2. **How did each party to the disagreement try to get the other person to change his or her thinking?**

   | (convince) |
   | --- |
   | |

3. **What was the end result?**

   | (resolve, conclude) |
   | --- |
   | |

Name _____ Date _____

# Unit 2: Short Stories
# Big Question Vocabulary—2

**The Big Question: Is conflict always bad?**

One kind of conflict is games or sports, which are played according to rules. Most people agree that games or sports are "good" conflict.

**challenge:** *n.* something that tests a person's strength, skill or ability; *v.* to question whether something is fair or right

**compete:** to try to gain something, or to be better or more successful at something than someone else

**game:** an activity or sport in which people play against one another according to agreed rules

**lose:** to not be best or first at something

**win:** to be best or first at something

**DIRECTIONS:** *Using the words in parentheses, describe a game or sport that you are familiar with.*

**1. How do you play?**

> (game, challenge)

**2. Who plays?**

> (compete)

**3. What is the end result?**

> (win, lose)

Name _____ Date _____

# Unit 2: Short Stories
# Big Question Vocabulary—3

## The Big Question: Is conflict always bad?

Sometimes conflict can lead to violent battles or wars between opposing groups. The following words can help you talk about these kinds of conflict.

**battle:** encounter in which opposing groups compete, fight, or argue to try to win

**defend:** to act in support of someone being hurt or criticized

**negotiate:** to discuss something to reach an agreement

**resist:** to stop yourself from doing something you would very much like to do

**survival:** the state of continuing to exist when there is a risk that you might die

**DIRECTIONS:** *Answer the questions below using the words in parentheses in the boxes.*

When the early settlers came to America, the Native Americans were already living here.

1. What were two ways the settlers could have dealt with the problem of sharing land with the Native Americans?

2. What are possible results of each decision?

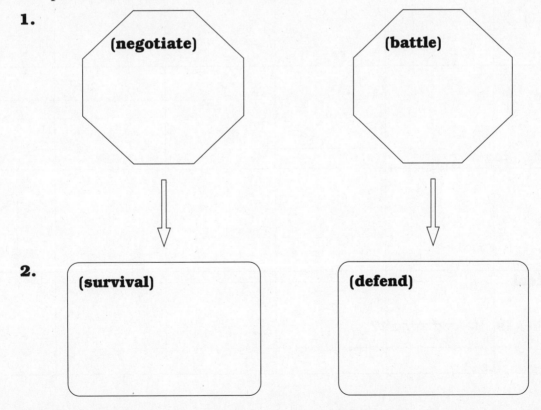

Name _____ Date _____

# Unit 2: Short Stories
# Applying the Big Question

 **Is conflict always bad?**

**DIRECTIONS:** *Complete the chart below to apply what you have learned about the "pros and cons" of conflict. One row has been completed for you.*

| Example | Type of Conflict | How the conflict is resolved | What is bad about the conflict | What is good about the conflict | What I learned |
|---|---|---|---|---|---|
| **From Literature** | In "The Circuit," a boy wants to stay in one place, but his family must often move. | Panchito must accept the hardships of his family's life. | Panchito feels uncomfortable in school; he has to leave a new friend. | Panchito sees how others live; he learns something new with each new experience. | Some conflicts cannot be resolved; conflicts can be a source of courage. |
| **From Literature** | | | | | |
| **From Science** | | | | | |
| **From Social Studies** | | | | | |
| **From Real Life** | | | | | |

Name _____ Date _____

## Jean Craighead George
# Listening and Viewing

### Segment 1: Meet Jean Craighead George
• Why do you think Jean Craighead George chose to write about nature?

_____

_____

_____

_____

### Segment 2: Short Story
• How does Jean Craighead George determine when to use the short-story form? Why did she choose to write the story about the wolf?

_____

_____

_____

_____

### Segment 3: The Writing Process
• Why do you think research is such an important part of Jean Craighead George's writing?

_____

_____

_____

_____

### Segment 4: The Rewards of Writing
• What reward does Jean Craighead George hope to receive from writing? How is her audience also rewarded?

_____

_____

_____

_____

Name _____ Date _____

# Learning About Short Stories

The short story is a form of fiction. This chart outlines its basic elements.

| Elements of Short Story | Examples |
|---|---|
| **CHARACTERS**<br>The characters are the people or animals in the story. | A character's **traits** are his or her qualities, such as honesty.<br>A character's **motives** are the reasons he or she acts, such as a desire to be liked. |
| **PLOT**<br>The plot is the series of events. | The plot contains a **conflict,** or problem, between opposing forces. One or more characters must solve the conflict.<br><br>An **internal conflict** takes place inside a character's mind, such as when a man struggles to make a decision.<br><br>An **external conflict** is one in which a character struggles with an outside force. |
| **SETTING**<br>The setting is the time and place of the story's action. | An example of setting might be a small village in England in the winter of 1765. |
| **THEME**<br>The theme is a message about life. | A **stated theme** is expressed directly by the author, such as when a fable ends with the moral "Look before you leap."<br><br>An **implied theme** is suggested by what happens to the characters, such as when a thief ends up in jail. The implied theme is that crime doesn't pay. |

**DIRECTIONS:** *The following are examples of short story elements. Underline the term that correctly identifies each.*

1. A deer tries to survive a forest fire.

    internal conflict    external conflict

2. A character says, "Honesty is very important."

    stated theme    implied theme

3. A man always turns everything into a joke.

    character trait    character motive

4. Relax and make discoveries during a vacation.

    theme    setting

5. A man must find a way to return from outer space.

    character    plot

Name _____ Date _____

"The Wounded Wolf" by Jean Craighead George
# Model Selection: Short Story

Like other fiction, a short story contains plot, characters, setting, and theme. The plot contains a **conflict,** or problem, that one or more characters must solve. An **internal conflict** occurs inside a character's mind. The character struggles to make a decision or overcome an obstacle. An **external conflict** is one in which a character struggles with an outside force or enemy.

As the conflict deepens, the plot builds to a **climax.** This is the point of greatest tension. Then there is a **resolution,** the solving of the problem. Then the story ends.

Characters have certain **character traits,** or qualities. For example, a character might be brave. They also have **character motives.** These are the reasons why they act. For example, a character might do something in order to win a prize.

The **setting** is the time and place in which the story takes place. Often, the setting plays an important role. For example, the setting of a burning building would certainly affect the characters' actions.

**A. DIRECTIONS:** *"The Wounded Wolf" is a short story. Answer these questions about its plot, characters, and setting.*

1. What character traits does Roko have? _____

2. What character motives lead him to act in certain ways?

   _____

3. Does Roko face an internal or an external conflict? Explain.

   _____

   _____

4. What is the setting of the story? _____

5. How does the setting affect Roko's actions?

   _____

   _____


**B. DIRECTIONS:** *Many short stories carry a **theme,** a message about life. It might be stated by the author or a character. Or, it might be suggested by the characters' actions. Answer the questions about theme.*

1. Does "The Wounded Wolf" have a stated theme or a suggested theme? Explain.

   _____

   _____

2. What might the theme of "The Wounded Wolf" be? Support your answer with details from the story. _____

   _____

Name _____ Date _____

"**The Tail**" by Joyce Hansen
# Writing About the Big Question

**Is conflict always bad?**

## Big Question Vocabulary

| | | | | |
|---|---|---|---|---|
| argue | battle | challenge | compete | conclude |
| convince | defend | game | issue | lose |
| negotiate | oppose | resolve | survival | win |

**A.** *Use one or more words from the list above to complete each sentence.*

1. One way to entertain a child is to play a _____ with him or her.

2. Parents and children are likely to _____ with each other.

3. It often seems important to both sides to _____ an argument.

4. Sometimes it is possible to _____ an outcome that makes everyone happy.

**B.** *Respond to each item with a complete sentence.*

1. Describe two arguments you have had with someone in your family.

_____

_____

2. Explain how you managed to negotiate an agreement in one of the arguments you had. Use at least two of the Big Question vocabulary words.

_____

_____

**C.** *Complete this sentence. Then, write a brief paragraph in which you connect this sentence to the Big Question.*

Conflicts between kids and their parents can have positive outcomes when

_____

_____

_____

_____

_____

_____

Name _____ Date _____

"**The Tail**" by Joyce Hansen
# Reading: Use Details to Make Inferences

When you **make inferences,** you make logical assumptions about something that is not directly stated in the text. To make inferences, use the **details** that the author provides.

**Details in the text + What you know = Inference**

Look at the details, shown in italics, in the following sentence.

Arnie *ran* to the mailbox *as fast as he could* to see if Jim's letter had *finally* arrived.

You can make two inferences from the details and from what you know.

• From *finally,* you can infer that Arnie has been waiting to hear from Jim.
• Because Arnie runs fast, you can infer that he is eager to get the letter.

**DIRECTIONS:** *As you read "The Tail," find details that help you make three inferences. Write two details and your logical inference in each row of boxes below.*

**A.**

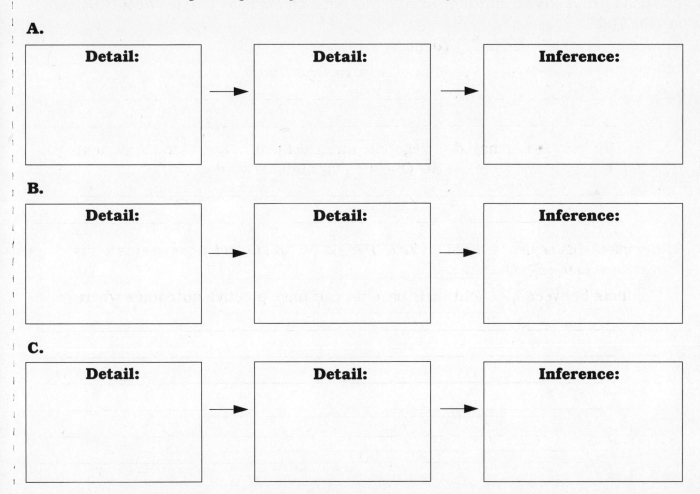

**Detail:** → **Detail:** → **Inference:**

**B.**

**Detail:** → **Detail:** → **Inference:**

**C.**

**Detail:** → **Detail:** → **Inference:**

Name _____ Date _____

# Literary Analysis: Characterization

**Characterization** is the way writers develop and reveal information about characters.

- **Direct characterization:** a writer makes direct statements about a character.
- **Indirect characterization:** a writer suggests information through a character's thoughts, words, and actions as well as what other characters say and think about the character.

In this passage from "The Tail," the writer uses Tasha's thoughts to give an indirect characterization that Junior is cute, but very troublesome.

> Junior held her hand and stared up at her with an innocent look in his bright brown eyes, which everyone thought were so cute. Dimples decorated his round cheeks as he smiled and nodded at me every time Ma gave me an order. I knew he was just waiting for her to leave so he could torment me.

**DIRECTIONS:** *In each part of the pyramid below, jot down direct statements as well as Tasha's and other characters' words, thoughts, and actions that tell about Tasha in "The Tail."*

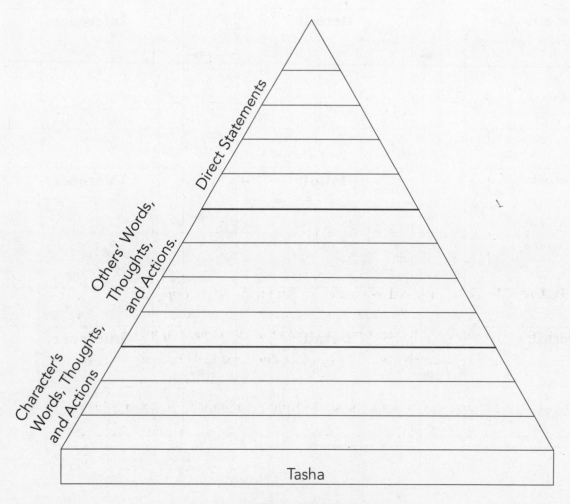

Name _____  Date _____

"Zlateh the Goat" by Isaac Bashevis Singer
"The Old Woman Who Lived With the Wolves" by Chief Luther Standing Bear

# Integrated Language Skills: Support for Writing a Persuasive Speech

Pretend that you are either Aaron or Marpiyawin. Then, in the chart below, list at least three reasons for your life-changing decision. Use details from the story to support the reasons, and explain why each reason was necessary and what either your family or tribe must do now.

| Reasons | Details That Support the Reason | Why the Reason Is Convincing |
|---|---|---|
|  |  |  |
|  |  |  |
|  |  |  |
|  |  |  |
|  |  |  |

Now, use the reasons you have written to write your persuasive speech.

Name _____ Date _____

# Writing About the Big Question

**Is conflict always bad?**

## Big Question Vocabulary

| | | | | |
|---|---|---|---|---|
| argue | battle | challenge | compete | conclude |
| convince | defend | game | issue | lose |
| negotiate | oppose | resolve | survival | win |

**A.** *Use one or more words from the list above to complete each sentence.*

1. In a baseball _____, two teams play.

2. The two teams _____ each other, one on each side.

3. One team will _____, and the other will _____.

4. The losing team must _____ to do better next time.

**B.** *Respond to each item with a complete sentence.*

1. Describe a game you have played that was hard-fought.

   _____

   _____

2. Explain whether you won or lost, and why. Use at least two Big Question
   vocabulary words in your response.

   _____

   _____

**C.** *Complete this sentence. Then, write a brief paragraph in which you connect this
sentence to the Big Question.*

   When a person uses force in a conflict to get what he or she wants, _____

   _____

   _____

   _____

   _____

   _____

   _____

**"Becky and the Wheels-and-Brake Boys"** by James Berry
**"The Southpaw"** by Judith Viorst

# Literary Analysis: Comparing Characters' Traits and Motives

The qualities that make a character unique are called **character traits**. A **character's motives** are the reasons behind a character's thoughts, feelings, and actions. These motivations can be based on internal and external factors.

- *Internal factors* include thoughts and feelings, such as love, pride, or anger.
- *External factors* are events or actions, such as a natural disaster or winning a prize.

**A. DIRECTIONS:** *Read the following passage. Then, answer the questions.*

> Then, going home with the noisy flock of children from school, I had such a new, new idea. If Mum thought I was scruffy, Nat, Aldo, Jimmy, and Ben might think so, too. I didn't like that.
> After dinner I combed my hair in the bedroom.

1. What character traits does Becky reveal in this passage?

_____

2. What external factor motivates the narrator, Becky, to comb her hair?

_____

3. What internal factor motivates Becky to comb her hair?

_____

**B. DIRECTIONS:** *Read the following passages. Then, write a response.*

> Dear Richard,
>     I wasn't kicking exactly. I was kicking back.
>                 Your former friend,
>                     Janet
>
> P.S. In case you were wondering, my batting average is .345.

> Dear Janet,
>
>     Alfie is having his tonsils out tomorrow. We might be able to let you catch next week.
>                     Richard

1. What character traits does Janet reveal in her note?

_____

2. What character traits does Richard reveal in his note?

_____

3. Alfie is mentioned in Richard's letter to Janet. Write a short letter from Alfie to Richard that explains the external motivation that will cause him to miss a baseball game.

_____

_____

_____

**"Becky and the Wheels-and-Brake Boys"** by James Berry
**"The Southpaw"** by Judith Viorst
# Vocabulary Builder

## Word List

| | | | | |
|---|---|---|---|---|
| enviable | envied | envy | former | menace |
| reckless | recklessly | recklessness | unreasonable | |

**A. DIRECTIONS:** *Write a sentence to answer each question. In your sentence, use a word from the Word List that has a similar meaning to the underlined word or words. The first one is done for you as an example.*

1. Who was your piano teacher in the <u>past</u>?

   My former piano teacher was Mr. Ruiz.

2. What habit is a <u>danger</u> to your health?

   _____

3. What rule might you find <u>unfair</u>?

   _____

4. What action might you expect from a <u>careless</u> truck driver?

   _____

5. When have you felt <u>unhappiness because you wanted something that belonged to someone else</u>?

   _____

**B. DIRECTIONS:** *Choose another form of the underlined word in each sentence. Use the new form in your answer.*

1. What might you <u>envy</u> about someone else's life?

   _____

2. What kind of <u>reckless</u> behavior have you seen?

   _____

3. What kind of talent have you <u>envied</u>?

   _____

4. Why do you think people sometimes act with <u>recklessness</u>?

   _____

Name _____ Date _____

**"Becky and the Wheels-and-Brake Boys"** by James Berry
**"The Southpaw"** by Judith Viorst

# Integrated Language Skills: Support for Writing an Essay

Before you draft your essay comparing and contrasting the traits and motives of Becky and Janet, complete the graphic organizer below. In the first row, write what each girl wants. In the second row, tell what motivates each girl to try to get what she wants. Then, in the third row, tell whether their character traits help or hinder each girl as she strives to reach her goal.

|  | **Becky** | **Janet** |
|---|---|---|
| What She Wants | | |
| What Motivates Her to Try to Get What She Wants? | | |
| What Traits Help Her? What Traits Hinder Her? | | |

Now, use your notes to write a brief essay comparing and contrasting the motives and traits of Becky and Janet.

### "The Circuit" by Francisco Jiménez
# Writing About the Big Question

### Is conflict always bad?

## Big Question Vocabulary

| | | | | |
|---|---|---|---|---|
| argue | battle | challenge | compete | conclude |
| convince | defend | game | issue | lose |
| negotiate | oppose | resolve | survival | win |

**A.** *Use one or more words from the list above to complete each sentence.*

1. When you are the new kid at school, the first day is a real _____.

2. You have to _____ to try to fit in and make friends.

3. You can _____ other kids that you are interesting and fun.

4. They will _____ that you would make a good friend.

**B.** *Respond to each item with a complete sentence.*

1. Describe an experience you have had being a new kid at school, or imagine what it would be like.

   _____

   _____

2. Tell what you did or would do at a new school to make friends. Use at least two Big Question vocabulary words in your response.

   _____

   _____

**C.** *Complete this sentence. Then, write a brief paragraph in which you connect this experience to the Big Question.*

   When I talk through conflicts with my family, _____.

   _____

   _____

   _____

   _____

   _____

   _____

   _____

Name _____ Date _____

"The Circuit" by Francisco Jiménez
# Reading: Draw Conclusions

A conclusion is a decision or opinion based on details in a literary work. To **identify the details** that will help you draw conclusions, **ask questions,** such as

- Why is this detail included in the story?
- Does this information help me understand the story better?

Example from "The Circuit":

The thought of having to move to Fresno and knowing what was in store for me there brought tears to my eyes.

You might ask what the narrator expects to happen in Fresno. The thought brings tears to his eyes. You can draw the conclusion that something in Fresno makes him sad.

**A. DIRECTIONS:** *The following passages from "The Circuit" are told from Panchito's point of view. Use details from each passage to draw a conclusion to answer the question.*

1. Suddenly I noticed Papa's face turn pale as he looked down the road. "Here comes the school bus," he whispered loudly in alarm. Instinctively, Roberto and I ran and hid in the vineyards.
   Does Papa want Roberto and Panchito to go to school? How do you know? _____
   _____

2. He walked up to me, handed me an English book, and asked me to read. "We are on page 125," he said politely. When I heard this, I felt my blood rush to my head; I felt dizzy.
   What makes Panchito feel dizzy? _____
   _____

3. Mr. Lema was sitting at his desk correcting papers. When I entered he looked up at me and smiled. I felt better. I walked up to him and asked if he could help me with the new words.
   How does Panchito feel about asking the teacher for help? _____
   _____

**B. DIRECTIONS:** *Underline details in this passage from "The Circuit" that help you draw the conclusion that the family is preparing to move. Then tell why these details help you draw this conclusion.*

I thought they were happy to see me, but when I opened the door to our shack, I saw that everything we owned was neatly packed in cardboard boxes.

**Conclusion:**

_____

_____

Name _____ Date _____

"The Circuit" by Francisco Jiménez
# Literary Analysis: Theme

The **theme,** or central idea of a story, is a thought about life that the story conveys. Sometimes the theme is stated directly. Other times you must figure it out by considering events in the story, characters' thoughts and feelings, and the story's title.

**A. DIRECTIONS:** *Write a statement about the theme of "The Circuit."*

**Theme:** _____

_____

**B. DIRECTIONS:** *In the chart below, write the details from each passage that tell about or support the theme of "The Circuit." The first one is started for you as an example.*

| Passage From "The Circuit" | What the Details Tell About Theme |
|---|---|
| **1.** Yes, it was that time of year. When I opened the front door to the shack, I stopped. Everything we owned was neatly packed in cardboard boxes. Suddenly I felt even more the weight of hours, days, weeks, and months of work. | The word *shack* indicates that the family is poor. Packed boxes indicate a change or move. |
| **2.** He was not going to school today. He was not going tomorrow, or next week, or next month. He would not go until the cotton season was over, . . . | |
| **3.** I thought they were happy to see me, but when I opened the door to our shack, I saw that everything we owned was neatly packed in cardboard boxes. | |

Name _____ Date _____

# Vocabulary Builder

## Word List

accompanied    drone    enroll    instinctively    savoring    surplus

**A. DIRECTIONS:** *Each sentence below features a word from the list. For each sentence, explain why the underlined word does or does not make sense in the sentence.*

1. There was a <u>surplus</u> of food for the party, so everyone was still hungry.

   _____

2. The <u>drone</u> of the television made it hard to concentrate.

   _____

3. Megan went home after school so she could <u>enroll</u> in a school club.

   _____

4. Carlos <u>instinctively</u> ducked when the ball came toward his face.

   _____

5. Jaime ate so fast he almost choked, <u>savoring</u> every bite.

   _____

6. Maria <u>accompanied</u> her sister to the fair.

   _____

**B. WORD STUDY:** *The Latin root -com- means "to move or to wander." Answer each question by paying attention to each of the underlined words with the root -com-. Then, explain your answer.*

1. Could you <u>combine</u> peanut butter and jelly to make a sandwich?

   _____

2. Could a pet ever be a good <u>companion</u> for a lonely person?

   _____

3. If you <u>compress</u> the items in a suitcase, is it harder to close it?

   _____

Name _____ Date _____

"The All-American Slurp" by Lensey Namioka
# Writing About the Big Question

## Is conflict always bad?

### Big Question Vocabulary

| | | | | |
|---|---|---|---|---|
| argue | battle | challenge | compete | conclude |
| convince | defend | game | issue | lose |
| negotiate | oppose | resolve | survival | win |

**A.** *Use one or more words from the list above to complete each sentence.*

1. The family dinner table is often the site of a _____ over food.

2. What to eat is often an _____ that family members fight about.

3. Parents try to _____ children that they should eat healthful food.

4. Children try to _____ with their parents so they can have something sweet to eat.

**B.** *Respond to each item with a complete sentence.*

1. Describe an issue involving food that your family has faced or that you have noticed in someone else's home.

_____

_____

2. Explain how the food issue was resolved. Use at least two of the Big Question vocabulary words.

_____

_____

**C.** *Complete this sentence. Then, write a brief paragraph in which you explain how differences in a new country can lead to a conflict.*

Getting used to differences in a new country _____

_____

_____

_____

_____

_____

_____

Name _____ Date _____

**"The All-American Slurp"** by Lensey Namioka
# Reading: Draw Conclusions

A conclusion is a decision or opinion based on details in a literary work. To **identify the details** that will help you draw conclusions, **ask questions,** such as

- Why is this detail included in the story?
- Does this information help me understand the story better?

Example from "The All-American Slurp":

> After arriving at the house, we shook hands with our hosts and packed ourselves into a sofa. As our family of four sat stiffly in a row, my younger brother and I stole glances at our parents for a clue as to what to do next.

You might ask what the visiting family is feeling in this scene. They are sitting stiffly and unsure of what to do. You can draw the conclusion that they are nervous and feel out of place.

**A. DIRECTIONS:** *The following passages from "The All-American Slurp" are told from the point of view of the narrator. Use details from each passage to draw a conclusion to answer the question.*

1. To my left, my parents were taking care of their own stalks. *Z-z-zip, z-z-zip, z-z-zip.* Suddenly I realized that there was dead silence except for our zipping.
Why is the dinner party suddenly quiet? _____

_____

2. The Gleasons' dinner party wasn't so different from a Chinese meal after all. My mother also puts everything on the table and hopes for the best.
What does the narrator realize about Chinese and American cultures? _____

_____

3. In this perfumed ladies' room, with its pink-and-silver wallpaper and marbled sinks, I looked completely out of place. What was I doing here? What was our family doing in the Lakeview Restaurant? In America?
What emotions is the narrator feeling? _____

_____

_____

**B. DIRECTIONS:** *Underline details in this passage from "The All-American Slurp" that help you draw the conclusion that the family is adjusting to American life. Then tell why these details help you draw this conclusion.*

> Next day we took the bus downtown and she bought me a pair of jeans. In the same week, my brother made the baseball team of his junior high school. Father started taking driving lessons, and Mother discovered rummage sales.

**Conclusion:** _____

_____

_____

Name _____ Date _____

# Literary Analysis: Theme

The **theme,** or central idea of a story, is a thought about life that the story conveys. Sometimes the theme is stated directly. Other times you must figure it out by considering events in the story, characters' thoughts and feelings, and the story's title.

**A. DIRECTIONS:** *Write a statement about the theme of "The All-American Slurp."*

**Theme:** _____

_____

**B. DIRECTIONS:** *In the chart below, write the details from each passage that tell about or support the theme of "The All-American Slurp." The first one is started for you as an example.*

| Passage | What Details Tell About Theme |
|---|---|
| **1.** But I had another worry, and that was my appearance. My brother didn't have to worry, since Mother bought him blue jeans for school, and he dressed like all the other boys. But she insisted that girls had to wear skirts. | The narrator is worried about her appearance. |
| **2.** Of course Chinese etiquette forced Father to say that I was a very stupid girl and Mother to protest that the teacher was showing favoritism toward me. But I could tell they were both very proud. | |
| **3.** "Do you always slurp when you eat a milkshake?" I asked, before I could stop myself.<br>   Meg grinned. "Sure. All Americans slurp." | |

Name _____    Date _____

### "The All-American Slurp" by Lensey Namioka
# Vocabulary Builder

**Word List**

acquainted    consumption    emigrated    etiquette    smugly    systematic

**A. DIRECTIONS:** *Each sentence below features a word from the list. For each sentence, explain why the underlined word does or does not make sense in the sentence.*

1. Proper <u>etiquette</u> says you will thank your host after a party.

   _____

2. Charley had a <u>consumption</u> after he ate too many candies.

   _____

3. Luis's <u>systematic</u> method of studying resulted in his failing the test.

   _____

4. The girls glanced at Rachel and smiled <u>smugly</u>, causing Rachel to feel grateful for their kind thoughts.

   _____

5. Margarita's family <u>emigrated</u> from Chile to America.

   _____

6. Marly and June got <u>acquainted</u> on their first day of school.

   _____

**B. WORD STUDY:** *The Latin root -migr- means "to move or to wander." Answer each question by paying attention to each of the underlined words with the root -migr-. Then, explain your answer.*

1. Could an <u>emigrant</u> move to a place where he or she would have to speak a new language?

   _____

2. When scientists study bird <u>migration</u>, are they looking at the birds' nests?

   _____

3. Did <u>immigrants</u> settle in North America in the 1600s and 1700s?

   _____

## "The Circuit" by Francisco Jiménez
## "The All-American Slurp" by Lensey Namioka
# Integrated Language Skills: Grammar

### Simple Verb Tenses

A **verb** is a word that expresses an action or a state of being. A **verb tense** shows the time of the action or state of being. The **simple verb tenses** show present, past, and future time. Form the past tense of regular verbs with *-ed* or *-d*. Memorize the past tense of irregular verbs. Form the future tense of all verbs with the helping verb *will*.

| Tenses | Regular Verb: Ask | Irregular Verb: Eat | Irregular Verb: Be |
|---|---|---|---|
| Present | I *ask.* | I *eat.* | I *am.* |
| Past | I *asked.* | I *ate.* | I *was.* |
| Future | I *will ask.* | I *will eat.* | I *will be.* |

**A. PRACTICE:** *Underline the verb in each sentence. Then, on the line before the sentence, write whether the verb is in the* present, past, *or* future *tense.*

_____ 1. We grow corn, carrots, tomatoes, and beans on our farm.

_____ 2. We will pick the vegetables in late summer and fall.

_____ 3. We always display the vegetables on a small farm stand.

_____ 4. The tomatoes sell better than the other crops.

_____ 5. Next year, we will grow more tomatoes.

_____ 6. Last year, we also planted parsnips.

_____ 7. It was a bumper year for parsnips.

_____ 8. We ate parsnips in our soup all winter long.

**B. Writing Application:** *Write a sentence about a sports event using verbs in the past tense. Then, rewrite the sentence using verbs in the present tense. Finally, rewrite the sentence using verbs in the future tense. Study these examples:*

**PAST TENSE:** Rodrigo <u>pitched</u> the ball to the second batter.
**PRESENT TENSE:** Rodrigo <u>pitches</u> the ball to the second batter.
**FUTURE:** Rodrigo <u>will pitch</u> the ball to the second batter.

_____

_____

_____

Name _____ Date _____

"**The Circuit**" by Francisco Jiménez
"**The All-American Slurp**" by Lensey Namioka

# Integrated Language Skills: Support for Writing a Character Description

Choose a character from "The Circuit" or "The All-American Slurp." Then, use the chart below to list details that describe that character. Include information from the story that illustrates the details used.

**Name of Character:** _____

| Details That Describe the Character | Examples From the Story |
|---|---|
|  |  |
|  |  |
|  |  |
|  |  |

Use the details that describe the character and examples from the story to write your character description.

Name _____ Date _____

# Writing About the Big Question

**Is conflict always bad?**

## Big Question Vocabulary

| | | | | |
|---|---|---|---|---|
| argue | battle | challenge | compete | conclude |
| convince | defend | game | issue | lose |
| negotiate | oppose | resolve | survival | win |

**A.** *Use one or more words from the list above to complete each sentence.*

1. Sometimes on the playground, bigger kids will _____ little kids and try to take something away from them.

2. The little kids are not able to _____ themselves.

3. It is very difficult for someone small to _____ someone bigger.

4. A small child cannot _____ with a bigger child physically.

**B.** *Answer each question with a complete sentence.*

1. Describe a time when you were challenged by someone bigger or stronger. What were you battling over?

   _____

   _____

2. Explain the outcome of the incident. Who won? Who lost? Why? Use at least two Big Question vocabulary words in your response.

   _____

   _____

**C.** *Complete this sentence. Then, write a brief paragraph in which you write about how stealing can lead to conflict.*

   If someone tried to steal my friend's property, I would _____

   _____

   _____

   _____

   _____

   _____

   _____

Name _____ Date _____

*"The King of Mazy May"* by Jack London
# Reading: Use Prior Knowledge to Draw Conclusions

**Drawing conclusions** means making decisions or forming opinions about what has happened in a literary work. You make your conclusions using details from the text and your own **prior knowledge**—what you know from your own experience. You bring prior knowledge with you whenever you read a story.

Example from "The King of Mazy May":

He has never seen a train of cars nor an elevator in his life, and for that matter he has never once looked upon a cornfield, a plow, a cow, or even a chicken. He has never had a pair of shoes on his feet, nor gone to a picnic or a party, nor talked to a girl.

Details from the passage tell you what Walt Masters has never done or seen. Your own prior knowledge about what the author describes tells you that Walt does not live in a city or on a farm. You can conclude that Walt lives somewhere very isolated from civilization.

**A. DIRECTIONS:** *Fill in this chart with your own prior knowledge and the conclusions you can draw. The first one has been done for you as an example.*

| Story Details | Prior Knowledge | Conclusion |
|---|---|---|
| **1.** The Mazy May creek is beginning to reward the prospectors for their hard work. | Prospectors came to the Yukon to find gold. | The prospectors are beginning to find gold. |
| **2.** Walt is able to stay by himself, cook his own meals, and look after the claim. | | |
| **3.** The days are short and the nights are long when the story takes place. | | |
| **4.** The stampeders try to kill Walt to keep him from reaching Dawson. | | |

**B. DIRECTIONS:** *Write about another conclusion that you can make on your own from "The King of Mazy May." Explain your conclusion by telling the details and the prior knowledge you used.*

_____

_____

_____

_____

Name _____ Date _____

### "The King of Mazy May" by Jack London
# Literary Analysis: Setting

The **setting** of a literary work is the time and place of the action. The time may be established as a historical era, the present or future, the season of the year, or the hour of the day. The place can be as general as planet Earth or as specific as a room in a house. As you read, notice how characters and events in a story are affected by the setting of the story.

Example from "The King of Mazy May":

> But he has seen the sun at midnight, watched the ice jams on one of the mightiest of rivers, and played beneath the northern lights . . .

This passage tells you that the story takes place in the far north, which is where you can see the sun at midnight and the northern lights.

**A. DIRECTIONS:** *Use the chart to tell about the setting of "The King of Mazy May." In column two, record your answer and the details from the story that help you answer each question.*

| Questions About the Setting of the Story | Answer and Story Details |
|---|---|
| **1.** Where does the first part of "The King of Mazy May" take place? | |
| **2.** When does the first part of "The King of Mazy May" take place? | |
| **3.** Where does the chase take place? | |
| **4.** When does the chase take place? | |

**B. DIRECTIONS:** *Use the information in your chart to help you answer the following questions.*

How important is the setting in this story? Why is it important?

_____

_____

_____

_____

_____

_____

_____

Name _____ Date _____

## Word List

abruptly    declined    endured    liable    pursuing    summit

**A. DIRECTIONS:** *Provide an answer and an explanation for each question.*

1. If you have *endured* the experience of watching a movie, did you enjoy the film?

   _____

2. If a friend *declined* an invitation to a party, would he or she be going to it?

   _____

3. If a teacher is *liable* to spring a pop quiz on your class, should you expect a quiz?

   _____

4. If a hiker reached the *summit* of a mountain, how much farther is it to the top?

   _____

5. If you left a party *abruptly,* would you be in a hurry?

   _____

6. If someone was *pursuing* you, would you feel nervous?

   _____

**B. WORD STUDY:** *The Latin root -clin- means "lean." Think about the meaning of the root -clin- in each underlined word. Then, write two reasons for each statement.*

1. You are going up a steep <u>incline</u>. Why?

   _____

   _____

2. You have <u>declined</u> a piece of cake. Why?

   _____

   _____

3. You have <u>reclined</u> on the couch. Why?

   _____

   _____

Name _____ Date _____

"**Aaron's Gift**" by Myron Levoy
# Writing About the Big Question

**Is conflict always bad?**

## Big Question Vocabulary

| | | | | |
|---|---|---|---|---|
| argue | battle | challenge | compete | conclude |
| convince | defend | game | issue | lose |
| negotiate | oppose | resolve | survival | win |

**A.** *Use one or more words from the list above to complete each sentence.*

1. A parent and child may _____ about the child's choices.

2. A friend who gets into trouble may be an _____ that causes an argument.

3. It can be hard to _____ your choice of a friend.

4. You must try to _____ your parent that your choice is a good one.

**B.** *Answer each question with a complete sentence.*

1. Why do you think a parent might disapprove of a child's friend?

   _____

   _____

2. Imagine you had to defend your choice of a friend to a parent. What would you say? Use at least two Big Question vocabulary words in your response.

   _____

   _____

**C.** *Complete this sentence. Then, write a brief paragraph about how children and parents can resolve conflicts.*

   Children may not always agree with their parents, but _____

   _____

   _____

   _____

   _____

   _____

   _____

   _____

   _____

**All-in-One Workbook**
**106**

**"Aaron's Gift"** by Myron Levoy

# Reading: Use Prior Knowledge to Draw Conclusions

**Drawing conclusions** means making decisions or forming opinions about what has happened in a literary work. You make your conclusions using details from the text and your own **prior knowledge**—what you know from your own experience. You bring prior knowledge with you whenever you read a story.

Example from "Aaron's Gift":

> Aaron skated back and forth on the wide walkway of the park, pretending he was an aviator in an air race zooming around pylons, which were actually two lamp posts.

Details from the passage tell you that Aaron invents stories when he plays. Your own prior knowledge about inventing stories might tell you that a person who invents stories has a good imagination. You can conclude that Aaron has a good imagination.

**A. DIRECTIONS:** *Fill in this chart with your own prior knowledge and the conclusions you can draw. The first one has been done for you as an example.*

| Story Details | Prior Knowledge | Conclusion |
|---|---|---|
| **1.** Aaron treats the wounded pigeon very gently. | People who like animals are gentle with them. | Aaron likes animals. |
| **2.** Aaron's father is amazed at how he set the pigeon's wing and calls him a genius. | | |
| **3.** Aaron's mother wants him to stay away from the gang of older boys. | | |
| **4.** Aaron wants to give his grandmother a wonderful present. | | |

**B. DIRECTIONS:** *Write about another conclusion that you can make on your own from "Aaron's Gift." Explain your conclusion by telling the details and the prior knowledge you used.*

_____

_____

_____

_____

**"Aaron's Gift"** by Myron Levoy
# Literary Analysis: Setting

The **setting** of a literary work is the time and place of the action. The time may be established as a historical era, the present or future, the season of the year, or the hour of the day. The place can be as general as planet Earth or as specific as a room in a house. As you read, notice how characters and events in a story are affected by the setting of the story.

Example from "Aaron's Gift":

> Aaron Kandel had come to Tompkins Square Park to roller-skate, for the streets near Second Avenue were always too crowded with children and peddlers and old ladies and baby buggies.

This passage tells you that the story takes place in New York City (where Tompkins Square Park and Second Avenue are). It hints that the time is in the past because it refers to "peddlers."

**A. DIRECTIONS:** *Use the chart to tell about the setting of "Aaron's Gift." In column two, record your answer and the details from the story that help you answer each question.*

| Questions About the Setting of the Story | Answer and Story Details |
|---|---|
| **1.** Where does the main story of "Aaron's Gift" take place? | |
| **2.** When does the main story of "Aaron's Gift" take place? | |
| **3.** Where does the story of the pogrom take place? | |
| **4.** When does the story of the pogrom take place? | |

**B. DIRECTIONS:** *Use the information in your chart to help you answer the following questions.*

How important is the setting in this story? Why is it important? _____

_____

_____

_____

_____

Name _____ Date _____

"Aaron's Gift" by Myron Levoy
# Vocabulary Builder

## Word List

coaxed     consoled     hesitated     pleaded     temporarily     thrashing

**A. DIRECTIONS:** *Provide an answer and an explanation for each question.*

1. If a small animal is *thrashing* in your hands, how does it probably feel?

   _____

2. If a boy *hesitated* before climbing a tree, do you think he enjoyed heights?

   _____

3. If a friend needs to be *consoled* after running a race, did she win the race?

   _____

4. If a girl *pleaded* to be allowed to go to a party, how much did she want to go?

   _____

5. If you *coaxed* a dog out of its hiding place, how would you act toward it?

   _____

6. If your phone is *temporarily* out of order, when would you expect it to work again?

   _____

**B. WORD STUDY:** *The Latin root -tempor- means "time." Think about the meaning of the root -tempor- in each underlined word. Then, write two reasons for each statement.*

1. This detour is <u>temporary</u>. Why?

   _____

   _____

2. It is hard to give an <u>extemporaneous</u> speech. Why?

   _____

   _____

3. Fashion magazines show <u>contemporary</u> clothes. Why?

   _____

   _____

Name _____ Date _____

# Integrated Language Skills: Grammar

## Perfect Tenses

The **perfect tenses** of verbs combine a form of the helping verb *have* with the past participle of the main verb. The past participle usually ends in *-ed* or *-d*.

- The **present perfect tense** shows an action that began in the past and continues into the present.
- The **past perfect tense** shows a past action or condition that ended before another past action began.
- The **future perfect tense** shows a future action or condition that will have ended before another begins.

| Present Perfect | Past Perfect | Future Perfect |
|---|---|---|
| have, has + past participle | had + past participle | will have + past participle |
| They *have arrived.* | They *had arrived* before we came. | They *will have arrived* before the show starts. |

**A. PRACTICE:** *Complete each sentence by using the form of the verb requested in parentheses. Write the verb on the line provided.*

(travel-past perfect)     1. Joe _____ to Alaska after gold was discovered there.

(remain-present perfect) 2. He _____ in Alaska ever since.

(reside-future perfect)   3. By this May, he _____ here for ten years.

(live-present perfect)    4. His wife _____ in Alaska all her life.

(propose-past perfect)    5. They wed after he _____ to her for the fifth time.

(finish-future perfect)   6. Next month, they _____ work on their new igloo.

**B. Writing Application:** *Write a paragraph about a valuable object or experience. Use verbs in the present perfect, past perfect, and future perfect tenses. Use each of the three perfect tenses at least once.*

_____

_____

_____

_____

_____

**"The King of Mazy May"** by Jack London
**"Aaron's Gift"** by Myron Levoy

# Integrated Language Skills:
# Support for Writing a Personal Narrative

Use a timeline to help you list the events you will describe in your personal narrative. Write your events on the left-hand side of the write-on line. Write details that describe the events on the right-hand side. Be sure to place the events in correct time order.

**First Event**

1.

**Events**                                                                 **Details**

2. _____

3. _____

4. _____

5. _____

6. _____

**Final Event**

7.

Now use the details from your timeline to write your personal narrative.

Name _____ Date _____

"**The Fun They Had**" by Isaac Asimov
"**Feathered Friend**" by Arthur C. Clarke
# Writing About the Big Question

**Is conflict always bad?**

## Big Question Vocabulary

| | | | | |
|---|---|---|---|---|
| argue | battle | challenge | compete | conclude |
| convince | defend | game | issue | lose |
| negotiate | oppose | resolve | survival | win |

**A.** *Use one or more words from the list above to complete each sentence.*

1. Bullying is an important _____ in many schools.

2. Students facing bullies alone are often unable to _____ themselves.

3. Sometimes students can work together to _____ a bully.

4. A strong group can _____ a bully to back down.

**B.** *Respond to each item with a complete sentence.*

1. Describe an incident you have seen or heard about in which someone was bullied.

   _____

   _____

2. What are some ways to stop bullying? Use at least two Big Question vocabulary
words in your answer.

   _____

   _____

**C.** *Complete this sentence. Then, write a brief paragraph in which you connect this idea
to the Big Question.*

   When humans rely on animals or computers to do their work, _____

   _____

   _____

   _____

   _____

   _____

   _____

Name _____  Date _____

### "The Fun They Had" by Isaac Asimov
### "Feathered Friend" by Arthur C. Clarke
# Literary Analysis: Comparing Setting and Theme

**Setting** is the time and place of a story's action. In most stories, the setting serves as a background for the plot and creates a feeling or atmosphere. Setting can be real or make-believe. Details of setting can include the year, the time of day, or even the weather. The time may be a historical era, the present, or the future. The place may be a specific home, neighborhood, or state, or even outer space.

The **theme**, or central idea, of a story is the thought, message, or lesson about life that the story conveys. A theme can be expressed in a sentence, such as "Hard work leads to success" or "Every member of a team counts." Sometimes the theme is directly stated, and sometimes it is not. To determine the theme, consider the events; the characters' thoughts, words, actions, and feelings; and the title.

**A. DIRECTIONS:** *Read the following passage from "The Fun They Had" by Isaac Asimov. Write the details of the setting.*

> Margie went into the schoolroom. It was right next to her bedroom, and the mechanical teacher was on and waiting for her. It was always on at the same time every day except Saturday and Sunday, because her mother said little girls learned better if they learned at regular hours.
>
> The screen was lit up, and it said: "Today's arithmetic lesson is on the addition of proper fractions. Please insert yesterday's homework in the proper slot."

Past, Present, or Future? _____

Place: _____

Time of Day and Week: _____

**B. DIRECTIONS:** *Read the following passage from "Feathered Friend" by Arthur C. Clarke. Then, list three events or details that suggest the story's theme. On the last line, write a sentence stating the theme.*

> For the last few minutes, something had been tugging at my memory. My mind seemed to be very sluggish that morning, as if I was still unable to cast off the burden of sleep. I felt that I could do with some of that oxygen—but before I could reach the mask, understanding exploded in my brain. I whirled on the duty engineer and said urgently:
>
> "Jim! There's something wrong with the air! That's why Claribel's passed out. I've just remembered that miners used to carry canaries down to warn them of gas."

Detail: _____

Detail: _____

Detail: _____

Theme: _____

Name _____ Date _____

**"The Fun They Had"** by Isaac Asimov
**"Feathered Friend"** by Arthur C. Clarke
# Vocabulary Builder

**Word List**

calculated    ceased    fusing    loftily    nonchalantly    regulation

**DIRECTIONS:** *Use a thesaurus to find a* **synonym,** *a word with nearly the same meaning, for each word in the Word List. Use each synonym in a sentence that makes the meaning of the word clear. The first one is done for you as an example.*

1. regulation

    Synonym: <u>rule</u>

    Sentence: The new <u>rule</u> stated that no dogs were allowed in the park.

2. calculated

    Synonym: _____

    Sentence: _____

3. loftily

    Synonym: _____

    Sentence: _____

4. nonchalantly

    Synonym: _____

    Sentence: _____

5. regulation

    Synonym: _____

    Sentence: _____

6. fusing

    Synonym: _____

    Sentence: _____

7. ceased

    Synonym: _____

    Sentence: _____

Name _____ Date _____

"The Fun They Had" by Isaac Asimov
"Feathered Friend" by Arthur C. Clarke

# Integrated Language Skills: Support for Writing an Essay

Before you draft your essay comparing the themes, complete this graphic organizer. In the first row, write the nonhuman helper in each story. In the second row, describe the helper's usefulness. In the third row, describe any problems the helper causes. Finally, write a possible theme about the usefulness of animals and computers.

|  | "The Fun They Had" | "Feathered Friend" |
|---|---|---|
| Nonhuman helper |  |  |
| Usefulness |  |  |
| Problems |  |  |
| Theme |  |  |

Now, use your notes to write an essay comparing the theme each story presents about the usefulness of animals and computers.

## BQ Tunes

### We Won't Stop Listening, performed by VladG the Kt-Fav

(If you think you know, you got another thing comin')
It's so hard to really tell the difference...
**Distinguish** what you know from what you think you know
The **concept's** easy, see if you could dig this...
The idea is simple, we just got to take it slow

Cause when people **judge**, and they think they know, I get angry...
They're **narrow** minded, the light can't make it through...
There's no **limit** to our **knowledge**, can ya feel me
No boundary to our understanding, and that's all right!

We can't stop listening
We can feel everything
We can't stop questioning
We won't stop listening

Well I **guess** I know, I'm not sure, but I'll check it out
The answers to the **questions** that you're askin'
We'll **examine** the facts, look closely, **study** all the time...
There's a **purpose** – our aim is to get it right and win

You could **measure** a man, size him up, by what he doesn't know
Or test him by what he can watch, **observe** and learn
I'm talkin' about the **source** of my confusion, yea the cause of our illusions
I'm **referring** to the fact, saying that, we can get it right.

We can't stop listening
We can feel everything
We can't stop questioning
We won't stop listening

---

Song Title: **Can't Stop Listening**
Artist / Performed by VladG the Kt-Fav
Vocals: Nina Zeitlin
Lyrics by VladG with Keith London
Music composed / produced by VladG the Kt-Fav
Post-Production: Mike Pandolfo, Wonderful
Executive Producer: Keith London, Defined Mind

Name _____ Date _____

# Unit 3: Types of Nonfiction
# Big Question Vocabulary—1

### The Big Question: What is important to know?

Often, in order to learn about something, we must put in some effort. The words that follow are used to describe that effort.

**concept:** an idea of how something is or how something should be done

**examine:** to look carefully at something in order to learn more about it

**knowledge:** the information and understanding that you have gained through learning and experience

**question:** a sentence used to ask for information

**study:** *n.* a piece of work done to find out more about a subject or problem; *v.* to watch and examine something carefully over a period of time to find out more about it

**DIRECTIONS:** *Complete the blanks in the story that follows using the vocabulary words above. You will use all of the words, some of them more than once.*

Ms. Walsh was asking about some scientific (1) _____ that Derrick did not understand. He raised his hand to ask Ms. Walsh a (2) _____ .

"Yes, Derrick?" Ms. Walsh called on him.

"I do not understand that (3) _____, Ms. Walsh," Derrick said.

"Well," said Ms. Walsh, "Let's (4) _____ your (5)_____, Derrick. Have you been paying attention to what has been going on in class today?"

Derrick's face reddened and he shook his head. He had been distracted.

"It's okay, Derrick," said Ms. Walsh. "If you (6) _____ pages 32–34 in the science textbook tonight, you will gain the same (7) _____ that the rest of the class gained in our class discussion today."

**DIRECTIONS:** *Answer the following question in full sentences, using at least three of the vocabulary words in your answer.*

8. You discover an interesting yellow and green insect in your backyard. It is about the size and shape of your pinky finger and it has many legs. You really want to know more about this insect. What do you do?

_____

_____

_____

# Unit 3: Types of Nonfiction
# Big Question Vocabulary—2

### The Big Question: What is important to know?

How do we form our opinions? Sometimes our opinions are based on knowledge, and sometimes they are based on an instinct or a feeling. It is important to be open to learning facts that might change your opinion.

**distinguish:** to recognize or understand the difference between two similar things or people

**guess:** to answer a question or make a judgment without knowing all the facts

**judge:** to form or give an opinion about something or someone

**observe:** to watch someone or something carefully in order to learn something

**purpose:** the aim or result that an activity or event is supposed to achieve

How do you choose your friends?

Write sentences in the chart below describing how some people might choose friends on each basis listed. Use the word in parentheses in your sentences. Put a star next to the way that you like to choose friends.

| Some people choose friends based on: | |
|---|---|
| 1.  their hobbies   **(distinguish)** | |
| 2.  how they look   **(judge)** | |
| 3.  what they see others doing or hear them saying   **(observe)** | |
| 4.  what they might want to learn from others **(purpose)** | |
| 5.  a feeling   **(guess)** | |

Name _____ Date _____

# Unit 3: Types of Nonfiction
# Big Question Vocabulary—3

## The Big Question: What is important to know?

There is so much information available in so many forms that sometimes it is difficult to determine which information is useful to you and which information should be disregarded.

**limit:** the greatest or least amount of something that is allowed

**measure:** to judge something's importance, value, size, weight, or true nature

**narrow:** limited in scope or amount

**refer:** to mention or speak about someone or something

**source:** a person, book, or document that supplies you with information

**DIRECTIONS:** *Read the passage. Then, complete the list below, using the words in parentheses.*

You have been assigned a research project. You are to research the state where you live. You get on the Internet and you begin to do your research, but there is so much information! What should you do?

Make a list of strategies to help you figure out what to include.

1. **(narrow)** *In order to make this report manageable, I will*
_____

_____

2. **(limit, source)** *When researching, I will make sure to*
_____

_____

3. **(measure)** *I have to remember to*
_____

_____

4. **(refer)** *I will not*
_____

_____

Name _____ Date _____

# Unit 3: Types of Nonfiction
# Applying the Big Question

**What is important to know?**

**DIRECTIONS:** *Complete the chart below to apply what you have learned about what is important to know. One row has been completed for you.*

| Example | Something important to know | Source of this knowledge | Why knowing this is important | Ways this knowledge can be used | What I learned |
|---------|------------------------------|---------------------------|-------------------------------|----------------------------------|----------------|
| **From Literature** | Things have names, as in "Water." | Helen learned from her teacher. | She could communicate thoughts and feelings. | to connect with others | Language is an important tool in communicating with others. |
| **From Literature** | | | | | |
| **From Science** | | | | | |
| **From Social Studies** | | | | | |
| **From Real Life** | | | | | |

Name _____ Date _____

## Zlata Filipović
# Listening and Viewing

**Segment 1: Meet Zlata Filipović**
• What influences helped Zlata Filipović decide to keep a diary? Why do you think it is a good idea to write daily in a journal or diary?

_____
_____
_____
_____

**Segment 2: Zlata Filipović Introduces *Zlata's Diary***
• How did the content of Zlata's diary change over time? What do you think you could learn by reading a diary written during wartime?

_____
_____
_____
_____

**Segment 3: The Writing Process**
• How did Zlata's diary become a published book? How did the publication of her diary significantly change her life?

_____
_____
_____
_____

**Segment 4: The Rewards of Writing**
• How do you think Zlata's journal has had an impact on others? Why is *Zlata's Diary* important to society?

_____
_____
_____
_____

# Learning About Nonfiction

Nonfiction writing is about real people, places, ideas, and experiences. This chart shows many of the common elements and types of nonfiction.

| Elements/Types of Nonfiction | Definitions and Examples |
|---|---|
| Organization | • **chronological:** presents details or events in time order<br>• **cause-and-effect:** shows the relationships among events<br>• **comparison-and-contrast:** shows how two or more subjects are alike and different |
| Author's role | • An **author's influences** include his or her heritage, culture, experiences, and personal beliefs.<br>• An **author's style** is the way he or she puts ideas into words.<br>• The author's influences and style have a strong impact on the **mood,** or overall feeling, of the writing.<br>• An **author's purpose,** or reason, for writing can include to entertain, to inform, to explain how to do something, and to persuade. |
| Types | • **biography and autobiography:** life stories of real people<br>• **letters, journals, and diaries:** personal thoughts and reflections<br>• **media accounts:** nonfiction in newspapers, magazines, TV, or radio<br>• **reference materials/textbooks:** information, explanations, instructions<br>• **essays and articles:** short nonfiction that focuses on a particular subject, such as historical accounts, persuasive essays, etc. |

**DIRECTIONS:** *Answer the following questions by underlining each correct answer.*

1. Which pattern of organization would be best for an article that explains why thunder booms?
   chronological      cause-and-effect      comparison-and-contrast

2. Which pattern of organization would be best for an article that explains the differences between parrots and parakeets?
   chronological      cause-and-effect      comparison-and-contrast

3. What purpose would an author have for writing a funny article about his dog?
   to persuade      to entertain      to explain how to do something

4. Where would you be most likely to find a media account of a meeting between leaders?
   in an encyclopedia      in an essay      in a newspaper

5. Which type of nonfiction would be most likely to contain personal thoughts and reflections?
   a diary      a biography      a reference book

Name _____  Date _____

*from* **Zlata's Diary** by Zlata Filipović
# Model Selection: Nonfiction

In her diary, Zlata Filipović tells about living as a child in Sarajevo during the spring of 1992. Her writing contains many of the common elements of nonfiction, shown in this chart.

| Elements of Nonfiction | Definitions and Examples |
|---|---|
| Organization | • **chronological:** presents details or events in time order (first to last or sometimes last to first)<br>• **cause-and-effect:** shows the relationships among events (one event causes another event to happen)<br>• **comparison-and-contrast:** shows how two or more subjects are alike and different (moths and butterflies; spring and fall) |
| Author's role | • An **author's influences** include his or her heritage, culture, experiences and personal beliefs.<br>• An **author's style** is the way he or she puts ideas into words. That style might be formal, friendly, or humorous.<br>• The author's influences and style have a strong impact on the **mood**, or overall feeling, of the writing. It might be happy, sad, or triumphant.<br>• An **author's purpose**, or reason, for writing will also affect the content and mood. Common purposes include to entertain, to inform, to explain how to do something, and to persuade. |

**DIRECTIONS:** *Answer the following questions.*

1. Which method of organization does the structure of the diary follow? Explain what clues led to your answer. _____

   _____

2. What information does Zlata include about her heritage and culture?

   _____

   _____

3. What words would you use to describe Zlata's style of writing? Explain why.

   _____

   _____

4. Use details from the diary entries to support this statement: *The mood at the beginning of the diary is different from the mood at the end.*

   _____

   _____

Name _____ Date _____

"**Water**" by Helen Keller

# Writing About the Big Question

## What is important to know?

**Big Question Vocabulary**

| | | | | |
|---|---|---|---|---|
| concept | distinguish | examine | guess | judge |
| knowledge | limit | measure | narrow | observe |
| purpose | question | refer | source | study |

**A.** *Write down one or more words from the list above that help describe how you might learn each piece of information.*

1. the length of a line _____

2. the best CD player to buy _____

3. how birds build nests _____

4. the scientist who discovered penicillin _____

**B.** *Answer each question in full sentences. Include at least two words from the list above.*

1. What is the most effective way to gather facts for a research report?

   _____

   _____

   _____

2. What could a person do to learn about important issues in his or her community?

   _____

   _____

   _____

**C.** *Complete the sentence below. Then, write a short paragraph in which you connect your point of view to the Big Question, telling how people can increase their knowledge through careful communication skills.*

   To communicate with others clearly, it is important to _____

   _____

   _____

   _____

   _____

   _____

"Water" by Helen Keller

# Reading: Recognize Details That Indicate Author's Purpose

An **author's purpose** is the main reason the author writes a work. An author's general purpose may be to entertain, to inform, to persuade, or to reflect. (*To reflect* means "to think carefully or seriously about something after it has happened.") The author also has a specific purpose. For example, in an article about teachers, the general purpose may be to inform, and the specific purpose may be to persuade the reader to consider teaching as a career.

**Learn to recognize details** that indicate the author's purpose. Look at these examples of how details can indicate purpose.

- Facts, statistics, and technical terms are used to inform or persuade.
- Stories about experiences are used to entertain.
- Opinions and thoughts are used to reflect on an experience.

An author can have more than one purpose. For example, an author may inform and entertain in the same piece of writing.

**DIRECTIONS:** *Use the chart to help you recognize the details Helen Keller uses to achieve her purpose for writing. Read each detail from "Water." In the center column, note the kind of detail. Is it a fact or technical term? An incident or event? An opinion or a thought? In the column at the right, note the general purpose of the detail. Is it to entertain? To inform? To persuade? To reflect?*
*The first one is done for you as an example.*

| Detail from "Water" | Kind of Detail | General Purpose of Detail |
|---|---|---|
| **1.** That living word awakened my soul, gave it light, hope, joy, set it free! | a thought | to reflect |
| **2.** The morning after my teacher came she led me into her room and gave me a doll. | | |
| **3.** But my teacher had been with me for several weeks before I understood that everything has a name. | | |
| **4.** We walked down the path to the well-house, attracted by the fragrance of the honeysuckle. . . . | | |
| **5.** Everything had a name, and each name gave birth to a new thought. | | |

Name _____ Date _____

"**Water**" by Helen Keller
# Literary Analysis: Autobiographical Essay

In a **narrative essay,** the author narrates, or tells in order, the true story of real events that happened to real people. An **autobiographical essay** tells about an event or a time in the author's own life. Because the author is writing about personal experiences, his or her own thoughts, feelings, and reactions can also be included.

Writers choose to include particular events, thoughts, and feelings to achieve a purpose. For example, writers may choose to tell about overcoming a challenge in their life to encourage others to take on their own challenges.

**DIRECTIONS:** *Complete the graphic organizer below to help you understand the author's choices in the autobiographical essay "Water" by Helen Keller. Reread "Water" to find more information about the events listed in the arrows on the left. Then write the author's thoughts or feelings at the time and her specific purpose for including that event. The first one is done for you as an example.*

| Events | Purpose | Author's Thoughts/Feelings |
|---|---|---|
| **1.** Miss Sullivan slowly spelled into my hand the word "d-o-l-l." | To show that she was imitating without understanding | pleased and proud |
| **2.** I knew I was going out into the warm sunshine. | | |
| **3.** I left the well-house eager to learn. | | |
| **4.** I remembered the doll I had broken. | | |
| **5.** I lay in my crib at the close of that eventful day. | | |

Name _____ Date _____

"**Water**" by Helen Keller
# Vocabulary Builder

## Word List

barriers    fragments    imitate    persisted    repentance    sentiment

**A. DIRECTIONS:** *Complete each item for the vocabulary words shown above. The first item is started as an example.*

1. **barriers** Definition: <u>obstructions, such as fences</u>; Synonym: _____
   Sentence: _____

2. **fragments** Definition: _____ Synonym: _____
   Sentence: _____

3. **imitate** Definition: _____ Synonym: _____
   Sentence: _____

4. **persisted** Definition: _____ Synonym: _____
   Sentence: _____

5. **repentance** Definition: _____ Synonym: _____
   Sentence: _____

6. **sentiment** Definition: _____ Synonym: _____
   Sentence: _____

**B. WORD STUDY:** The Latin suffix *-ance* means "the act or process of doing, being, or feeling." Answer each of these questions using one of these words containing *-ance*: *attendance, assistance, acceptance.*

1. Would a sixth grader be able to give *assistance* to a young child learning to spell? Explain why or why not.

   _____

2. What types of animals might be in *attendance* at a farm?

   _____

3. If you won an award, what might be the first sentence in your *acceptance* speech?

   _____

Name _____ Date _____

"Hard as Nails" by Russell Baker
# Writing About the Big Question
### What is important to know?

## Big Question Vocabulary

| | | | | |
|---|---|---|---|---|
| concept | distinguish | examine | guess | judge |
| knowledge | limit | measure | narrow | observe |
| purpose | question | refer | source | study |

**A.** *Use one or more words from the list above to complete each set of related words.*

1. read, research, review, _____

2. idea, notion, plan, _____

3. goal, aim, mission, _____

4. ask, challenge, dispute, _____

**B.** *Answer the questions. Write your responses in complete sentences. Use at least two words from the list above.*

1. What do you feel is important for a young child to know before he or she enters kindergarten?

_____

_____

2. In your opinion, what important lessons did Russell Baker learn from his first job?

_____

_____

**C.** *Complete the sentence below. Then, write a short paragraph in which you explain how specific bits of knowledge can help people to prepare for, and complete, a job or project.*

When you start to do any new job, the most important thing to remember is

_____

_____

_____

_____

_____

_____

_____

"**Hard as Nails**" by Russell Baker
# Reading: Recognize Details That Indicate Author's Purpose

An **author's purpose** is the main reason the author writes a work. An author's general purpose may be to entertain, to inform, to persuade, or to reflect. (*To reflect* means "to think carefully or seriously about something after it has happened.") The author also has a specific purpose. For example, in an article about a first job, the general purpose may be to entertain, and the specific purpose may be to reflect on the valuable lessons learned in the first job.

**Learn to recognize details** that indicate the author's purpose. Look at the examples of how details can indicate purpose.

- Facts, statistics, and technical terms are used to inform or persuade.
- Stories about experiences are used to entertain.
- Opinions and thoughts are used to reflect on an experience.

An author can have more than one purpose. For example, an author may inform and persuade in the same piece of writing.

**A. DIRECTIONS:** *Use the chart to help you recognize the details Russell Baker uses to achieve his purpose for writing. Read each detail from "Hard as Nails." In the center column, note the kind of detail. Is it a fact or technical term? An incident or event? An opinion or a thought? In the column at the right, note the general purpose of the detail. Is it to entertain? To inform? To persuade? To reflect? The first one is done for you as an example.*

| Detail from "Hard as Nails" | Kind of Detail | General Purpose of Detail |
|---|---|---|
| **1.** As we walked back to the house, she said I couldn't have a paper route until I was twelve. | an incident | to entertain |
| **2.** This move of hers to Baltimore was a step toward fulfilling a dream. | | |
| **3.** So, as soon as it was legal, I went into newspaper work. | | |
| **4.** I had often gazed with envy at paperboys; to be one of them at last was happiness sublime. | | |
| **5.** I never quit believing it was a great life. | | |

Name _____ Date _____

# Literary Analysis: Autobiographical Essay

In a **narrative essay,** the author narrates, or tells in order, the true story of real events that happened to real people. An **autobiographical essay** tells about an event or a time in the author's own life. Because the author is writing about personal experiences, his or her own thoughts, feelings, and reactions can also be included.

Writers choose to include particular events, thoughts, and feelings to achieve a purpose. For example, writers may choose to tell about an experience in their lives in order to share with the reader what they learned from the experience.

**DIRECTIONS:** *Complete the graphic organizer below to help you understand the author's choices in the autobiographical essay "Hard as Nails" by Russell Baker. Reread "Hard as Nails" to find more information about the events listed in the arrows on the left. Then write the author's thoughts or feeling at the time and his specific purpose for including that event. The first one is done for you as an example.*

| Events | Purpose | Thoughts/Feelings |
|---|---|---|
| **1.** I had to sit beside Deems throughout the meal. | to show how young and inexperienced he is | panicked, horrified, afraid to make mistakes |
| **2.** He asked if I would like to join a small group of boys he was taking to visit the *News-Post* newsroom. | | |
| **3.** Riding home on the streetcar that night, I realized I was a lucky boy. | | |
| **4.** You're a member of the fourth estate. | | |
| **5.** Deems quit. | | |

Name _____ Date _____

### "Hard as Nails" by Russell Baker
# Vocabulary Builder

## Word List

embedded    exhaust    fulfilling    idle    immense    sublime

**A. DIRECTIONS:** *Complete each item for the vocabulary words shown above. The first item is started as an example.*

1. **embedded** Definition: <u>firmly fixed in a surrounding material;</u> Synonym: <u>set</u>
   Sentence: _____

2. **exhaust** Definition: _____ Synonym: _____
   Sentence: _____

3. **fulfilling** Definition: _____ Synonym: _____
   Sentence: _____

4. **idle** Definition: _____ Synonym: _____
   Sentence: _____

5. **immense** Definition: _____ Synonym: _____
   Sentence: _____

6. **sublime** Definition: _____ Synonym: _____
   Sentence: _____

**B. WORD STUDY:** The Latin suffix *-ity* means "the condition or state of." Answer each of these questions using one of these words containing *-ity: probability, activity, unity.*

1. If everyone in our group disagrees, do we have a *unity* of opinion? Explain why or why not.

   _____

2. During the summer, is there a high *probability* that the weather will be hot? Explain why or why not.

   _____

3. What is your favorite *activity*? Explain why you favor it.

   _____

Name _____ Date _____

**"Water"** by Helen Keller
**"Hard as Nails"** by Russell Baker
# Integrated Language Skills: Grammar

## Adjectives and Articles

An **adjective** is a word that describes a person, place, or thing. An adjective answers one of the following questions: *What kind? Which one? How many? How much?* In the following sentences, the adjectives are underlined.

- We saw <u>beautiful</u> paintings. *Beautiful* is an adjective that answers the question "**What kind** of paintings?"
- She did well in <u>that</u> class. *That* is an adjective that answers the question "**Which** class?"
- Dave spelled <u>ten</u> words correctly. *Ten* is an adjective that answers the question **"How many?"**
- I learned only a <u>few</u> words in Spanish. *Few* is an adjective that answers the question **"How much?"**

An **article** is a special kind of adjective. There are three articles: *a, an,* and *the.*

- Use *a* before a word that begins with a consonant. <u>A</u> dog answers the question **"How many?"**
- Use *an* before a word beginning with a vowel. <u>An</u> apple answers the question **"How many?"**
- Use *the* before a word beginning with either a consonant or vowel. <u>The</u> teacher answers the question **"Which one?"**

**A. PRACTICE:** *Underline the adjectives in the following sentences. On the line following the sentence, tell what the adjective describes. Then, circle the articles in the sentence. The first sentence is done for you as an example.*

1. Ray was (a) <u>new</u> student at (the) school.

   <u>*New* tells what kind of student</u>.

2. We need five minutes to talk about the problem.

   _____

3. Diane performed a long cheer she had learned.

   _____

4. He quickly opened a math book.

   _____


**B. Writing Application:** *Write a short paragraph about a first job. Choose four of these adjectives to include in your paragraph:* young, lucky, great, little, difficult, exciting, easy, *and a number such as* ten *or* fifty. *Use other adjectives too to help you write an interesting paragraph. Underline each adjective and circle each article that you use.*

_____

_____

Name _____ Date _____

# Integrated Language Skills: Support for Writing a Letter

Young Russell Baker and Helen Keller lived in the days before computer e-mail. Choose one of these characters and write a letter from his or her point of view. Use this model to help you construct your letter.

| | |
|---|---|
| **Heading** ————— | 123 Wayside Street<br>Franklin, MD 11485<br>October 9, 2010 |
| **Greeting** ————— | Dear [fill in name], |
| **Body of Letter** ——— | You may not remember me, but I want to let you know how much you influenced my life. |
| **Closing** ————— | Sincerely yours, |
| **Signature** ————— | [name of character] |

**DIRECTIONS:** In your letter, describe an event that happened in the narrative. Use this chart to gather details for your letter.

| **Paragraph 1:** Describe the event and explain how it made you feel. | Notes on how you think the main character feels: |
|---|---|
| **Paragraph 2:** Conclude your letter with an explanation of what you learned from your experience. | Notes on what you learned: |

Now, use your notes to write a letter.

Name _____   Date _____

**"Jackie Robinson: Justice at Last"** by Geoffrey C. Ward and Ken Burns
# Writing About the Big Question
### What is important to know?

## Big Question Vocabulary

| | | | | |
|---|---|---|---|---|
| concept | distinguish | examine | guess | judge |
| knowledge | limit | measure | narrow | observe |
| purpose | question | refer | source | study |

**A.** *Use one or more words from the list above to complete each sentence.*

1. To find the meaning of a word, _____ to a dictionary.

2. It is the duty of every person to _____ between right and wrong.

3. Be sure to _____ your topic so that you can cover it well in one paragraph.

4. A newspaper is a great _____ for facts about current events.

**B.** *Follow the directions. Write your responses in complete sentences. Use at least two words from the list above.*

1. List two important ways that you have used to gain knowledge. _____
   _____
   _____

2. Explain how facts can help you judge if someone's opinion is fair and accurate.
   _____
   _____

**C.** *Complete the sentence below. Then, write a short paragraph in which you explain how knowledge can help people to be confident.*

   If people are unfair to you, it's important to remember that _____
   _____
   _____
   _____
   _____
   _____
   _____
   _____

Name _____   Date _____

"Jackie Robinson: Justice at Last" by Geoffrey C. Ward and Ken Burns

# Reading: Ask Questions to Understand Author's Purpose

An **author's purpose** is his or her main reason for writing. One way to understand an author's specific purpose is to ask questions, such as

- What kind of details am I given?
- How are the details presented?
- Why does the author present the details in this way?

Sometimes a work may have a combination of purposes. You may need to look at several passages before you decide on the general purpose of the work. Answering the questions on a graphic organizer will help you determine the author's purpose.

**DIRECTIONS:** *Read each passage from the selection. Then, answer the questions to complete each graphic organizer. The first one is started for you.*

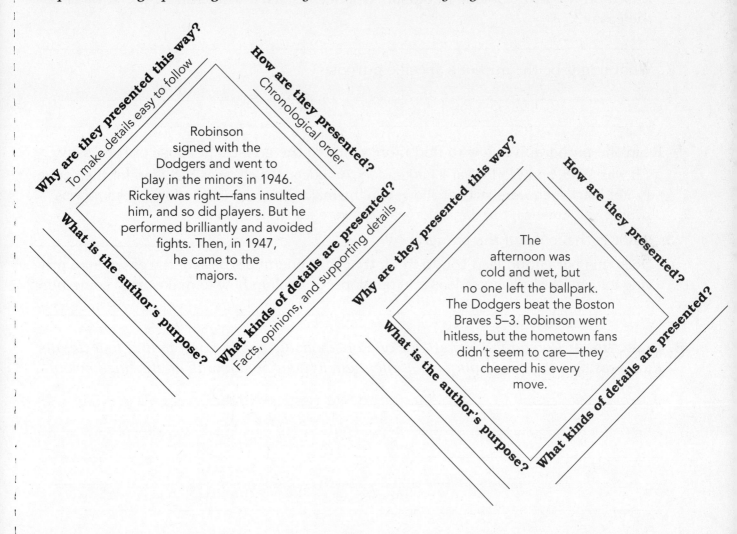

**Why are they presented this way?** To make details easy to follow

**How are they presented?** Chronological order

Robinson signed with the Dodgers and went to play in the minors in 1946. Rickey was right—fans insulted him, and so did players. But he performed brilliantly and avoided fights. Then, in 1947, he came to the majors.

**What kinds of details are presented?** Facts, opinions, and supporting details

**What is the author's purpose?**

**Why are they presented this way?**

**How are they presented?**

The afternoon was cold and wet, but no one left the ballpark. The Dodgers beat the Boston Braves 5–3. Robinson went hitless, but the hometown fans didn't seem to care—they cheered his every move.

**What kinds of details are presented?**

**What is the author's purpose?**

Name _____ Date _____

"**Jackie Robinson: Justice at Last**" by Geoffrey C. Ward and Ken Burns
# Literary Analysis: Expository Essay

An **essay** is a short piece of nonfiction about a specific subject. An **expository essay** has one or more of the following general purposes.

- to provide information
- to discuss ideas and opinions
- to explain how to make or do something

As you read an expository essay, notice how the subject of the essay gives a specific focus to one or more of these general purposes.

**A. DIRECTIONS:** *To help you find the general purpose, the subject, and the author's specific purpose in writing this expository essay, answer the following questions.*

1. Based on the title, "Jackie Robinson: Justice at Last," what will be the subject of the essay?

   _____

2. What might be the author's specific purpose?

   _____

   _____

   Read the paragraph below to find more clues to the general purpose of the essay.

   It was 1945, and World War II had ended. Americans of all races had died for their country. Yet black men were still not allowed in the major leagues. The national pastime was loved by all America, but the major leagues were for white men only.

3. What is the focus of the paragraph? _____

4. Does this paragraph lead you to think that the general purpose of the essay is to provide information, discuss ideas and opinions, or explain how to make or do something?

   _____

**B. DIRECTIONS:** *Reread the essay "Jackie Robinson: Justice at Last" to find four details that develop the writer's purpose. Write them in your own words on the lines below.*

   _____

   _____

   _____

   _____

   _____

   _____

   _____

Name _____ Date _____

### "Jackie Robinson: Justice at Last" by Geoffrey C. Ward and Ken Burns
# Vocabulary Builder

**Word List**

dignity     integrate     petition     prejudiced     retaliated     superb

**A. DIRECTIONS:** *In each item below, think about the meaning of the italicized word, and then answer the question.*

1. Parents have suggested that the middle school *integrate* its athletic teams so girls and boys will play on the same team. Is this a good idea? Why or why not?

   _____

   _____

2. Imagine that you could start a *petition* to ask your school principal to make a change in school rules. What would be the subject of your petition?

   _____

   _____

3. If a student *retaliated* against bullying from another student, what would have been a good course of action for the first student?

   _____

   _____

4. A student has some incorrect ideas that lead him to be *prejudiced* against people from foreign countries. What could you say to him to set him straight?

   _____

5. Your best friend has asked you to recommend a *superb* book for him or her to read. What book would you recommend? Explain your choice.

   _____

6. Before a field trip to a senior citizens' center, a teacher reminded her students to treat each senior citizen with *dignity*. What type of behavior does the teacher expect from her students?

   _____

**B. WORD STUDY:** The Latin prefix *sup-* or *super-* means "greater than normal." Answer each of these questions using a word containing *sup-* or *super-*.

1. How is a superhighway different from a country road?

   _____

2. Is the Supreme Court a higher court than a county court? What clues led to your answer?

   _____

3. Which do you think is larger, a grocery store or a superstore? Explain your answer.

   _____

Name _____ Date _____

**"The Shutout"** by Patricia C. McKissack and Frederick McKissack, Jr.

# Writing About the Big Question

**What is important to know?**

## Big Question Vocabulary

concept     distinguish     examine     guess     judge
knowledge     limit     measure     narrow     observe
purpose     question     refer     source     study

**A.** *Use one or more words from the list above to complete each sentence.*

1. To draw a conclusion, you make a good _____ based on facts and events.

2. When doing research, first _____ the reliability of each source.

3. The _____ of a thesaurus is to provide synonyms and antonyms.

4. Use many sources for facts. Do not _____ your search to only one source.

**B.** *Follow the directions. Write your responses in complete sentences. Use at least two words from the list above.*

1. List two topics or activities that you would enjoy learning more about. For each one, describe one way that you might increase your knowledge. _____

   _____

   _____

   _____

   _____

   _____

2. Imagine that you needed to learn more about the health of a pet. Where would you turn for information? _____

   _____

**C.** *Complete the sentence below. Then, give an example of a problem someone might face, and provide knowledge that would help him or her solve it.*

   Knowing ways to solve problems is important because _____

   _____

   _____

   _____

Name _____   Date _____

**"The Shutout"** by Patricia C. McKissack and Fredrick McKissack, Jr.
# Reading: Ask Questions to Understand Author's Purpose

An **author's purpose** is his or her main reason for writing. Authors often write to inform, to entertain, to persuade, or to reflect. One way to understand an author's specific purpose is to ask questions, such as

- What kind of details am I given?
- How are the details presented?
- Why does the author present the details in this way?

Sometimes, a work may have a combination of purposes. You may need to look at several passages before you decide on the general purpose of the work. Answering the questions on a graphic organizer will help you determine the author's purpose.

**DIRECTIONS:** *Read each passage from the selection. Then, answer the questions to complete each graphic organizer. The first one is started for you.*

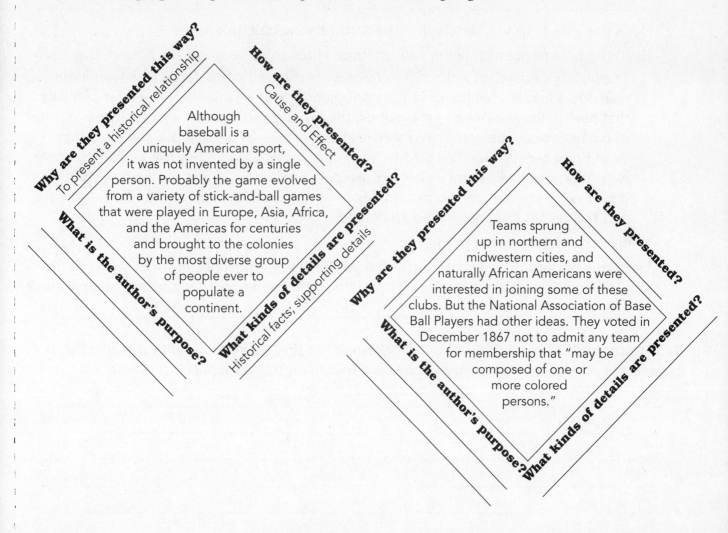

**Why are they presented this way?**
To present a historical relationship

**How are they presented?**
Cause and Effect

Although baseball is a uniquely American sport, it was not invented by a single person. Probably the game evolved from a variety of stick-and-ball games that were played in Europe, Asia, Africa, and the Americas for centuries and brought to the colonies by the most diverse group of people ever to populate a continent.

**What is the author's purpose?**

**What kinds of details are presented?**
Historical facts; supporting details

**Why are they presented this way?**

**How are they presented?**

Teams sprung up in northern and midwestern cities, and naturally African Americans were interested in joining some of these clubs. But the National Association of Base Ball Players had other ideas. They voted in December 1867 not to admit any team for membership that "may be composed of one or more colored persons."

**What is the author's purpose?**

**What kinds of details are presented?**

*"The Shutout"* by Patricia C. McKissack and Fredrick McKissack, Jr.

# Literary Analysis: Expository Essay

An **essay** is a short piece of nonfiction about a specific subject. An **expository essay** has one or more of the following general purposes.

- to provide information
- to discuss ideas and opinions
- to explain how to make or do something

As you read an expository essay, notice how the subject of the essay gives a specific focus to one or more of these general purposes.

**A. DIRECTIONS:** *To help you find the general purpose, the subject, and the author's specific purpose in writing this expository essay, answer the following questions.*

1. Based on the title, "The Shutout," what might the subject of the essay be?

   _____

2. Does the title help you determine the author's specific purpose? _____

   Read the first paragraph below to find more clues to the general purpose of the essay.

   > The history of baseball is difficult to trace because it is embroidered with wonderful anecdotes that are fun but not necessarily supported by fact. There are a lot of myths that persist about baseball—the games, the players, the owners, and the fans—in spite of contemporary research that disproves most of them. For example, the story that West Point cadet Abner Doubleday "invented" baseball in 1839 while at Cooperstown, New York, continues to be widely accepted, even though Doubleday never visited Cooperstown. A number of records and documents show that people were playing stick-and-ball games long before the 1839 date.

3. What is the focus of the paragraph? _____

4. Does this paragraph lead you to think that the general purpose of the essay is to provide information, discuss ideas and opinions, or explain how to make or do something?

   _____

**B. DIRECTIONS:** *Reread the essay "The Shutout" to find four details that develop the writer's purpose. Write them in your own words on the lines below.*

_____

_____

_____

_____

_____

**"The Shutout"** by Patricia C. McKissack and Fredrick McKissack, Jr.
# Vocabulary Builder

**Word List**

> anecdotes    composed    diverse    evolved    infamous    irrational

**A. DIRECTIONS:** *Think about the meaning of the italicized word. Then, answer the question.*

1. Is it possible for a baseball team to be *composed* of players who all want to be stars? Explain your answer.

   _____

   _____

2. Do you like to read *anecdotes* that you can finish quickly, or do you prefer longer stories with more characters and an exciting plot? Give a reason for your answer.

   _____

   _____

3. What might be considered an *irrational* reaction after a baseball player hits a home run?

   _____

   _____

4. Describe one change that happened as American baseball *evolved* over the years.

   _____

   _____

5. If a friend eats hot dogs every day, what suggestions can you make for a more *diverse* diet?

   _____

   _____

6. In your opinion, what character in history, stories, or movies was the most *infamous*? Explain your choice.

   _____

   _____

**B. WORD STUDY:**  The Latin prefix *ir-* often means "not." Answer each of these questions using a word containing *ir-*.

1. How is an *irreligious* person different from a *religious* person?

   _____

2. A shopper tried to redeem a coupon at the supermarket, but the clerk said that the coupon was *irredeemable.* What did the clerk mean?

   _____

3. When I broke my aunt's cup, she told me not to feel bad. "I can always buy a new cup," she said, "but you are *irreplaceable.*" What did she mean?

   _____

Name _____ Date _____

**"Jackie Robinson: Justice at Last"** by Geoffrey C. Ward and Ken Burns
**"The Shutout"** by Patricia C. McKissack and Fredrick McKissack, Jr.
# Integrated Language Skills: Grammar

## Comparisons With Adjectives

Most adjectives have different forms—the **positive** (strong), the **comparative** (stronger), and the **superlative** (strongest). *Comparative adjectives* are used to compare two people, places, or things. *Superlative adjectives* are used to compare three or more people, places, or things.

If a positive adjective contains one or two syllables, you can usually change it into a comparative or superlative adjective by adding the ending *-er* or *-est*. If the positive adjective contains three or more syllables, use the words *more* or *most*.

| Positive | Comparative | Superlative |
|---|---|---|
| tall | This player is *taller* than that one. | These players are the *tallest* of all. |
| funny | Your jokes are *funnier* than mine. | Her jokes are the *funniest* I've heard. |
| interesting | Her story was *more interesting* than her sister's. | The *most interesting* story is the last one in the book. |

**Exceptions:** There are a few adjectives that cannot take comparative or superlative forms. The adjective *unique* means "one of a kind" or "without equal." Something that is unique cannot be compared to anything else. Other adjectives that cannot be used in the comparative or superlative forms include the words *original, complete,* and *perfect.*

**A. PRACTICE:** *In each of the following sentences, underline the comparative or superlative form of the adjective. Write **C** on the line if the sentence contains a comparative, and **S** if it contains a superlative.*

____ 1. Those are the proudest fans I know.
____ 2. Of all those players, he performed most brilliantly.
____ 3. The catcher is nearer to us than the pitcher.
____ 4. Jackie Robinson had a closer acquaintance with racism than he liked.

**B. Writing Application:** *Write a paragraph of five or more sentences about a sport you enjoy playing or watching. Use the comparative or superlative form of an adjective in three of your sentences. Underline each comparative or superlative form that you use.*

_____

_____

_____

_____

Name _____ Date _____

**"Jackie Robinson: Justice at Last"** by Geoffrey C. Ward and Ken Burns
**"The Shutout"** by Patricia C. McKissack and Fredrick McKissack, Jr.

# Integrated Language Skills: Support for Writing a Persuasive Letter

Use the following chart to take notes for your persuasive letter, encouraging a friend to read either "The Shutout" or "Jackie Robinson: Justice at Last."

| Why the Essay Is Interesting and Worthwhile | Supporting Examples and Your Reactions |
|---|---|
| Reason 1: | |
| Reason 2: | |
| Reason 3: | |

Review your notes and organize them in a way that emphasizes the reasons that will be most important to your friend. Then use your notes to write your persuasive letter.

*from* **Something to Declare** by Julia Alvarez
**"A Backwoods Boy"** by Russell Freedman
# Writing About the Big Question

## What is important to know?

### Big Question Vocabulary

| | | | | |
|---|---|---|---|---|
| concept | distinguish | examine | guess | judge |
| knowledge | limit | measure | narrow | observe |
| purpose | question | refer | source | study |

**A.** *Use a word from the list above to answer each question.*

1. Which word means the opposite of *answer*? _____

2. Which word could name both a person and an action? _____

3. Which word means almost the same as *wisdom* and *learning*?

   _____

4. A palindrome is a word that is spelled the same both backward and forward. Which word is a palindrome? _____

**B.** *Answer the questions. Write your responses in complete sentences. Use at least two words from the list above.*

1. What do you do to **distinguish** between facts and opinions? _____

   _____

   _____

   _____

   _____

2. What is the most important thing to know about how to make and keep friends?

   _____

   _____

**C.** *Complete the sentence below. Then, give an example of a nonfiction book that you enjoyed, and provide details about the knowledge that it gave you.*

When I read a work of nonfiction, I enjoy learning about _____

_____

_____

_____

_____

All-in-One Workbook
**144**

*from* **Something to Declare** by Julia Alvarez
**"A Backwoods Boy"** by Russell Freedman

# Literary Analysis: Comparing Biography and Autobiography

**Biography** is a form of nonfiction in which a writer tells the life story of another person. Biography uses the pronouns *he* or *she* and often relies on historical facts. It explains the challenges, successes, or failures a person faced. "A Backwoods Boy," for example, gives facts about the early life of Abraham Lincoln.

In contrast, **autobiography** is a form of nonfiction in which a person tells his or her own life story. Autobiography uses the pronoun *I* and relies on firsthand thoughts and experiences. It often explains the author's actions or gives insights into certain events. For example, the selection from *Something to Declare* gives important insights into Julia Alvarez's work as a writer.

**A. DIRECTIONS:** *Read each passage and answer the questions that follow.*

**from *Something to Declare* by Julia Alvarez**

. . . Jessica Peet, a high-school student, read my first novel, *How the García Girls Lost Their Accents,* in her Vermont Authors class and wanted to know if I considered myself a Vermonter. The Lane Series, our local arts and entertainment series, wanted to know what I might have to say about opera. Share Our Strength was putting together a fund-raising anthology. Did I have anything at all to declare about food?

1. Is this passage biography or autobiography? _____
2. Give three reasons why you know the passage is from a biography or an autobiography.

   A. _____

   B. _____

   C. _____

**from "A Backwoods Boy" by Russell Freedman**

Yes, the law intrigued him. It would give him a chance to rise in the world, to earn a respected place in the community, to live by his wits instead of by hard physical labor.

Yet Lincoln hesitated, unsure of himself because he had so little formal education. That was no great obstacle, his friend Stuart kept telling him.

3. Is this passage biography or autobiography? _____
4. Give three reasons why you know the passage is from a biography or an autobiography.

   A. _____

   B. _____

   C. _____

Name _____ Date _____

# Vocabulary Builder

## Word List

concludes    intrigued    perplexities    quandaries    regarded    treacherous

**A. DIRECTIONS:** *Complete each sentence with a Word List word. Use each word or a form of the word only once.*

1. Her description of the new science-fiction movie _____ me.

2. The guide promised that the steep mountain hike was safe, but it looked _____ to me.

3. "Thanks for coming, folks!" said the announcer. "That last singer _____ our show!"

4. Reading the game's instructions only led to greater _____.

5. Josh _____ his older sister as an expert in basketball.

6. "This _____ will be easily solved," I told Fred as he tried to choose between a hedgehog and a puppy for a pet.

**B. DIRECTIONS:** *Answer each question and provide an explanation for your answer. Include the underlined word or a form of the word in your answer.*

1. When a movie <u>concludes</u>, do you watch the rolling credits at the end? _____

   _____

2. When might going for a walk be considered a <u>treacherous</u> activity? _____

   _____

3. Do you prefer a homework assignment with or without <u>perplexities</u>? _____

   _____

4. If a person was <u>intrigued</u> by a book, would he or she continue to read it? _____

   _____

5. What <u>quandaries</u> might a person face in a foreign country? _____

   _____

6. What would someone have to do to be <u>regarded</u> as a hero? _____

   _____

Name _____ Date _____

from **Something to Declare** by Julia Alvarez
**"A Backwoods Boy"** by Russell Freedman
# Integrated Language Skills: Support for Writing to Compare Literary Works

Before you draft your essay comparing and contrasting what you learned about Julia Alvarez and what you learned about Abraham Lincoln, complete the graphic organizer below.

| | **Julia Alvarez** | **Abraham Lincoln** |
|---|---|---|
| **Important Facts I Learned About the Person** | | |
| **Important Opinion or Beliefs Held by the Person** | | |
| **My Overall Impression of the Person** | | |

Now, use your notes to write an essay comparing and contrasting what you learned about the subject of each selection. Which subject, Alvarez or Lincoln, do you feel you know better? Why?

Name _____ Date _____

# Writing About the Big Question

**What is important to know?**

## Big Question Vocabulary

| | | | | |
|---|---|---|---|---|
| concept | distinguish | examine | guess | judge |
| knowledge | limit | measure | narrow | observe |
| purpose | question | refer | source | study |

**A.** *Use a word from the list above to complete each sentence.*

1. A dictionary is an example of a(n) _____.

2. "The earth is flat" was a(n) _____ that Columbus set out to prove wrong.

3. A seismograph is a device used to _____ the force of an earthquake.

4. A telescope is a device used to _____ stars and planets.

**B.** *Answer the questions. Write your responses in complete sentences. Use at least two words from the list above.*

1. What wild animals do you often **observe** in your local environment? _____

   _____

   _____

2. What mistakes do humans do that **limit** the chances of wild animals' survival?

   _____

   _____

**C.** *Complete the sentences below. Then, explain why our knowledge of endangered animals is important.*

People who work to save animals from extinction must **study** _____.

The **knowledge** they gain from their studies can be used to _____

_____

_____

_____

_____

_____

_____

**"Turkeys"** by Bailey White
# Reading: Identify Key Details to Determine the Main Idea

The **main idea** is the most important point in a literary work or passage. Sometimes the author states the main idea directly. Other times, however, you must figure it out by **identifying key details** in the text. Asking the following three questions can help you find the key details.

- What is this literary work about?
- What details are repeated throughout the selection?
- What details are related to other details in the selection?

For example, an essay about a person's real-life experience with wild turkeys might include details such as when and why the event happened, a description of the wild turkeys, and how the person thought and felt about the event during and after it happened. The key details might point to a main idea of *Wild turkeys are a symbol of wilderness* or *The experience with turkeys gave me a connection to wildlife I'll never forget*. Note that not every paragraph will contain a key detail. To help you find the key details, ask the three questions listed above.

**DIRECTIONS:** *Use the graphic organizer below to record key details as you read "Turkeys." The details will help you determine the main idea. The first key detail is done for you.*

| 1. Key detail |
|---|
| In those days, during the 1950s, the big concern of ornithologists in our area was the wild turkey. |

| 2. Key detail |
|---|
|  |

| 3. Key detail |
|---|
|  |

| 4. Main idea |
|---|
|  |

"**Turkeys**" by Bailey White

# Literary Analysis: Author's Influences

An **author's influences** are the cultural and historical factors that affect his or her writing. These factors may include the time and place of an author's birth, the author's cultural background, or world events that happened during the author's lifetime. For example, growing up on a farm near a small town in the South during the 1950s might have influenced Bailey White's ideas about nature. As you read, look for details that indicate an author's influences.

**DIRECTIONS:** *Three of the factors that may have influenced Bailey White are listed below. Answer the questions following each one.*

1. **Bailey White still lives in the house where she was born and raised.**

   How do you think this factor might have influenced White's writing?

   _____

   _____

   _____

2. **White's mother was a farmer and her father was a writer.**

   A. How do you think these factors might have influenced White's writing?

   _____

   _____

   _____

   B. How do you know that White's mother had an unusual closeness to nature?

   _____

   _____

   _____

3. **White lives close to nature in the pinewoods of southern Georgia.**

   Find one detail in the essay that shows how she feels about nature. Write it on the lines below.

   _____

   _____

   _____

Name _____ Date _____

"Turkeys" by Bailey White
# Vocabulary Builder

## Word List

demise     descendants     dilution     incubator
methods     sensible     vigilance

**A. DIRECTIONS:** *Circle the letter of the word or phrase that is closest in meaning to each word in CAPITAL LETTERS.*

1. SENSIBLE:
   A. loving      B. sensitive      C. careless      D. wise

2. METHODS:
   A. ways      B. studies      C. questions      D. traits

3. VIGILANCE:
   A. attack      B. nonsense      C. watchfulness      D. guardianship

4. DILUTION:
   A. enlarge      B. sensitive      C. intelligence      D. process of weakening

5. DEMISE:
   A. beginning      B. death      C. health      D. sickness

6. INCUBATOR:
   A. heated container      B. refrigerator      C. wastebasket      D. suitcase

7. DESCENDANTS:
   A. grandparents      B. ancestors      C. offspring      D. neighbors

**B. WORD STUDY:** The Latin suffix *-ible* means "tending to or capable of." Use the context of the sentence and what you know about the suffix *-ible* to answer each question.

1. The teacher handed back my paper and said, "I can't read this. Please rewrite it so that it is *legible*." What did she mean?

   _____

2. Which is more *flexible*—a log or a thin stick? Explain your answer.

   _____

3. Is sixteen *divisible* by four? Explain why or why not.

   _____

"**Langston Terrace**" by Eloise Greenfield
# Writing About the Big Question

**What is important to know?**

## Big Question Vocabulary

| | | | | |
|---|---|---|---|---|
| concept | distinguish | examine | guess | judge |
| knowledge | limit | measure | narrow | observe |
| purpose | question | refer | source | study |

**A.** *Use one or more words from the list above to complete each set of related words.*

1. conclude, answer, decide, _____

2. inspect, analyze, search, _____

3. decrease, restrict, lessen, _____

4. watch, see, look, _____

**B.** *Follow the directions. Write your responses in complete sentences. Use at least two words from the list above.*

1. Describe a piece of writing that you have done. What was its **purpose**? _____

   _____

   _____

   _____

2. How did you achieve your purpose, and what **knowledge** helped you do that?

   _____

   _____

   _____

   _____

**C.** *Complete the sentence below. Then, explain why such knowledge would be important to learn before the move.*

Before a family moves to a new neighborhood, they might **question** people who already live there about _____

_____

_____

_____

_____

Name _____  Date _____

"**Langston Terrace**" by Eloise Greenfield

# Reading: Identify Key Details to Determine the Main Idea

The **main idea** is the most important point in a literary work or passage. Sometimes the author states the main idea directly. Other times you can figure out the main idea by **identifying key details** in the text. Asking the following three questions can help you find the key details.

- What is this literary work about?
- What details are repeated throughout the selection?
- What details are related to other details in the selection?

For example, an essay about moving to a house in a new neighborhood might include details about why the move is necessary, how the neighborhood looks, and what the new house is like. The key details might point to a main idea of *The new neighborhood is friendly* or *We found a home at last.* Note that not every paragraph will contain a key detail. To help you find the key details, ask the three questions listed above.

**DIRECTIONS:** *Use this organizer to record key details as you read "Langston Terrace." The details will help you determine the main idea. The first key detail is done for you.*

**1. Key detail**

    I fell in love with Langston Terrace the very first time I saw it.

**2. Key detail**

**3. Key detail**

**4. Key detail**

**5. Main idea**

"**Langston Terrace**" by Eloise Greenfield
# Literary Analysis: Author's Influences

An **author's influences** are the cultural and historical factors that affect his or her writing. These factors may include the time and place of an author's birth, the author's cultural background, or world events that happened during the author's lifetime. For example, the Great Depression, which lasted through much of the 1930s, might have influenced the ideas of an author who grew up at that time. As you read, look for details that indicate an author's influences.

**DIRECTIONS:** *Two of the cultural and historical factors that may have influenced Eloise Greenfield are listed below. Read the information about each possible influence and answer the questions that follow.*

1. **Growing up during the Great Depression**

   Eloise Greenfield was born in 1929 at the beginning of the Great Depression. The years 1929–1940 were a period of financial hardship for many people in the United States. Businesses and banks closed. People lost their jobs, their savings, and their houses. They stood in long lines waiting to get bread. Many were homeless and starving. The Great Depression affected many people, especially racial minorities who were "last hired, first fired."

   **A.** Write one detail from the information above that tells you that the Greenfield family had little money.

   _____

   **B.** Now think about the selection "Langston Terrace." How do you think the event of the Great Depression influenced Greenfield's writing?

   _____

2. **Growing up in a working-class African American family**

   Greenfield was the oldest of five children in a close family with many relatives. Both of her parents were high school graduates who had grown up in the South. For many years, Greenfield went back to the South every summer to visit family members there. Like most African Americans at that time, Greenfield attended segregated schools and lived in segregated housing at Langston Terrace. She graduated from high school right after the end of World War II.

   **A.** Write one detail from the information above that tells you something about Greenfield's family.

   _____

   **B.** Think again about the selection "Langston Terrace." How do you think the time and place of Greenfield's childhood influenced her writing?

   _____

   _____

"**Langston Terrace**" by Eloise Greenfield
# Vocabulary Builder

**Word List**

applications    choral    community    homey    resident    reunion

**A. DIRECTIONS:** *Circle the letter of the word or phrase that is closest in meaning to the word in CAPITAL LETTERS.*

1. APPLICATIONS:
   A. jobs
   B. requests
   C. tools
   D. methods

2. RESIDENT:
   A. member
   B. manager
   C. officer
   D. inhabitant

3. REUNION:
   A. annual meeting
   B. coming together again
   C. show of support
   D. charity event

4. COMMUNITY:
   A. resort
   B. courage
   C. city
   D. happiness

5. CHORAL:
   A. singing
   B. dancing
   C. reading
   D. artistic

6. HOMEY:
   A. ugly
   B. beautiful
   C. modern
   D. cozy

**B. WORD STUDY:** The suffix *-ent* can form an adjective. It means "has," "shows," or "does." Use the context of the sentence and what you know about the suffix *-ent* to answer each question.

1. The coach told me I'd pitch in tomorrow's baseball game. "You're a great pitcher," he said. "I'm *confident* that you'll do a great job." What did he mean?

   _____

2. If a building catches on fire, is there an *urgent* need to call for help? Explain your answer.

   _____

3. Is getting a perfect score on a test *dependent* upon having all the answers correct? Explain.

   _____

Name _____ Date _____

**"Turkeys"** by Bailey White
**"Langston Terrace"** by Eloise Greenfield
# Integrated Language Skills: Grammar

## Adverbs

An **adverb** is a word that modifies or describes a verb, an adjective, or another adverb. Adverbs answer the questions *how, when, where,* and *to what extent*. Many adverbs end in the suffix *-ly*.

| Adverb | Word It Modifies | Question It Answers |
|---|---|---|
| We waited <u>patiently</u>. | waited (verb) | How did we wait? |
| He <u>often</u> travels by train. | travels (verb) | When does he travel by train? |
| The pigeons flew <u>away</u>. | flew (verb) | Where did the pigeons go? |
| Jane was <u>very</u> tired from her trip. | tired (adjective) | To what extent was she tired? |

**A. PRACTICE:** *Underline the adverb in each sentence. Then, circle the word that the adverb modifies.*

1. Paul accidentally forgot his best friend's birthday.
2. At the end of the day, we were quite tired.
3. We were extremely disappointed to learn that the show had been cancelled.
4. I will finish my exams tomorrow.
5. He patiently taught the children how to read and write.

**B. Writing Application:** *Describe something that happened at school. Use at least three adverbs in your description.*

_____

_____

_____

_____

_____

_____

_____

_____

_____

_____

**"Turkeys"** by Bailey White
**"Langston Terrace"** by Eloise Greenfield

# Integrated Language Skills: Support for Writing a Journal Entry

For your journal entry, first decide on the event from the essay about which you want to write. Then, use the graphic organizer below to jot down words and phrases that describe your thoughts and feelings about the event.

The event: _____

feel that

think that

**Author's reaction, . . .**

feel that

think that

Use your notes to write a journal entry that describes the event and your reactions as one of the writers. Remember to write from the point of view of one of the writers.

Name _____ Date _____

"La Leña Buena" by John Phillip Santos
# Writing About the Big Question

**What is important to know?**

## Big Question Vocabulary

| | | | | |
|---|---|---|---|---|
| concept | distinguish | examine | guess | judge |
| knowledge | limit | measure | narrow | observe |
| purpose | question | refer | source | study |

**A.** *Use one or more words from the list above to complete each sentence.*

1. A knife is used to cut. This job is the knife's _____.

2. Because there are not many cookies, I will _____ each child's share to two.

3. How do you _____ a leopard from a tiger? One has spots, and the other has stripes.

4. An almanac is an excellent _____ for facts about different nations of the world.

**B.** *Follow the directions. Write your responses in complete sentences. Use at least two words from the list above.*

1. List two different times when another person helped you increase your knowledge.
   _____
   _____

2. Pick one of these experiences. Explain why this knowledge was important to you.
   _____
   _____
   _____

**C.** *Complete the sentence below. Then, explain why the topics of study would be helpful to you.*

   If I wanted to be an expert at _____, I would **study** _____.
   _____
   _____
   _____
   _____
   _____

Name _____  Date _____

"La Leña Buena" by John Phillip Santos

# Reading: Determine Main Idea by Distinguishing Between Important and Unimportant Details

The **main idea** is the most important point in a literary work. Individual paragraphs or sections may also have a central idea that supports the main idea of the work. To determine the main idea, look at details in the story and **distinguish between important and unimportant details**. Important details are also called supporting details. They are minor pieces of information that tell more about the main idea.

- Ask yourself questions about details in a literary work. For example: *Why did the author include this detail? Does this detail help readers better understand the main idea?*
- Keep in mind that not all details support the main idea.

**DIRECTIONS:** *From the title and the opening paragraph of "La Leña Buena," you know that the main idea has something to do with "good wood." Read the example passage below. The important details, especially those about trees or wood, have been underlined.*

**Example:** Mesquite, and even better, cedar—these are noble, hard woods. They burn hot and long. Their smoke is fragrant. And if you know how to do it, they make exquisite charcoal.

*Now read passages 1 and 2 below, and underline the details that seem important to you. Then, complete the chart that follows the passages.*

1. Good wood is like a jewel, and old Tío Abrán knew wood the way a jeweler knows stones. In northern Coahuila, from Múzquiz to Rosita, his charcoal was highly regarded for its sweet, long-burning fire.

2. Abrán was one of the last of the Garcias to come north. Somewhere around 1920, he finally had to come across the border with his family. He was weary of the treacheries along the roads that had become a part of life in the sierra towns since the beginning of the revolution ten years earlier. Most of the land near town had been deforested and the only wood he could find around Palaú was huisache.

| | One Important Detail | One Unimportant Detail |
|---|---|---|
| Example | Mesquite and cedar are hardwoods that make good charcoal. | Their smoke is fragrant. |
| Passage 1 | | |
| Passage 2 | | |

What is the main idea of the two passages from "La Leña Buena"? _____

_____

Name _____ Date _____

"La Leña Buena" by John Phillip Santos
# Literary Analysis: Mood

**Mood** is the overall feeling a literary work produces in a reader. For example, the mood of a work may be happy, sad, scary, or hopeful. To create a particular mood, writers carefully choose words and create word pictures that appeal to the senses.

Some literary works present a single mood throughout a selection. In other works, the mood may change as the piece progresses.

**A. DIRECTIONS:** *Read the following passages, and circle the words, phrases, or details that help create a certain mood for the reader. On the line below each passage, write a sentence to describe the mood.*

1. Good wood is like a jewel, Tío Abrán, my great-grandfather Jacobo's twin brother, used to say. Huisache burns fast, in twisting yellow flames, engulfing the log in a cocoon of fire. It burns brightly, so it is sought after for Easter bonfires.

   Mood: _____

2. Most of the land near town had been deforested and the only wood he could find around Palaú was huisache. To find any of the few pastures left with arbors of mesquite trees, he had to take the unpaved mountain road west from Múzquiz, along a route where many of the militantes had their camps.

   Mood: _____

**B. DIRECTIONS:** *Use the organizer below to record other details in "La Leña Buena" that help to create a mood. Use the space in the center to name the mood or feeling that you get when you read the selection. Then, jot down three details that contribute to this mood.*

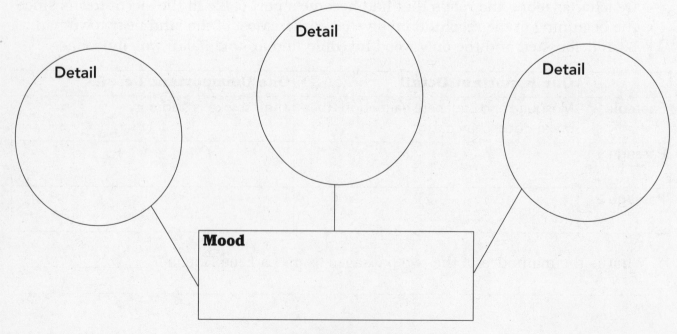

Name _____  Date _____

"La Leña Buena" by John Phillip Santos
# Vocabulary Builder

**Word List**

confiscated    engulfing    fragrant    reluctantly    revolution    treacheries

**A. DIRECTIONS:** *Use a dictionary or a thesaurus to help you find a* **synonym,** *a word that means the same or nearly the same, for each vocabulary word. Then, use each vocabulary word in a sentence that makes the meaning of the word clear.*

Example: **exquisite**    synonym: beautiful
Sentence: The antique ring had one <u>exquisite</u> pearl set in gold.

1. **engulfing**    synonym: _____
Sentence: _____

2. **fragrant**    synonym: _____
Sentence: _____

3. **confiscated**    synonym: _____
Sentence: _____

4. **reluctantly**    synonym: _____
Sentence: _____

5. **revolution**    synonym: _____
Sentence: _____

6. **treacheries**    synonym: _____
Sentence: _____

**B. WORD STUDY:** The Latin root *-volv-* means "to roll or turn." Answer each question.

1. What turn or change took place because of the American *Revolution*?

_____

2. Why do we describe the moon as *revolving* around Earth?

_____

3. What happens to a problem if it turns from a simple one to an *involved* one?

_____

Name _____  Date _____

# Writing About the Big Question

**What is important to know?**

## Big Question Vocabulary

| | | | | |
|---|---|---|---|---|
| concept | distinguish | examine | guess | judge |
| knowledge | limit | measure | narrow | observe |
| purpose | question | refer | source | study |

**A.** *Give an example of each of the following.*

1. A **concept** about our planet: _____

2. A reliable Internet research **source**: _____

3. A device used to **measure**: _____

4. Something that you often **observe** on your way to school _____

**B.** *Answer the questions. Write your responses in complete sentences. Use at least two words from the list above.*

1. What steps do you follow to study for a social studies or science test?

_____

_____

_____

_____

2. How do these steps help you remember the facts you need to complete the test well?

_____

_____

_____

_____

**C.** *Complete the sentence below. Then, suggest a new rule that you would put in place at school if you were the principal.*

The **purpose** of having rules at school is _____

_____

_____

_____

_____

Name _____ Date _____

*from* **The Pigman & Me** by Paul Zindel

# Reading: Determine Main Idea by Distinguishing Between Important and Unimportant Details

The **main idea** is the most important point in a literary work. Individual paragraphs or sections may also have a central idea that supports the main idea of the work. To determine the main idea, look at details in the story and **distinguish between important and unimportant details.** Important details are also called supporting details. They are minor pieces of information that tell more about the main idea.

- Ask yourself questions about details in a literary work. For example: *Why did the author include this detail? Does this detail help readers better understand the main idea?*
- Keep in mind that not all details support the main idea.

**DIRECTIONS:** *Read the example from* The Pigman & Me. *The important details, those that have something to do with trouble that is about to happen, have been underlined.*

**Example:** When trouble came to me, it didn't involve anybody I thought it would. It involved the nice, normal, smart boy by the name of John Quinn. Life does that to us a lot. Just when we think something awful's going to happen one way, it throws you a curve and the something awful happens another way.

*Now read passages 1 and 2 below, and underline the details that seem important to you. Then, complete the chart that follows the passages.*

1. What I didn't know was that you were allowed to sign out the paddles for only fifteen minutes per period so more kids could get a chance to use them. I just didn't happen to know that little rule, and Richard Cahill didn't think to tell me about it. Richard was getting a drink from the water fountain when John Quinn came up to me and told me I had to give him my paddle.

2. That was when I did something berserk. I was so wound up and frightened that I didn't think, and I struck out at him with my right fist. I had forgotten I was holding the paddle, and it smacked into his face, giving him an instant black eye. John was shocked. I was shocked. Richard Cahill came running back to me and he was shocked.

| | **One Important Detail** | **One Unimportant Detail** |
|---|---|---|
| **Example** | It involved the nice, normal, smart boy by the name of John Quinn. | Life does that to us a lot. |
| **Passage 1** | | |
| **Passage 2** | | |

What is the main idea of the two passages from *The Pigman & Me?* _____

_____

Name _____ Date _____

*from* **The Pigman & Me** by Paul Zindel
## Literary Analysis: Mood

**Mood** is the overall feeling a literary work produces in a reader. For example, the mood of a work may be happy, sad, scary, or hopeful. To create a particular mood, writers carefully choose words and create word pictures that appeal to the senses.

Some literary works present a single mood throughout a selection. In other works, the mood may change as the piece progresses.

**A. DIRECTIONS:** *Read the following passages, and circle the words, phrases, or details that help create a certain mood for the reader. On the line below each passage, write a sentence to describe the mood.*

1. That was all he had to say, and I spilled out each and every horrifying detail. Nonno Frankie let me babble on and on. He looked as if he understood exactly how I felt and wasn't going to call me stupid or demented or a big yellow coward. When I didn't have another word left in me, I just shut up and stared down at the ground.

   Mood: _____

2. "Yes, you curse this John Quinn. You tell him, 'May your left ear wither and fall into your right pocket!' And you tell him he looks like a fugitive from a brain gang! And tell him he has a face like a mattress! And that an espresso coffee cup would fit on his head like a sombrero. And then you just give him the big Sicilian surprise!"

   Mood: _____

**B. Directions:** *Use the organizer below to record other details in* The Pigman & Me *that help to create a mood. Use the space in the center to name the mood or feeling you get when you read the selection. Then, jot down three details that contribute to this mood.*

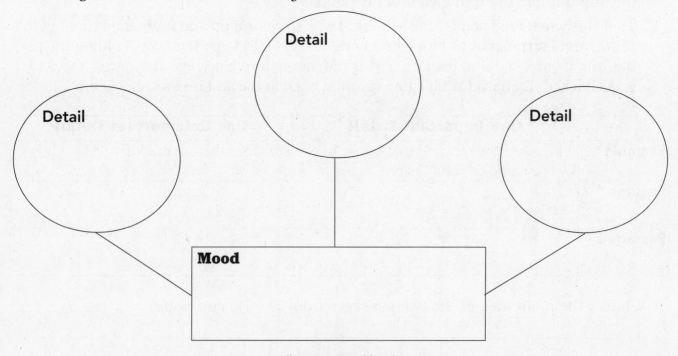

Name _____ Date _____

*from* **The Pigman & Me** by Paul Zindel
# Vocabulary Builder

## Word List

condemnation    demented    distorted    exact    observant    undulating

**A. DIRECTIONS:** *Use a dictionary or a thesaurus to help you find a* **synonym,** *a word that means the same or nearly the same, for each vocabulary word. Then, use each vocabulary word in a sentence that makes the meaning of the word clear.*

Example: **berserk**    synonym: crazy

Sentence: Berserk with anger, the bear fought off the attack on her cub.

1. **exact** (used as a verb)    synonym: _____

   Sentence: _____

2. **undulating**    synonym: _____

   Sentence: _____

3. **distorted** (used as an adjective)    synonym: _____

   Sentence: _____

4. **demented**    synonym: _____

   Sentence: _____

5. **observant**    synonym: _____

   Sentence: _____

6. **condemnation**    synonym: _____

   Sentence: _____

**B. WORD STUDY:** The Latin root *-tort-* means "to twist out of shape." Answer each question.

1. When a snake coils up to rest, it is in a *tortile* position. What does that word mean?

   _____

2. *Tortellini* are pieces of pasta twisted into little pouches. Why were they given that name?

   _____

3. If you suddenly got good news, how might you *contort* your face to show your feelings?

   _____

Name _____ Date _____

"**La Leña Buena**" by John Phillip Santos
*from* **The Pigman & Me** by Paul Zindel
# Integrated Language Skills: Grammar

## Conjunctions and Interjections

**Conjunctions:** A **conjunction** is a word that connects other words or groups of words.

- A **coordinating conjunction** connects similar kinds or groups of words. The coordinating conjunctions are *and, but, for, or, nor, so,* and *yet.*
- A **subordinating conjunction** connects ideas by making one dependent on the other. Common subordinating conjunctions are *after, although, as, as if, because, before, if, since, when, where, whenever, wherever, while, unless,* and *until.*

**A. Practice:** *Circle the conjunction in each sentence. On the line, write* C *if it is a coordinating conjunction or* S *if it is a subordinating conjunction.*

____ 1. Mrs. White loved to cook, so she made pies for everyone.

____ 2. Randi saw the eggs hatching when she visited the farm.

____ 3. Bailey felt as if she had done something important.

____ 4. Linda ran down the hill, and her dog ran too.

**Interjections:** An **interjection** is a word or group of words that expresses sudden excitement or strong feeling. A strong interjection is followed by an exclamation point. A comma follows a mild interjection. When the interjection is followed by a comma, it is connected to the sentence that follows it.

**Strong interjection—separated from following sentence:** *Please!* Won't you help us?

**Mild interjection—connected to following sentence:** *Well,* maybe it is time to go.

**B. Practice:** *Circle the interjection in each of the following sentences. Then, write whether it is a strong interjection or mild interjection.*

1. Cool! Those turkeys were born to fly. _____

2. Oh, no! I can't see them anymore! _____

3. Hey, we always knew they could do it. _____

**C. Writing Application:** *Write a brief account of an experience you had with an animal or insect. Use at least two coordinating conjunctions, two subordinating conjunctions, and two interjections in your account. Underline those parts of speech.*

_____

_____

_____

_____

_____

Name _____ Date _____

"**La Leña Buena**" by John Phillip Santos
*from* **The Pigman & Me** by Paul Zindel
# Integrated Language Skills: Support for Writing
# a Problem-and-Solution Essay

Use the following chart to write your problem-and-solution essay to help a newcomer adjust to either a new school or a new country. Write a problem that the newcomer might face on the line provided. Then, list the possible solutions in the chart. Include evidence to support each solution.

**Problem:** _____

_____

| Solutions to the Problem |
|---|
|  |
|  |
|  |
|  |
|  |
|  |
|  |
|  |

Name _____     Date _____

"**Letter from a Concentration Camp**" by Yoshiko Uchida
"**Letter to Scottie**" by F. Scott Fitzgerald

# Writing About the Big Question

**What is important to know?**

## Big Question Vocabulary

| concept | distinguish | examine | guess | judge |
|---|---|---|---|---|
| knowledge | limit | measure | narrow | observe |
| purpose | question | refer | source | study |

**A.** *Write a word or phrase that is an antonym (opposite) for each of the words shown.*

1. question _____

2. narrow _____

3. knowledge _____

4. observe _____

**B.** *Answer the questions. Write your responses in complete sentences. Use at least two words from the list above.*

1. What would you ask if you had the chance to **question** the author of these selections?

   _____

   _____

2. How might the author's answer increase your knowledge and understanding?

   _____

   _____

**C.** *Complete the sentence below. Then, explain why such knowledge would be important to you.*

   If somebody I care about was far away and wrote me a letter, I would want to know _____

   _____

   _____

   _____

   _____

   _____

   _____

   _____

## "Letter From a Concentration Camp" by Yoshiko Uchida
### "Letter to Scottie" by F. Scott Fitzgerald
# Literary Analysis: Comparing Authors' Styles

An **author's style** is his or her usual way of writing. Style is influenced by

- **Words** (or diction): Writers choose words that are formal or informal, ornate or plain, technical or ordinary. Words such as *anyway* and *stuff* in "Letter From a Concentration Camp" show the author's use of informal words.
- **Arrangement of Words:** Words can be organized into short, clipped sentences or long, thoughtful ones.
- **Emotion/Tone:** The author's attitude toward a subject affects style. In "Letter to Scottie," the author's style shows both serious concern and playful affection for his daughter.
- **Figurative Language:** Some writers use poetic "word pictures" to present ideas in fresh ways. Others use words that mean exactly what they say. To give a clear picture of life in the camp in "Letter From a Concentration Camp," the author uses plain words.

**DIRECTIONS:** *Read the passages. Then, answer the questions that follow.*

### *from* "Letter From a Concentration Camp" by Yoshiko Uchida

Hey, do me a favor? Go pet my dog, Rascal, for me. He's probably wondering why I had to leave him with Mrs. Harper next door. Tell him I'll be back to get him for sure. It's just that I don't know when. There's a rumor we're getting shipped to some desert—probably in Utah. But don't worry, when this stupid war is over, I'm coming home to California and nobody's ever going to kick me out again! You just wait and see!

### *from* "Letter to Scottie" by F. Scott Fitzgerald

All I believe in in life is the rewards for virtue (according to your talents) and the *punishments* for not fulfilling your duties, which are doubly costly. If there is such a volume in the camp library, will you ask Mrs. Tyson to let you look up a sonnet of Shakespeare's in which the line occurs *"Lilies that fester smell far worse than weeds."*

1. A. Which writer uses a more informal style? _____

   B. Write two words or phrases from the informal passage that contribute to this style.

   _____

2. A. Which writer uses a more formal style? _____

   B. Write two words or phrases from the formal passage that contribute to this style.

   _____

3. An author's sentences might be short, clipped sentences or long, thoughtful sentences.

   A. Uchida's sentences are _____ and _____.

   B. Fitzgerald's sentences are _____ and _____.

4. Which writer's style shows greater emotion? Why? _____

   _____

**"Letter From a Concentration Camp"** by Yoshiko Uchida
**"Letter to Scottie"** by F. Scott Fitzgerald
# Vocabulary Builder

## Word List

composed    documentation    hearing    misery    regret    rudimentary

**A. DIRECTIONS:** *Match each word to its definition. Write the letter of the definition on the line to the left of the word.*

___ 1. documentation        A. great sorrow
___ 2. rudimentary          B. chance to give evidence
___ 3. regret               C. be sorry for
___ 4. hearing              D. supporting evidence
___ 5. composed             E. not fully developed
___ 6. misery               F. made up

**B. DIRECTIONS:** *Answer each question and provide an explanation for your answer. Use the underlined word in your answer.*

1. Which group would hold a <u>hearing</u>—a rock band or a town council?

   _____

2. Why would you not give a piano concert if you had <u>rudimentary</u> piano skills?

   _____

3. Would you feel <u>regret</u> if you said something rude to a friend?

   _____

4. Do you need to show <u>documentation</u> to enter your own home?

   _____

5. Might a soccer team be <u>composed</u> of a field, a ball, and a goal?

   _____

6. Would discovering gold cause <u>misery</u> for an explorer?

   _____

Name _____ Date _____

**"Letter From a Concentration Camp"** by Yoshiko Uchida
**"Letter to Scottie"** by F. Scott Fitzgerald

# Integrated Language Skills: Support for Writing to Compare Literary Works

Before you draft your essay comparing and contrasting the two writers' styles, complete the graphic organizers below.

| Formal or Conversational Style? | |
|---|---|
| Uchida: _____ | Fitzgerald: _____ |
| Examples: <br><br> 1. <br><br><br> 2. <br><br><br> 3. | Examples: <br><br> 1. <br><br><br> 2. <br><br><br> 3. |

| Images (or "Word Pictures") Used | |
|---|---|
| Uchida | Fitzgerald |
| Examples: <br><br> 1. <br><br><br> 2. <br><br><br> 3. | Examples: <br><br> 1. <br><br><br> 2. <br><br><br> 3. |

| Writer's Personality | |
|---|---|
| Uchida | Fitzgerald |
| Details that show personality: <br><br> 1. <br><br><br> 2. <br><br><br> 3. | Details that show personality: <br><br> 1. <br><br><br> 2. <br><br><br> 3. |

Now, use your notes to write an essay comparing and contrasting the two writers' styles.

 **BQ Tunes**

## Between Us, performed by Natalia DiSario

We don't, need words no we don't

Between us, between you and me oh

I can't survive the way you stare at me cause

I can, I can read your eyes

They're telling, showing what's inside and

Showing all the things you're scared to share with me

**Verse 1:**

I can tell when our eyes joined that we made a **connection**, first time in a long time that I fell for perfection / And every part of your persona caught my attention cause it **corresponds** with mine, with similar perspectives / And I know we haven't yet shared any **dialogue**, but don't need conversation to get caught off guard / Every time you smile I feel my heart stop and all the smiles I share just means I like you a lot / See, our **communication** has a lot of expressions, and if you like we can exchange thoughts every second / Some of your **gestures** and body language keep me guessin while your striking eyes leave a branding impression / We have our own **language** when we communicate with each other makes me wanna take time to know one another / But for now we're good with **nonverbal** relations cause we don't need words or have to give explanations /

We don't, need words no we don't

Between us, between you and me oh

I can't survive the way you stare at me cause

I can, I can read your eyes

They're telling, showing what's inside and

Showing all the things you're scared to share with me

**Verse 2:**

See I'm just waiting on you to **reveal** your emotions, show me how you feel without any caution / **Share** every piece of my mind, every part, every portion, cause I see depth in your eyes that I wanna get lost in / Every **expression** between us declares how we feel, without **verbalizing** any words that it's real / It's like we symbolize something ideal, we represent a chemistry that can't be concealed / Words could never quote or refer to what we have, or how my heart feels every time that we laugh / Wish I could **convey** the message that I'm glad, but I think you get the idea with the fun that we have / Not everybody loves unconditional, but when I see you everyone else is minimal / Would

*Continued*

have never seen this coming but now I have a **visual,** cause even without words what's
between us is visible /

We don't, need words no we don't
Between us, between you and me oh
I can't survive the way you stare at me cause
I can, I can read your eyes
They're telling, showing what's inside and
Showing all the things you're scared to share with me

_____

Song Title: **Between Us**
Artist / Performed by Natalia DiSario
Lyrics by Natalia DiSario
Music composed by Mike Pandolfo, Wonderful
Produced by Mike Pandolfo, Wonderful
Executive Producer: Keith London, Defined Mind

All-in-One Workbook
**173**

# Unit 4: Poetry
# Big Question Vocabulary—1

### The Big Question: Do we need words to communicate well?

One of the main ways in which people exchange information is by using words. Words can be a clear way of telling others what is on your mind.

**communicate:** to exchange information with people using words, signs, or writing

**dialogue:** a conversation or a discussion between two or more people

**language:** a system of communication by written or spoken words that is used by the people of a particular country or area

**quote:** to repeat exactly what someone said or wrote

**verbal:** words spoken rather than written

**DIRECTIONS:** Answer the questions using the number of vocabulary words specified. You can use words more than once, but you must use all five vocabulary words.

"Use your own words!" Rosa shouted at Phil. He insisted on always copying the words of others. How was Rosa supposed to know what Phil was really thinking if they couldn't have a real conversation?

1. What problem is Rosa having with her friend Phil? Use at least two of the vocabulary words in your answer.

   _____

   _____

   _____

"Don't shout at me and walk away," Phil responded.  "Let's talk about this!"

2. What was Phil suggesting? Use at least one vocabulary word in your answer.

   _____

   _____

Rosa sat across the table from Phil. She began speaking. She told him that he should have confidence in his ability to express himself in words. Phil listened and agreed to speak his mind instead of hiding behind the words of others.

3. What did Phil agree to do? Use at least two vocabulary words in your answer.

   _____

   _____

   _____

Name _____ Date _____

# Unit 4: Poetry
# Big Question Vocabulary—2

**The Big Question: Do we need words to communicate well?**

Communication between people takes place in many ways that do not involve words or speaking. Although we may not be aware of it, we are reading and interpreting signals from people all through the day.

**expression:** a look on someone's face or what someone writes, says, or does that shows you what he or she feels or thinks

**gesture:** n. a movement of a person's arms, hands, or head that shows what he or she means or feels; v. to move your arms, hands, or head to tell someone something

**nonverbal:** not involving words

**symbolize:** to represent something

**visual:** able to be seen

**DIRECTIONS:** Finish the following story in the first person. Use your imagination and all five vocabulary words listed above.

> You wake up extra late on a Saturday morning and stretch luxuriously in your bed. You have a day of fun ahead of you. You are planning to go bowling with your friends and then go to the best pizza place in town for a slice. First, you will have to talk to your parents about your plans and ask them for a ride to the bowling alley.  But that should be no problem. You hear your whole family talking and having breakfast. You get up, get dressed, and brush your teeth, and then you join your family at the breakfast table. "Good morning," your Dad says cheerily. You grin and open your mouth to answer, but nothing happens. No sound comes out. You try again. Still no sound. What is wrong with you? And, more important, how are you going to ask your parents about your plans?

_____

_____

_____

_____

_____

_____

_____

Name _____     Date _____

# Unit 4: Poetry
# Big Question Vocabulary—3

**The Big Question: Do we need words to communicate well?**

People become friends and feel close when they trust one another enough to share secrets. The communication that happens between people who are close is a special kind of communication.

**connection:** a situation in which two people understand and like each other

**correspond:** to communicate by letter

**message:** a spoken or written piece of information that you send to another person

**reveal:** to make a secret known

**share:** to tell others about an idea or a problem

**DIRECTIONS:** Think about someone that you are very close to. It could be a friend or a family member. Put the person's name in the center circle. Then, fill in information in the surrounding circles using the words in parentheses.

Brian told his old friend Steve,

**1. (isolate, culture)**

Steve advised Brian to find others with similar interests so that he will meet people. He said

**2. (involve, group)**

Brian was grateful for Steve's advice.  Brian understood him because they shared a similar past. He said

**3. (history)**

Name _____  Date _____

# Unit 4: Poetry
# Applying the Big Question

**Do we need words to communicate well?**

**DIRECTIONS:** *Complete the chart below to apply what you have learned about types of communication. One row has been completed for you.*

| Example | Type of information | How it is communicated | Main idea | Another way to communicate this | What I learned |
|---|---|---|---|---|---|
| **From Literature** | Poem: "Life Doesn't Frighten Me" | by words on a page | A person is strong and confident. | through proud facial expression or with hands on hips | Words are not always needed to show a person's strength and confidence. |
| **From Literature** | | | | | |
| **From Science** | | | | | |
| **From Social Studies** | | | | | |
| **From Real Life** | | | | | |

Name _____ Date _____

## Gary Soto
# Listening and Viewing

### Segment 1: Meet Gary Soto
- How did the popular songs of Gary Soto's youth inspire him to write poetry? What music could inspire you to write?

_____

_____

_____

_____

### Segment 2: Poetry
- How does Gary Soto "make things new" in his poetry? Why do you think Gary Soto likes to use both made-up and factual details in a poem?

_____

_____

_____

_____

### Segment 3: The Writing Process
- Why does Gary Soto use strong images in his poems? According to Gary Soto, no one can write poetry without reading it. Do you agree or disagree with him? Why?

_____

_____

_____

_____

### Segment 4: The Rewards of Writing
- How does Gary Soto like to connect with his audience? How do you think literature can bring all people together?

_____

_____

_____

_____

# Learning About Poetry

Poetry is different from other types of writing in its appearance, its use of words, and its musical qualities. Two major elements of poetry are **sound devices** and **figurative language.**

| Elements of Poetry | Types and Examples |
|---|---|
| **Sound devices** can add a musical quality to poetry. | **Rhyme:** the repetition of sounds at the ends of words (*clown, down*)<br>**Rhythm:** the beat created by the pattern of stressed and unstressed syllables (*Ă moúse lives ín mỹ hoúse.*)<br>**Repetition:** the use of a sound, word, or group of words more than once (*Sunny thoughts filled a sunny day.*)<br>**Onomatopoeia:** the use of words that imitate sounds (*splash, meow*)<br>**Alliteration:** the repetition of consonant sounds at the beginning of words (*a round red rose*) |
| **Figurative language** is writing or speech that is not meant to be taken literally. The many types of figurative language are called **figures of speech.** | **Metaphors:** describe one thing as if it were something else (*Courage is a fire that burns in your heart.*)<br>**Similes:** use *like* or *as* to compare two unlike things (*The baby's skin was as soft as silk.*)<br>**Personification:** gives human qualities to a nonhuman thing (*The flowing brook sang a happy song.*) |

**A. DIRECTIONS:** *Each of the following items contains an example of an element of poetry. Underline the correct term.*

| | | |
|---|---|---|
| rhyme | rhythm | 1. Fleet Street |
| alliteration | onomatopoeia | 2. the crunch of snow under our feet |
| repetition | alliteration | 3. a crafty, crawly critter |

**B. DIRECTIONS:** *Follow the directions for each item. Use complete sentences.*

1. Use a simile to write about a big dog.

_____

2. Use a metaphor to write about happiness.

_____

3. Use alliteration to write about a snake.

_____

**The Poetry of Gary Soto**
# Model Selection: Poetry

"Oranges" and "Ode to Family Photographs" contain **sound devices** and **figurative language.** This chart reviews these two major elements of poetry.

| Elements of Poetry | Types and Examples |
|---|---|
| **Sound devices** can add a musical quality to poetry. | **Rhyme:** the repetition of sounds at the ends of words (*clown, down*)<br>**Rhythm:** the beat created by the pattern of stressed and unstressed syllables (*Ă moúse lives ín mý house.*)<br>**Repetition:** the use of a sound, word, or group of words more than once (*Sunny thoughts filled a sunny day.*)<br>**Onomatopoeia:** the use of words that imitate sounds (*splash, meow*)<br>**Alliteration:** the repetition of consonant sounds at the beginning of words (*a round red rose*) |
| **Figurative language** is writing or speech that is not meant to be taken literally. The many types of figurative language are called **figures of speech.** | **Metaphors:** describe one thing as if it were something else (*Courage is a fire that burns in your heart.*)<br>**Similes:** use *like* or *as* to compare two unlike things (*The baby's skin was as soft as silk.*)<br>**Personification:** gives human qualities to a nonhuman thing (*The flowing brook sang a happy song.*) |

**DIRECTIONS:** *Answer these questions about the elements in Gary Soto's poems.*

1. What figure of speech is used in "I turned to the candies / Tiered like bleachers"?

_____

2. In "Oranges," a tiny bell brings the saleslady. Give two examples of onomatopoeia that could be used to describe the sound of the bell.

_____

3. "The saleslady's eyes met mine, / And held them, knowing / Very well what it was all / About." What figure of speech is used in these lines?

_____

4. Use stress marks to mark the rhythm in the line "This is the pond, and these are my feet."

_____

**Poetry Collection**
Ogden Nash, Rosemary and Stephen Vincent Benet, Jack Prelutsky
# Writing About the Big Question
**Do we need words to communicate well?**

## Big Question Vocabulary

| | | | | |
|---|---|---|---|---|
| communicate | connection | correspond | dialogue | expression |
| gesture | language | monologue | nonverbal | quote |
| reveal | share | symbolize | verbal | visual |

**A.** *Write one or more words from the list above to complete each sentence.*

1. The communication animals use is always _____.

2. How do people _____ with animals?

3. Sometimes a _____ or _____ can give more information than words.

4. All animals _____ the ability to communicate in one way or another.

**B.** *Follow the directions in responding to each of the items below.*

1. List two different times that you used **nonverbal communication.**

   _____

   _____

2. Write two sentences about one of the experiences in which you describe how effective your nonverbal communication was. Use at least two Big Question vocabulary words.

   _____

   _____

**C.** *Complete the sentence below. Then, write a short paragraph in which you connect this idea to the Big Question.*

   Verbal and nonverbal communications are effective in different kinds of situations because _____

   _____

   _____

   _____

   _____

Name _____ Date _____

# Reading: Ask Questions to Use Context Clues

When you come across a word you do not know or a word used in an unusual way, you can sometimes figure out the meaning by using context clues. **Context clues** are found in the words, phrases, and sentences surrounding an unfamiliar word. They may be words that have the same meaning or that describe or explain the word. To use context clues, **ask questions** such as these:

- *What kind of word is it?*
- *What word can I use in place of it?*
- *Which other words in the sentence explain it?*

**DIRECTIONS:** *Use this chart to figure out the meaning of some words that you may not know or that are used in an unusual way in the poems in this collection. For each item, write the question you would ask to figure out the meaning of the underlined word or words. Then, answer the question. Finally, write the meaning of the word or expression. The first item has been done for you.*

| Word in Context | Question | Answer | Meaning |
|---|---|---|---|
| **1.** there wasn't a thing on its <u>minuscule</u> mind | Which words explain what the unfamiliar word means? | "there wasn't a thing on its . . . mind" | little |
| **2.** its tail was a <u>cudgel</u> of gristle and bone | | | |
| **3.** "These birds are very <u>trying</u>. / I'm sick of hearing them. . . ." | | | |
| **4.** They sometimes skinned their noses. / For learning how to rule the air / Was <u>not a bed of roses</u>— | | | |
| **5.** The witch's face was <u>cross</u> and wrinkled | | | |

Name _____ Date _____

# Literary Analysis: Rhythm and Rhyme

Poets often use **rhythm** and **rhyme** to add a musical quality to their poems. **Rhythm** is the sound pattern created by stressed and unstressed syllables. Stressed syllables receive more emphasis than unstressed syllables. In this example, capital letters indicate the stressed syllables:

CLANK-i-ty CLANK-i-ty CLANK-i-ty CLANK! (4 stressed syllables, 6 unstressed syllables)

AN-ky-lo-SAUR-us was BUILT like a TANK (4 stressed syllables, 6 unstressed syllables)

**Rhyme** is the repetition of sounds at the ends of words, such as *clank* and *tank*. Once a rhyme pattern, or rhyme scheme, has been established, you come to expect the upcoming rhymes. Many traditional poems have rhyming words at the ends of lines.

**DIRECTIONS:** *Rewrite each of the following lines from the poems to show their rhythm and rhyme. Write each syllable separately, as in the example above. Use capital letters to show stressed syllables. Then, circle the words that rhyme.*

1. Ankylosaurus was best left alone / Its tail was a cudgel of gristle and bone

   _____

   _____

2. They glided here, they glided there, / They sometimes skinned their noses. /—For learning how to rule the air / Was not a bed of roses—

   _____

   _____

   _____

   _____

3. The giant was hairy, the giant was horrid, / He had one eye in the middle of his forehead. Good morning Isabel, the giant said, / I'll grind your bones to make my bread.

   _____

   _____

   _____

   _____

Name _____ Date _____

**Poetry Collection:** Ogden Nash, Jack Prelutsky, Rosemary and Stephen Vincent Benét
# Vocabulary Builder

**Word List**

    cavernous    horrid    inedible    minuscule    rancor    ravenous

**A. DIRECTIONS:** *Answer each question using a complete sentence. In your answer, use a word from the Word List in place of the underlined words.*

1. When would someone be <u>greedily hungry</u>?

_____

_____

2. What terrible thing might cause someone to feel <u>bitter hate</u>?

_____

_____

3. What kind of food would be considered <u>not fit to be eaten</u>?

_____

_____

4. What room in a house might be <u>large and hollow</u>?

_____

_____

5. What kind of villain would be <u>frightful</u>?

_____

_____

6. What is one animal that is <u>very small</u>?

_____

_____

**B. WORD STUDY:** *The root -min- means "very small." Answer each of the following questions using one of these words containing -min-: minimum, minor, minuscule.*

1. What is the *minimum* age for voting in the United States?

_____

2. If your paper has only *minor* errors, what kind of grade can you expect?

_____

3. If the portion of food you get in a restaurant is *minuscule*, how long will it be before you are hungry again?

_____

Name _____  Date _____

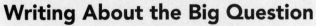
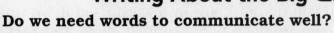

# Writing About the Big Question

**Do we need words to communicate well?**

## Big Question Vocabulary

| | | | | |
|---|---|---|---|---|
| communicate | connection | correspond | dialogue | expression |
| gesture | language | monologue | nonverbal | quote |
| reveal | share | symbolize | verbal | visual |

**A.** *Write a word from the list above to complete each sentence.*

1. In poems, objects can _____ ideas.

2. The _____ between objects and ideas can be a challenge to figure out.

3. Often poetic _____ is different from everyday speech.

4. Poems can _____ important truths about life.

**B.** *Follow the directions in responding to each of the items below.*

1. Describe a time when you used an **expression**, **gesture**, or another form of **nonverbal communication** to **share** an opinion.

   _____

   _____

2. Write two sentences about the effect of your expression or gesture. Use at least two Big Question vocabulary words.

   _____

   _____

**C.** *Complete the sentence below. Then, write a short paragraph in which you connect this idea to the Big Question.*

   Sometimes people fail to use language to state their real thoughts and feelings because _____

   _____

   _____

   _____

   _____

Name _____ Date _____

# Reading: Ask Questions to Use Context Clues

When you come across a word you do not know or a word used in an unusual way, you can sometimes figure out the meaning by using context clues. **Context clues** are found in the words, phrases, and sentences surrounding an unfamiliar word. They may be words that have the same meaning or that describe or explain the word. To use context clues, **ask questions** such as these:

- *What kind of word is it?*
- *What word can I use in place of it?*
- *Which other words in the sentence explain it?*

**DIRECTIONS:** *Use this chart to figure out the meaning of some words that you may not know or that are used in an unusual way in the poems in this collection. For each item, write the question you would ask to figure out the meaning of the underlined word or words. Then, answer the question. Finally, write the meaning of the word or expression. The first item has been done for you.*

| Word in Context | Question | Answer | Meaning |
|---|---|---|---|
| **1.** <u>Panthers</u> in the park / Strangers in the dark / No, they don't frighten me at all. | What kind of word is it? | It is a word that names an animal that frightens people. | kind of scary animal |
| **2.** Thus much let me <u>avow</u>— / You are not wrong | | | |
| **3.** I hold . . . / Grains of the golden sand— / How few! yet how they creep / Through my fingers to the <u>deep</u> | | | |
| **4.** can I not <u>grasp</u> / Them with a tighter clasp? | | | |
| **5.** The sun was shining on the sea, / . . . He did his very best to make / The <u>billows</u> smooth and bright | | | |

**Poetry Collection:** Edgar Allan Poe, Maya Angelou, Lewis Carroll
# Literary Analysis: Rhythm and Rhyme

Poets often use **rhythm** and **rhyme** to add a musical quality to their poems. **Rhythm** is the sound pattern created by stressed and unstressed syllables. Stressed syllables receive more emphasis than unstressed syllables. In this example, capital letters indicate the stressed syllables:)

The WAL-rus AND the CAR-pen-TER (4 stressed syllables, 4 unstressed syllables)

Were WALK-ing CLOSE at HAND (3 stressed syllables, 3 unstressed syllables)

**Rhyme** is the repetition of sounds at the ends of words, such as *wall* and *hall*. Once a rhyme pattern, or rhyme scheme, has been established, you come to expect the upcoming rhymes. Many traditional poems have rhyming words at the ends of lines.

**DIRECTIONS:** *Rewrite each of the following lines from the poems to show their rhythm and rhyme. Write each syllable separately, as in the example above. Use capital letters to show stressed syllables. Then, circle the words that rhyme.*

1. Don't show me frogs and snakes / And listen for my scream, /
   If I'm afraid at all / It's only in my dreams.

   _____

   _____

   _____

2. *All* that we see or seem / Is but a dream within a dream.

   _____

   _____

3. "The time has come," the Walrus said, / "To talk of many things: /
   Of shoes—and ships—and sealing wax— / Of cabbages—and kings—"

   _____

   _____

   _____

   _____

Name _____ Date _____

# Vocabulary Builder

**Word List**

amid    beseech    deem    dismal    pitiless    sympathize

**A. DIRECTIONS:** *Write the word from the Word List that best completes each sentence.*

1. My neighbor, a poet, said she would not _____ her barking dogs to be quiet.

2. The knight fought bravely _____ numerous foes.

3. After five days of _____ weather, we were ready for a sunny day.

4. The editors _____ the excellent poem worthy of publication.

5. I _____ with my friend who lost her dog.

6. The _____ king did not show his subjects any mercy.

**B. WORD STUDY:** *The root -mal- means "bad" or "evil." Answer each of the following questions using one of these words containing -mal-: dismal, malady, malfunction, malice, malign.*

1. What do you do if there is a *malfunction* of your computer?

   _____

2. If someone bears you *malice*, how does that person treat you?

   _____

3. What would be the normal reaction to a *dismal* story?

   _____

4. How would someone feel after a long *malady*?

   _____

5. What might someone do to *malign* an honest person?

   _____

**Poetry Collection 1:** Ogden Nash, Jack Prelutsky, Rosemary and Stephen Vincent Benét
**Poetry Collection 2:** Edgar Allan Poe, Maya Angelou, Lewis Carroll

# Integrated Language Skills: Grammar

## Sentences: Simple and Compound Subjects

A **sentence** is a group of words that has a subject and a verb and expresses a complete thought. A **simple sentence** expresses a single thought. It can contain a simple subject or a compound subject. A **subject** is the word or group of words that tells who or what the sentence is about. A **simple subject** is made up of one noun or pronoun. A **compound subject** is made up of two or more nouns or pronouns. The nouns or pronouns in a compound subject are connected by conjunctions such as *and, or,* or *nor.*

> **Simple subject:** Spring is my favorite season.
> **Compound subject:** Spring, summer, winter, and fall are the four seasons.

**A. PRACTICE:** *Underline the simple or compound subject in each sentence.*

1. Animals and people are good subjects for poems.
2. After dinner, will you or Robert put away the leftovers?
3. Everyone should come up with a plan.
4. Every spring, hungry deer and raccoons invade our garden in search of food.
5. On a counter in the kitchen, flour, sugar, and butter are waiting to be made into cookies.
6. Lewis Carroll may well be my favorite poet.

**B. Writing Application:** *If you could write a poem about any two subjects, what two subjects would you choose? In a brief paragraph, discuss the subjects you would use, and why. Include at least one sentence that has a simple subject and two sentences that have compound subjects. Underline the simple or compound subject in each sentence.*

_____

_____

_____

_____

_____

_____

_____

_____

_____

Name _____  Date _____

**Poetry Collection 1:** Ogden Nash, Jack Prelutsky, Rosemary and Stephen Vincent Benét
**Poetry Collection 2:** Edgar Allan Poe, Maya Angelou, Lewis Carroll

# Integrated Language Skills: Support for Writing a Letter to an Author

Use this form to draft a **letter to the author** of one of the poems in these two collections. Be sure to state your reaction to the poem and tell whether or not you like the poem. Include reasons for your reaction, and refer to the poem to support your reasons.

**Heading:** Your address and the date _____

_____

_____

_____

**Inside Address:** Where the letter will be sent _____

_____

_____

**Greeting**

Dear _____,

Begin **body** of letter. *State your over-all reaction.* _____

_____

_____

*State reasons for your reaction, and give examples to support reasons.* _____

_____

_____

_____

_____

_____

_____

**Closing** and **Signature** _____

_____

Now, write a final draft of your letter to the author of one of the poems in these collections.

Name _____ Date _____

# Writing About the Big Question

**Do we need words to communicate well?**

## Big Question Vocabulary

| | | | | |
|---|---|---|---|---|
| communicate | connection | correspond | dialogue | expression |
| gesture | language | monologue | nonverbal | quote |
| reveal | share | symbolize | verbal | visual |

**A.** *Write one or more words from the list above to complete each sentence.*

1. Poets _____ their ideas through carefully chosen words.

2. Can you _____ some lines from a famous poem?

3. When reading a poem aloud, one's voice and _____ should _____ to the meaning of the words.

**B.** *Follow the directions in responding to each of the items below.*

1. Describe a time when you failed to **communicate verbally** or **nonverbally** as well as you would have liked to.

   _____

   _____

2. Write two sentences that describe the problem caused by your inability to communicate fully. Use at least two Big Question vocabulary words.

   _____

   _____

**C.** *Complete the sentence below. Then, write a short paragraph in which you connect this idea to the Big Question by comparing nonverbal to spoken or written communication.*

Poets make connections between common and uncommon things in order to _____

_____

_____

_____

_____

_____

Name _____ Date _____

# Reading: Reread and Read Ahead to Find and Use Context Clues

**Context** is the situation in which a word or an expression is used. The words and phrases in the surrounding text give you clues to the meaning of the word. Sometimes a word has more than one meaning. You may recognize a word but not recognize the way in which it is used. **Reread and read ahead** to find and use context clues that clarify meanings of words with multiple meanings. Look at the following examples to see how context clarifies the meaning of *dips:*

The willow <u>dips</u> to the water. (*Dips* is an action the tree takes to reach the water.)

At the party we tasted many delicious <u>dips</u>. (*Dips* are something one eats at a party.)

As you read the poems, notice words that are used in unfamiliar or unusual ways. Use the context to help determine the meaning of the words.

**DIRECTIONS:** *Study the underlined word in each of the following lines from "Simile: Willow and Ginkgo" or "April Rain Song." Look for context clues in the lines that hint at the meaning of the word. On the line, write the context clues. Then, write two meanings for the word—first the meaning that fits the context and then a meaning that does* not *fit the context. The first item has been done for you.*

1. "The willow is like a nymph with <u>streaming</u> hair"

   **Context clues:** <u>"like a nymph," "hair"</u>

   **Meaning in context:** <u>long, flowing</u>     **Second meaning:** <u>moving quickly</u>

2. "Wherever it grows, there is green and gold and <u>fair</u>."

   **Context clues:** _____

   **Meaning in context:** _____   **Second meaning:** _____

3. "Let the rain beat upon your head with <u>silver</u> liquid drops."

   **Context clues:** _____

   **Meaning in context:** _____   **Second meaning:** _____

4. "The rain makes <u>still</u> pools on the sidewalk."

   **Context clues:** _____

   **Meaning in context:** _____   **Second meaning:** _____

**Poetry Collection:** Eve Merriam, Emily Dickinson, Langston Hughes
# Literary Analysis: Figurative Language

**Figurative language** is language that is not meant to be taken literally. Authors use figurative language to state ideas in fresh ways. They may use one or more of the following types of figurative language:

- **Similes** compare two different things using the word *like* or *as:* "The ginkgo is like a crude sketch."
- **Metaphors** compare two different things by stating that one thing is another: "Fame is a bee."
- **Personification** compares an object or animal to a human by giving it human characteristics: "Let the rain sing you a lullaby."

**A. DIRECTIONS:** *Underline each example of figurative language. Above it, write S if it is a simile, M if it is a metaphor, and P if it is personification.*

                                                                       P

It began to drizzle as I walked home. <u>The rain tapped me on the shoulder</u>. Gentle rain-drops fell like flower petals on my head and shoulders. The soft downpour was a surprising gift. I had been working like a machine, trying to finish my homework, and now the shower was a kindly messenger telling me to forget my worries.

**B. DIRECTIONS:** *In this chart, identify the type of figurative language. Then, tell what it does and what it shows. Look back at the poem if you need more context.*

| Figurative Language | Type | What It Does | What It Shows |
|---|---|---|---|
| **1.** The willow is like a nymph with streaming hair ("Simile: Willow and Ginkgo") | simile | It compares branches to hair. | It shows that the branches are long. |
| **2.** Like a city child, it grows up in the street. ("Simile: Willow and Ginkgo") | | | |
| **3.** the metal sky ("Simile: Willow and Ginkgo") | | | |
| **4.** Let the rain kiss you ("April Rain Song") | | | |

Name _____ Date _____

# Vocabulary Builder

**Word List**

    chorus    crude    precious    soprano    stubby    thrives

**A. DIRECTIONS:** *Think about the meaning of the underlined word in each item below. Then, answer the question, and explain your answer.*

1. If someone were a member of a <u>chorus</u>, would he or she sing alone or with a group?

_____

_____

2. Which animal <u>thrives</u> in the company of humans, a bear or a dog?

_____

_____

3. Is a <u>soprano</u> usually an adult male or an adult female?

_____

_____

4. Would someone with <u>stubby</u> legs take long or short strides?

_____

_____

5. Would a <u>crude</u> drawing show little detail or much detail?

_____

_____

6. Would a parent show a <u>precious</u> child favor or disfavor?

_____

_____

**B. WORD STUDY:** *The suffix -ness means "state or condition of being." Answer each of the following questions using one of these words containing -ness: preciousness, preparedness, tardiness.*

1. If you talk about the *preciousness* of someone, how do you feel about the person?

_____

2. What is a weather condition that would make *preparedness* necessary?

_____

3. What are some reasons people give for *tardiness*?

_____

**Poetry Collection**

Sandra Cisneros, Nikki Giovanni, Theodore Roethke

# Writing About the Big Question

**Do we need words to communicate well?**

## Big Question Vocabulary

| | | | | |
|---|---|---|---|---|
| communicate | connection | correspond | dialogue | expression |
| gesture | language | monologue | nonverbal | quote |
| reveal | share | symbolize | verbal | visual |

**A.** *Write one or more words from the list above to complete each sentence.*

1. Only one person can deliver a _____.

2. Two or more people can have a _____.

3. The tone of someone's voice should _____ with his or her feelings.

4. A crossword puzzle requires both _____ and _____ skills.

**B.** *Follow the directions in responding to each of the items below.*

1. Describe a situation in which you **communicated** your feelings of love or friendship in an unusual way.

   _____

   _____

2. Write two sentences that describe the reaction of the person who received your unusual communication. Use at least two Big Question vocabulary words.

   _____

   _____

**C.** *Complete the sentence below. Then, write a short paragraph in which you connect this idea to the Big Question.*

The way I communicate my love to the people close to me is _____

_____

_____

_____

_____

_____

Name _____ Date _____

# Reading: Reread and Read Ahead to Find and Use Context Clues

**Context** is the situation in which a word or an expression is used. The words and phrases in the surrounding text give you clues to the meaning of the word. Sometimes a word has more than one meaning. You may recognize a word but not recognize the way in which it is used. **Reread and read ahead** to find and use context clues that clarify meanings of words with multiple meanings. Look at the following examples to see how context clarifies the meaning of *flow:*

> a river would stop / its <u>flow</u> if only / a stream were there / to receive it (*Flow* describes an action the river takes.)

> The streams <u>flow</u> into the river. (*Flow* is an action taken by the streams.)

As you read the poems, notice words that are used in unfamiliar or unusual ways. Use the context to help determine the meaning of the words.

**DIRECTIONS:** *Study the underlined word in each of the following lines from "Abuelito Who" or "Child on Top of a Greenhouse." Look for context clues in the lines that hint at the meaning of the word. On the line, write the context clues. Then, write two meanings for the word—first the meaning that fits the context and then a meaning that does* not *fit the context. The first item has been done for you.*

1. "who is a <u>watch</u> and glass of water"

   **Context clues:** "glass of water" (something put on a table next to a bed) _____

   **Meaning in context:** small device for telling time **Second meaning:** to look at _____

2. "Who tells me in Spanish you are my <u>diamond</u> / who tells me in English you are my sky"

   **Context clues:** _____

   **Meaning in context:** _____ **Second meaning:** _____

3. "The wind billowing out the <u>seat</u> of my britches"

   **Context clues:** _____

   **Meaning in context:** _____ **Second meaning:** _____

4. "A <u>line</u> of elms plunging and tossing like horses"

   **Context clues:** _____

   **Meaning in context:** _____ **Second meaning:** _____

Name _____ Date _____

**Poetry Collection:** Sandra Cisneros, Nikki Giovanni, Theodore Roethke
# Literary Analysis: Figurative Language

**Figurative language** is language that is not meant to be taken literally. Authors use figurative language to state ideas in fresh ways. They may use one or more of the following types of figurative language:

- **Similes** compare two different things using the word *like* or *as:* "who throws coins like rain"
- **Metaphors** compare two different things by stating that one thing is another: "who is dough and feathers"
- **Personification** compares an object or animal to a human by giving it human characteristics: "The half-grown chrysanthemums staring up like accusers"

**A. DIRECTIONS:** *Underline each example of figurative language. Above the underlined phrase, write S if it is a simile, M if it is a metaphor, and P if it is personification. The first use of figurative language has been identified as an example.*

               P

The <u>pitiless sun</u> beat down on us like hammers as we walked home. The books in our

backpacks were as heavy as rocks. When we saw the fountain that welcomes visitors to the

park, we raced toward it. Our feet pounded on the stones leading to the center of the foun-

tain. We tore off our shoes and socks and splashed gratefully in the cool water. The fountain

was an oasis in the desert on that hot day.

**B. DIRECTIONS:** *Complete the following chart. First, identify the type of figurative language in each item. Then, tell what the figurative language does. Finally, tell what it shows. Look back at the poem if you need more context.*

| Figurative Language | Type | What It Does | What It Shows |
|---|---|---|---|
| **1.** who tells me in English you are my sky ("Abuelito Who") | metaphor | It compares the speaker to the sky. | It shows how much Abuelito loves the speaker. |
| **2.** an ocean would never laugh ("The World Is Not a Pleasant Place to Be") | | | |
| **3.** A line of elms plunging and tossing like horses ("Child on Top of a Greenhouse") | | | |

Name _____ Date _____

**Poetry Collection:** Sandra Cisneros, Nikki Giovanni, Theodore Roethke
# Vocabulary Builder

**Word List**
  accusers    billowing    pleasant    plunging    sour

**A. DIRECTIONS:** *Think about the meaning of the underlined word in each item below. Then, answer the question, and explain your answer.*

1. If you saw smoke <u>billowing</u> from the windows of a house, what would you do?

   _____

   _____

2. If you were in the market for a new computer and noticed <u>plunging</u> prices at an electronics store, would it be a good time to buy?

   _____

   _____

3. If the milk is <u>sour</u>, what would you do with it?

   _____

   _____

4. If you had a <u>pleasant</u> time somewhere, would you go back again?

   _____

   _____

5. If a defendant's <u>accusers</u> came to court, would they testify for or against him?

   _____

   _____

**B. WORD STUDY:** *The suffix -ant means "state or condition of being." Answer each of the following questions using one of these words containing -ant: vigilant, important, ignorant.*

1. Why does a doctor need to be *vigilant*?

   _____

2. Where would quietness be *important*?

   _____

3. Why would an *ignorant* person be prone to making mistakes?

   _____

Name _____ Date _____

# Integrated Language Skills: Grammar

## Sentence Functions

A **sentence** is a group of words that has a subject and a verb and expresses a complete thought. Sentences can be classified according to what they do—that is, according to their function or purpose. Notice that every sentence begins with a capital letter and ends with a punctuation mark. The kind of punctuation mark that is used depends on the function of the sentence.

| Type | Function and End Punctuation | Example |
|---|---|---|
| Declarative | makes a statement; ends with a period | These poems are interesting. |
| Interrogative | asks a question; ends with a question mark | Which poem do you like best? |
| Imperative | gives an order or a direction; ends with a period or an exclamation point | Let us read this poem. Please bring me that book. Catch it before it falls! |
| Exclamatory | expresses strong emotion; ends with an exclamation point | What a great poem to read aloud! |

**A. PRACTICE:** *Classify these sentences according to their function. On the line following each sentence, write* declarative, interrogative, imperative, *or* exclamatory.

1. What a wonderful poem that is! _____

2. Elena, please read the first poem in this collection. _____

3. These poems are about nature, and those are about people. _____

4. Noah, give us your opinion. _____

5. Does anyone have anything to add? _____

**B. Writing Application:** *Write a brief paragraph about any of the poems in your textbook. In your paragraph, use at least one of each kind of sentence. Write a* D *above each declarative sentence,* Int *above each interrogative sentence,* Imp *above each imperative sentence, and* E *above each exclamatory sentence. Be sure to capitalize and punctuate each sentence correctly.*

_____

_____

_____

_____

_____

Name _____ Date _____

# Integrated Language Skills: Support for Writing a Poem With Figurative Language

Use this cluster diagram to gather ideas for a **poem** you will write using figurative language. First, write your subject in the oval at the center of the diagram. Then, in each circle around the oval, jot down one quality of your subject. Add more circles if you need them.

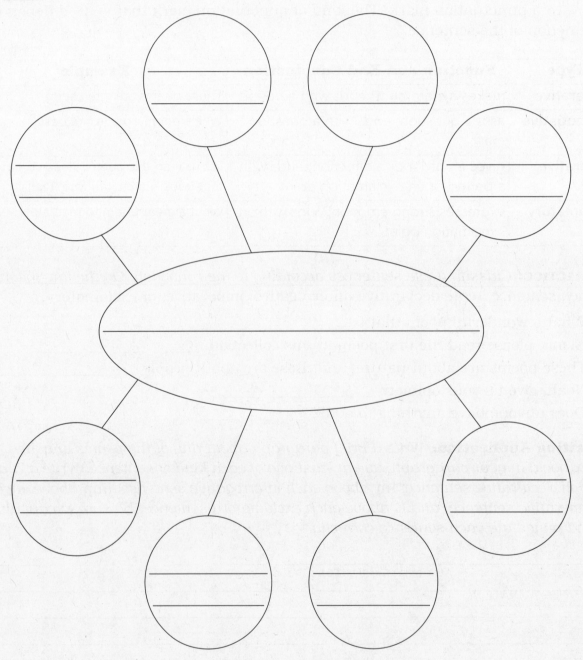

Now, use your notes to draft your poem. Be sure your poem has at least one simile, metaphor, or personification.

Name _____  Date _____

**Poetry** by Robert Frost and E.E. Cummings
# Writing About the Big Question

**Do we need words to communicate well?**

## Big Question Vocabulary

| | | | | |
|---|---|---|---|---|
| communicate | connection | correspond | dialogue | expression |
| gesture | language | monologue | nonverbal | quote |
| reveal | share | symbolize | verbal | visual |

**A.** *Write a word from the list above to complete each sentence.*

1. Do items in poems always _____ feelings and ideas?

2. Poetic images are _____ if they create pictures in readers' minds.

3. Sometimes it's easier to _____ feelings by writing them than by talking about them.

4. A person's _____ might appear sad even if he or she is content.

**B.** *Follow the directions in responding to each of the items below.*

1. Explain whether you more often read poems, which **communicate** through words, or look at paintings, which **communicate visually**.

   _____

   _____

2. Write two sentences that describe the difference between a poem and a painting that you find most striking. Use at least two Big Question vocabulary words.

   _____

   _____

**C.** *Complete the sentence below. Then, write a short paragraph in which you connect this idea to the Big Question.*

A visual image can be conveyed through words or pictures, but I prefer _____

_____

_____

_____

_____

**Poetry** by Robert Frost and E.E. Cummings
# Literary Analysis: Imagery

An **image** is a word or phrase that appeals to the five senses of sight, hearing, smell, taste, or touch. An image can also create a feeling of movement.

Writers use this sensory language—**imagery**—to create word pictures. The imagery in a word picture can appeal to more than one sense. For example, the images in the following lines appeal to the senses of both touch and taste:

Cold hands, warm mug;

sip of cocoa, mother's hug . . .

Imagery also helps a writer express mood. **Mood** is the feeling that a poem creates in a reader. A poem's mood might be fanciful, thoughtful, or lonely. In the lines above, the poet uses images that create a mood of cozy affection.

**A. DIRECTIONS:** *Listed below are images from Robert Frost's poem "Dust of Snow" and E.E. Cummings's poem "who knows if the moon's." For each image, list the senses that are involved. Choose from sight, hearing, smell, taste, touch. Also, explain whether the image creates a feeling of movement. Remember that each image can appeal to more than one sense.*

| "Dust of Snow" | |
|---|---|
| **Image** | **Senses** |
| **1.** crow shaking branches of tree | |
| **2.** dust of snow falling on speaker | |

| "who knows if the moon's" | |
|---|---|
| **Image** | **Senses** |
| **3.** the moon as a balloon | |
| **4.** a balloon filled with pretty people | |
| **5.** going up above houses and steeples and clouds | |
| **6.** flowers picking themselves | |

**B. DIRECTIONS:** *Tell what mood, or feeling, each poem's images help create.*

1. The mood of "Dust of Snow" is _____

2. The mood of "who knows if the moon's" is _____

**Poetry** by Robert Frost and E.E. Cummings
# Vocabulary Builder

**Word List**

    rued    steeples

**A. DIRECTIONS:** *Complete each sentence with a word from the Word List.*

1. Tall _____ can help travelers find a nearby village.
2. Sam _____ his poor brushing habits when the dentist found three cavities.

**B. DIRECTIONS:** *Revise each sentence so that the italicized vocabulary word is used correctly. Be sure to keep the vocabulary word in your revision.*

    Original Sentence: When the soup grew cold, it began to *simmer*.

    Revised Sentence: When the soup grew hot, it began to *simmer*.

1. When she saw the good grade on her paper, Kayla *rued* her preparation for the test.

_____

_____

2. It is difficult to see the churches' *steeples* from a distance.

_____

_____

**C. DIRECTIONS:** *On the line, write the letter of the word that is most nearly the same in meaning as the word in CAPITAL letters.*

____ 1. STEEPLES
    A. roads
    B. fences
    C. barrels
    D. towers

____ 2. RUED
    A. loved
    B. regretted
    C. viewed
    D. disturbed

Name _____ Date _____

**Poetry** by Robert Frost and E.E. Cummings
# Support for Writing a Comparative Essay

Before you draft your essay comparing the role of nature in each poem, complete the graphic organizer below.

| Nature | "Dust of Snow" | "who knows if the moon's" |
|---|---|---|
| Is nature seen as positive or negative? | | |
| Does nature play a central role or a background role? | | |
| Which words or phrases help create images of nature? | 1.<br><br>2.<br><br>3.<br><br>4. | 1.<br><br>2.<br><br>3.<br><br>4. |

Now, use your notes to write an essay comparing the role nature plays in each poem. Be sure to include examples from the poems to support your ideas.

Name _____ Date _____

**Poetry Collection**
Bashō, Lillian Morrison, Anonymous

# Writing About the Big Question

**Do we need words to communicate well?**

## Big Question Vocabulary

| | | | | |
|---|---|---|---|---|
| communicate | connection | correspond | dialogue | expression |
| gesture | language | monologue | nonverbal | quote |
| reveal | share | symbolize | verbal | visual |

**A.** *Write one or more words from the list above to complete each sentence.*

1. A shrug is a _____ that can _____ confusion.

2. With what question does this answer _____?

3. A direct _____ can make a magazine article more interesting.

**B.** *Follow the directions in responding to each of the items below.*

1. What might a person's reading preferences **reveal** about him or her?

_____

_____

2. Write two sentences that describe the genre of literature you like best. Use at least two Big Question vocabulary words.

_____

_____

**C.** *Complete the sentence below. Then, write a short paragraph in which you connect this idea to the Big Question by explaining how poetry uses words to communicate well.*

The language of poetry is unique because _____

_____

_____

_____

_____

_____

_____

_____

Name _____ Date _____

**Poetry Collection:** Bashō, Anonymous, Lillian Morrison
# Reading: Reread to Paraphrase

**Paraphrasing** is restating an author's words in your own words. Paraphrasing difficult or confusing passages in a poem helps you clarify the meaning. Use these steps to help you:

- First, stop and reread any difficult lines or passages.
- Next, identify unfamiliar words. Find their meaning and replace them with words that mean the same or nearly the same thing.
- Then, restate the lines in your own words, using everyday speech.
- Finally, reread the lines to see if your paraphrase makes sense in the poem.

A chart such as the one below can be useful in helping you paraphrase.

**DIRECTIONS:** *In the left column of the chart are passages from the poems in this collection. Underline unfamiliar words. Find the meanings of these words and write the meaning in the second column. In the third column, paraphrase the passage. The first one has been done for you as an example.*

| Passage | New Words | Paraphrase |
|---|---|---|
| **Example:** Skimming an asphalt sea | skimming: moving swiftly; asphalt: pavement | gliding swiftly over the sidewalk |
| **1.** I swerve, I curve, I sway; | | |
| **2.** An old silent pond . . . | | |
| **3.** A flea and a fly in a flue Were caught, | | |
| **4.** a flaw in the flue | | |

Name _____ Date _____

Poets use different **forms of poetry** suited to the ideas, images, and feelings they want to express. The following are three poetic forms:

- A **haiku** is a Japanese verse form with three lines. Line 1 has five syllables, line 2 has seven syllables, and line 3 has five syllables. Haiku often focuses on nature. It tries to capture a moment by giving you a few quick images or word pictures that help you see and hear something in a new way.
- A **limerick** is a short, funny poem of five lines. The first, second, and fifth lines rhyme and have three beats, or stressed syllables. The third and fourth lines rhyme and have two strong beats.
- A **concrete poem** has words arranged in a shape that reflects the subject of the poem.

**DIRECTIONS:** *Answer the questions about each form of poetry below.*

1. "Haiku" by Bashō

| | **What do you see?** | **What do you hear?** |
|---|---|---|
| An old silent pond . . . | | |
| A frog jumps into the pond, | | |
| splash! Silence again. | | |

2. "Limerick" by Anonymous

Underline each *stressed* syllable in each line. Then, identify the rhyme scheme or pattern by writing the letters *a* or *b* at the end of each line. Give each rhyme a different letter. For example, write the letter *a* at the end of the first line and *a* at the end of each line that rhymes with line one.

A flea and a fly in a flue _____

Were caught, so what could they do? _____

   Said the fly, "Let us flee." _____

   "Let us fly," said the flea. _____

So they flew through a flaw in the flue. _____

3. "The Sidewalk Racer" by Lillian Morrison

*Concrete* means "something real, something that can be touched," such as an apple, a tree, or a cellphone. List three subjects that you think might be good choices for a concrete poem.

_____

_____

_____

**Poetry Collection:** Bashō, Lillian Morrison, Anonymous
# Vocabulary Builder

## Word List

asphalt     flaw     flee     skimming

**A. DIRECTIONS:** *Revise each sentence to use the underlined vocabulary word logically. Be sure to keep the vocabulary word in your revision.*

1. Honesty is a <u>flaw</u> in his good character.

   _____

   _____

2. The skaters had a difficult time <u>skimming</u> over the smooth ice.

   _____

   _____

3. People use <u>asphalt</u> to surface buildings.

   _____

   _____

4. Since the roads were closed, it was easy for us to <u>flee</u> after hearing the flood warnings.

   _____

   _____

**B. WORD STUDY:** *The suffix* -less *means "without or not able." Answer each of the following questions using one of these words containing* -less: *careless, flawless, meaningless.*

1. On a scale of 1 to 10, what score should a diver receive for a *flawless* back flip?

   _____

2. What would make a book in a foreign language *meaningless* to you?

   _____

3. What do you look like if you are *careless* about your appearance?

   _____

**Poetry Collection**

Muso Soseki, Dorothi Charles, Anonymous

# Writing About the Big Question

**Do we need words to communicate well?**

## Big Question Vocabulary

| | | | | |
|---|---|---|---|---|
| communicate | connection | correspond | dialogue | expression |
| gesture | language | monologue | nonverbal | quote |
| reveal | share | symbolize | verbal | visual |

**A.** *Write a word from the list above to complete each sentence.*

1. Be sure to use quotation marks when you record characters' conversations, or
_____.

2. Make a _____ from the audience if I need to speak louder.

3. What does flying _____ in a dream?

4. Her _____ skills are excellent, so she is a skilled public speaker.

**B.** *Follow the directions in responding to each of the items below.*

1. In your opinion, what kind of **visual** art form does a limerick most closely resemble? Explain.

_____

_____

2. In two sentences explain why you do or do not like limericks. Use at least two Big Question vocabulary words.

_____

_____

**C.** *Complete the sentence below. Then, write a short paragraph in which you connect this idea to the Big Question by explaining how concrete poetry uses both the meaning of words and the pattern of words on a page to communicate.*

Concrete poetry uses visual means of communication similar to _____

_____

_____

_____

_____

Name _____  Date _____

**Poetry Collection:** Musō Soseki, Dorthi Charles, Anonymous
# Reading: Reread to Paraphrase

**Paraphrasing** is restating an author's words in your own words. Paraphrasing difficult or confusing passages in a poem helps you clarify the meaning. Use these steps to help you:

- First, stop and reread any difficult lines or passages.
- Next, identify unfamiliar words. Find their meaning and replace them with words that mean the same or nearly the same thing.
- Note that in a concrete poem, words are shaped to reflect the subject of the poem.
- Finally, reread the lines to see if your paraphrase makes sense in the poem.

A chart such as the one below can be useful in helping you paraphrase.

**DIRECTIONS:** *In the left column of the chart are passages from the poems in this collection. Underline unfamiliar words. Find the meanings of these words, and write the meanings in the second column. In the third column, paraphrase the passage. The first one has been done for you as an example.*

| Passage | New Words | Paraphrase |
|---|---|---|
| **Example:** winds <u>howl</u> in a <u>rage</u> | howl: make a loud wailing cry; rage: great anger | winds are so strong that they make a loud crying noise, like an angry person |
| **1.** with no leaves to blow. | | |
| **2.** There was a young fellow named Hall, | | |
| **3.** Who fell in the spring in the fall; | | |

All-in-One Workbook
© Pearson Education, Inc. All rights reserved.
**210**

**Poetry Collection:** Musō Soseki, Dorthi Charles, Anonymous
# Literary Analysis: Forms of Poetry

Poets use different **forms of poetry** suited to the ideas, images, and feelings they want to express. The following are three poetic forms:

- A **haiku** is a Japanese verse form with three lines. Line 1 has five syllables, line 2 has seven syllables, and line 3 has five syllables. Haiku often focuses on nature. It tries to capture a moment by giving you a few quick images, or word pictures, that help you see, hear, and feel something in a new way.
- A **limerick** is a short, funny poem of five lines. The first, second, and fifth lines rhyme and have three beats, or stressed syllables. The third and fourth lines rhyme and have two strong beats.
- In a **concrete poem,** words are arranged in a shape that reflects the subject of the poem.

**DIRECTIONS:** *Answer the questions about each form of poetry below.*

1. "Haiku" by Soseki

|  | **What do you see?** | **What do you hear?** | **What do you feel?** |
|---|---|---|---|
| Over the wintry |  |  |  |
| forest, winds howl in a rage |  |  |  |
| with no leaves to blow. |  |  |  |

2. "Limerick" Anonymous

   Underline each *stressed* syllable in each line. Then, identify the rhyme scheme or pattern by writing the letters *a* or *b* at the end of each line. Give each rhyme a different letter. For example, write the letter *a* at the end of the first line and *a* at the end of each line that rhymes with line one.

   There was a young fellow named Hall, _____

   Who fell in the spring in the fall; _____

   　'Twould have been a sad thing _____

   　If he'd died in the spring, _____

   But he didn't—he died in the fall. _____

3. "Concrete Cat" by Dorthi Charles

   *Concrete* means "something that can be touched," such as a tree or a cellphone.

   Name some other things that are concrete.

   _____

   _____

**Poetry Collection:** Musō Soseki, Dorthi Charles, Anonymous
# Vocabulary Builder

**Word List**

fellow    howl    rage    wintry

**A. DIRECTIONS:** *Revise each sentence to use the underlined vocabulary word logically. Be sure to keep the vocabulary word in your revision.*

1. I met a <u>fellow</u> named Mary Ann.

_____

_____

2. You expect <u>wintry</u> weather in August.

_____

_____

3. We sleep peacefully when the dogs <u>howl</u> at night.

_____

_____

4. When I fixed my brother's bicycle, he went into a <u>rage</u>.

_____

_____

**B. WORD STUDY:** *The suffix* -ship *means "all individuals in a certain category" or "the quality, condition or state of being." Answer each of the following questions using one of these words containing* -ship: *fellowship, leadership, partnership.*

1. What is one *fellowship* that you participate in at school?

_____

2. What are two different kinds of *partnership*?

_____

3. What are two important *leadership* qualities?

_____

**Poetry Collections:** Bashō, Lillian Morrison, Anonymous
Musō Soseki, Dorthi Charles, Anonymous

# Integrated Language Skills: Grammar

## Subject Complements: Direct and Indirect Objects

Most sentences need words beyond a subject and a verb to complete their meaning. Direct objects and indirect objects complete ideas and make sentences more specific.

- A **direct object** is a noun or pronoun that receives the action of the verb and answers the question *Whom?* or *What?*
- They recited their <u>poems</u>. *What* was recited? their poems

  *Poems* receives the action of the verb *recited.*
- The teacher greeted <u>them</u>. Greeted *whom?* them

  *Them* receives the action of the verb *greeted.*

- An **indirect object** is a noun or pronoun that names the person or thing to whom or for whom an action is done. An indirect object answers the question *To or for whom?* or *To or for what?*
- She sent <u>him</u> a poem. *To whom?* him *What?* a poem

  The indirect object is *him.*

  The direct object is *poem.*
- He wrote his <u>grandmother</u> and <u>grandfather</u> a limerick. *For whom?* grandmother and grandfather *What?* a limerick

  The compound indirect object is *grandmother* and *grandfather.*

  The direct object is *limerick.*

**A. PRACTICE:** *Underline the <u>direct object</u> once. Underline the <u>indirect object</u> twice. Then, write the question each object answers:* • What?   • To whom?   • For whom?

1. The new student gave the teacher his haiku.

   Direct object answers _____ Indirect object answers_____

2. The nurse offered Sally a cellphone.

   Direct object answers _____ Indirect object answers _____

3. Her mother sent the teacher a note about Sally's absence from school.

   Direct object answers _____ Indirect object answers _____

**B. Writing Application:** *Write four sentences about a shopping trip. Tell what you and an adult family member buy for you and others. Include a direct object and an indirect object in every sentence. Underline the direct objects once and the indirect objects twice. You may want to use some of the following verbs:* bought, gave, showed, paid, sold, asked, found.

_____

_____

_____

Name _____ Date _____

# Integrated Language Skills: Support for Writing a Poem

You have read examples of a haiku, a limerick, and a concrete poem. Now, try writing a poem of your own, using one of these forms.

What form of poetry will you use? _____

What do you need to remember about this form? Take notes here.

_____

_____

_____

_____

Use the lines below to jot down ideas for your poem. If you're writing a haiku, you will want to think about nature images. If you're writing a limerick, think up a silly character or start with place names that sound funny and will be easy to rhyme—for example, "Chicago." If you're writing a concrete poem, think of a real subject that suggests a shape—for example, a pizza or an ocean wave.

_____

_____

_____

_____

_____

_____

_____

_____

_____

_____

_____

_____

_____

_____

**Poetry Collection**

Shel Silverstein, Rachel Field, Octavio Paz

# Writing About the Big Question

**Do we need words to communicate well?**

## Big Question Vocabulary

communicate   connection   correspond   dialogue   expression
gesture        language      monologue    nonverbal  quote
reveal         share         symbolize    verbal     visual

**A.** *Write a word from the list above to complete each sentence.*

1. Wipe that nasty _____ off your face!

2. The main character will _____ the solution to the mystery.

3. Let's _____ by mobile phone when I'm on vacation.

4. I like to _____ with my arms when I talk.

**B.** *Follow the directions in responding to each of the items below.*

1. Why might a poet choose to use everyday **language** and **communicate** about common experiences?

   _____

   _____

2. In two sentences, describe a common experience you would like to write about in a poem. Use at least two Big Question vocabulary words.

   _____

   _____

**C.** *Complete the sentence below. Then, write a short paragraph in which you connect this idea to the Big Question by considering how poets communicate their ideas.*

When a poet writes about ordinary things, he or she is sharing _____

_____

_____

_____

_____

All-in-One Workbook
**215**

Name _____  Date _____

**Poetry Collection:** Shel Silverstein, Octavio Paz, Rachel Field
# Reading: Read Aloud According to Punctuation to Paraphrase

**Paraphrasing** is restating something in your own words. To paraphrase a poem, you must first understand it and then use simpler language to restate its meaning. **Reading aloud according to punctuation** will help you find clues to a poem's meaning.

- When you read a poem aloud, do not automatically stop at the end of each line.
- Pause only at punctuation marks, as if you were reading a prose passage.

Even when you read poetry silently to yourself, it will make more sense if you follow these rules:

- **No punctuation** at the ends of lines: don't stop
- **After a comma (,):** slight pause
- **After a colon (:), semicolon (;), or dash (—):** longer pause
- **After endmarks—a period (.), question mark (?), or exclamation point (!):** full stop

**A. DIRECTIONS:** *Below are the first six lines from the poem "Parade." For each line, write the letters* SP *for* slight pause, LP *for* longer pause, FS *for* full stop, *or* DS *for* don't stop. *The first line has been done for you as an example.*

Line 1: This is the day the circus comes          <u>DS</u>
Line 2: With blare of brass, with beating drums,     _____
Line 3: And clashing cymbals, and with roar        _____
Line 4: Of wild beasts never heard before          _____
Line 5: Within town limits. _____ Spick and span     _____
Line 6: Will shine each gilded cage and van;        _____

**B. DIRECTIONS:** *Briefly explain why a good reader will not pause between lines 3 and 4.*

_____

_____

_____

_____

_____

_____

_____

_____

_____

**Poetry Collection:** Shel Silverstein, Octavio Paz, Rachel Field
# Literary Analysis: Sound Devices

**Sound devices** are a writer's tools for bringing out the music in words and for expressing feelings. Sound devices commonly used in poetry include the following:

- **Repetition:** the use, more than once, of any element of language—a sound, word, phrase, clause, or sentence—as in *give me liberty, or give me death*
- **Alliteration:** the repetition of initial consonant sounds, such as the *r* sound in *rock 'n' roll* or the *sl* sound in *slipping and sliding*
- **Onomatopoeia:** the use of a word that sounds like what it means, such as *roar* and *buzz*

**A. DIRECTIONS:** *Underline the repetition, alliteration, and onomatopoeia in the following lines from the poetry collection. On the line after each item, write R for repetition, A for alliteration, and O for onomatopoeia. Some items will have more than one letter. The first one has been done for you.*

1. I've been <u>scratched and sprayed and bitten</u>     <u>R, A</u>
2. No more midnight meowing mews          _____
3. Water and wind and stone               _____
4. the water murmurs as it goes           _____
5. With blare of brass, with beating drums,  _____
6. And clashing cymbals, and with roar     _____

**B. DIRECTIONS:** *Find one example of repetition, one example of alliteration, and one example of onomatopoeia in this passage. Then, write the examples on the lines below.*

When we started feeding the feral cat, we did not know she was about to have kittens. When the kittens were born, they were very tiny. As they grew older, their purring sounded like a motorboat. Like squeaky, funny balls of fluff, they chased each other, pounced on each other, and raced with each other. We were lucky to find homes for them—and we kept Felicity, the feral cat, who is now as tame as tame can be.

1. Example of repetition: _____
2. Example of alliteration: _____
3. Example of onomatopoeia: _____

**Poetry Collection:** Shel Silverstein, Octavio Paz, Rachel Field
# Vocabulary Builder

## Word List
cuddly    dispersed    gilded    hollowed    leisurely    sculpted

**A. DIRECTIONS:** *Following the instructions, use each Word List word correctly.*

1. Use *dispersed* in a sentence about an election at school.

   _____

   _____

2. Use *cuddly* in a sentence about a teddy bear.

   _____

   _____

3. Use *leisurely* in a sentence about what might happen on a weekend.

   _____

   _____

4. Use *hollowed* in a sentence about a pumpkin.

   _____

   _____

5. Use *gilded* in a sentence about a king or queen.

   _____

   _____

6. Use *sculpted* in a sentence about pottery.

   _____

   _____

**B. WORD STUDY:** *The suffix -ly means "like, characteristic of, or in the manner of." Answer each of the following questions using one of these words containing -ly: cuddly, leisurely, simultaneously.*

1. What are two things that you can do *simultaneously*?

   _____

2. What makes something *cuddly*?

   _____

3. What might be a place where you would walk *leisurely*?

   _____

Name _____ Date _____

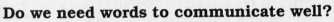

**Poetry Collection**

William Shakespeare, Diana Chang, Gwendolyn Brooks

# Writing About the Big Question

## Do we need words to communicate well?

### Big Question Vocabulary

| | | | | |
|---|---|---|---|---|
| communicate | connection | correspond | dialogue | expression |
| gesture | language | monologue | nonverbal | quote |
| reveal | share | symbolize | verbal | visual |

**A.** *Write a word from the list above to complete each sentence.*

1. What is the _____ between your answer and my question?

2. I like to text message to _____ with my friends.

3. Even though your words are pleasant, your _____ cues are not.

4. If we _____ the work, we'll finish quicker.

**B.** *Follow the directions in responding to each of the items below.*

1. Must a poem be about something you have experienced for you to make a **connection** to it? Why or why not?

   _____

   _____

2. In two sentences, describe the qualities you enjoy in a poem. Use at least two Big Question vocabulary words.

   _____

   _____

**C.** *Complete the sentence below. Then, write a short paragraph in which you connect this idea to the Big Question.*

Reading about someone else's experiences helps the reader to feel a connection to

_____

_____

_____

_____

_____

Name _____ Date _____

# Reading: Read Aloud According to Punctuation to Paraphrase

**Paraphrasing** is restating something in your own words. To paraphrase a poem, you must first understand it and then use simpler language to restate its meaning. **Reading aloud according to punctuation** will help you find clues to a poem's meaning.

- When you read a poem aloud, do not automatically stop at the end of each line.
- Pause only at punctuation marks, as if you were reading a prose passage.

Even when you read poetry silently to yourself, it will make more sense if you follow these rules:

- **No punctuation** at the ends of lines: don't stop
- **After a comma (,):** slight pause
- **After a colon (:), semicolon (;), or dash (—):** longer pause
- **After endmarks—a period (.), question mark (?), or exclamation point (!):** full stop

**A. DIRECTIONS:** *Below are the first five lines from the poem "Cynthia in the Snow." For each line, write the letters* SP *for slight pause,* LP *for longer pause,* FS *for full stop, or* DS *for don't stop. The first line has been done for you as an example.*

Line 1: It SUSHES.                            __FS__

Line 2: It hushes                              _____

Line 3: The loudness in the road.      _____

Line 4: It flitter-twitters,             _____

Line 5: And laughs away from me.     _____

**B. DIRECTIONS:** *Briefly explain why a good reader will not pause between lines 2 and 3.*

_____

_____

_____

_____

_____

_____

_____

_____

_____

_____

_____

**Poetry Collection:** William Shakespeare, Diana Chang, Gwendolyn Brooks
# Literary Analysis: Sound Devices

**Sound devices** are a writer's tools for bringing out the music in words and for expressing feelings. Sound devices commonly used in poetry include the following:

- **Repetition:** the use, more than once, of any element of language—a sound, word, phrase, clause, or sentence—as in *This land is your land/ This land is my land*
- **Alliteration:** the repetition of initial consonant sounds, such as the *b* sound in *beautiful big brown eyes* or the *cl* sound in *clattered* and *clashed*
- **Onomatopoeia:** the use of a word that sounds like what it means, such as *patter* and *roar*

**A. DIRECTIONS:** *Underline the repetition, alliteration, and onomatopoeia in the following lines from the poetry collection. On the line after each item, write R for repetition, A for alliteration, and O for onomatopoeia. Some items will have more than one letter. The first one has been done for you.*

1. You <u>spotted snakes</u> with double tongue     <u> A </u>
2. Lulla, lulla, lullaby, lulla, lulla lullaby     <u>    </u>
3. "Are you Chinese?"/ "Yes." / "American?"/ "Yes"     <u>    </u>
4. Not neither-nor / not maybe     <u>    </u>
5. It SUSHES     <u>    </u>
6. And whitely whirs away     <u>    </u>

**B. DIRECTIONS:** *Find one example of repetition, one example of alliteration, and one example of onomatopoeia in this passage. Then, write the examples on the lines below.*

     There would be no stargazing, no night hike, and no campfire until the weather cleared. We scrambled into our sleeping bags, determined to get some rest. The drip, drip, drip of the rain on the roof of the tent finally put us to sleep. We woke up suddenly when we heard Roy shouting outside. We unzipped the tent and saw a big, brown bear standing on its hind legs at the edge of the woods. We grabbed pans and banged on them as the bear crashed through the bushes to escape the noise.

1. Example of repetition: _____

2. Example of alliteration: _____

3. Example of onomatopoeia: _____

Name _____ Date _____

**Poetry Collection:** William Shakespeare, Diana Chang, Gwendolyn Brooks
# Vocabulary Builder

**Word List**

    hence    nigh    offense    thorny    whirs

**A. DIRECTIONS:** *Following the instructions, use each Word List word correctly.*

1. Use *nigh* in a sentence about a storm that is about to arrive.

_____

_____

2. Use *offense* in a sentence about a misunderstanding.

_____

_____

3. Use *hence* in a sentence about leaving a place.

_____

_____

4. Use *thorny* in a sentence about a porcupine.

_____

_____

5. Use *whirs* in a sentence about a breeze.

_____

_____

**B. WORD STUDY:** *The suffix -y forms adjectives that mean "having, full of, or characterized by." Answer each of the following questions using one of these words containing -y: hearty, stealthy, thorny.*

1. What is one plant that could be considered *thorny*?

_____

2. What would be someone's feelings toward you if that person gives you a *hearty* welcome?

_____

3. What kind of animal has a *stealthy* approach when hunting prey?

_____

Name _____ Date _____

**Poetry Collections:** Shel Silverstein, Octavio Paz, Rachel Field;
William Shakespeare, Diana Chang, Gwendolyn Brooks
# Integrated Language Skills: Grammar

## Predicate Nouns and Predicate Adjectives

Some sentences use linking verbs such as *be, is, were, feel, appear,* or *seems.* In those sentences, the **subject complements** that complete the idea of the subject and verb are called predicate nouns or predicate adjectives. A **predicate noun** renames or identifies the subject of a sentence. A **predicate adjective** describes the subject of a sentence.

Octavio Paz was a Mexican <u>poet</u>. (predicate noun—*identifies* the subject, Octavio Paz)
His poems seem <u>timeless</u>. (predicate adjective—*describes* poems)

**A. PRACTICE:** *Look at the underlined subject complement in each sentence. Draw an arrow to the word or phrase that the subject complement renames or describes. Then, write whether the subject complement is a predicate noun or a predicate adjective. The first one has been done for you.*

1. The sky was <u>cloudy</u> all day. <u>predicate adjective</u>

2. William Shakespeare's plays are <u>famous</u> all over the world. _____

3. Sacramento is the <u>capital</u> of California. _____

4. Kira and Naomi were the highest <u>scorers</u> in the game. _____

5. A sari is the traditional outer <u>garment</u> of an Indian woman. _____

6. Commercials on television are often <u>loud</u> and <u>annoying</u>. _____

**B. WRITING APPLICATION:** *Write five sentences to describe a place in nature that you have seen. Use predicate nouns or predicate adjectives in your sentences. Underline and number five predicate nouns and predicate adjectives. Then, write PN or PA next to the item number below your description.*

1. _____

2. _____

3. _____

4. _____

5. _____

   1. _____    2. _____    3. _____    4. _____    5. _____

Name _____  Date _____

**Poetry Collections:** Shel Silverstein, Octavio Paz, Rachel Field;
William Shakespeare, Diana Chang, Gwendolyn Brooks

# Integrated Language Skills: Support for Writing a Prose Description

Choose one of the poems, and use the chart to list details for a prose description of the picture the poet painted. The list will help you focus on details that appeal to the senses.

| Details I Might See: |
| --- |
| |
| **Details I Might Smell:** |
| |
| **Details I Might Hear:** |
| |
| **Details I Might Touch or Be Able to Feel:** |
| |
| **Details I Might Taste:** |
| |

Now, use the details you have collected to write your prose description.

Name _____ Date _____

# Writing About the Big Question

**Do we need words to communicate well?**

## Big Question Vocabulary

| | | | | |
|---|---|---|---|---|
| communicate | connection | correspond | dialogue | expression |
| gesture | language | monologue | nonverbal | quote |
| reveal | share | symbolize | verbal | visual |

**A.** *Write a word from the list above to complete each sentence.*

1. If you _____ someone, make sure you do it accurately.

2. Her donation to the museum was a generous _____.

3. I read his letter, but what was his _____ response?

4. His two-year-old sister uses the _____ of a much older child.

**B.** *Follow the directions in responding to each of the items below.*

1. Why do you think poets use sensory **language** to **communicate** in their poetry?

_____

_____

2. In two sentences, describe what sensory words can add to a poem. Use at least two Big Question vocabulary words.

_____

_____

**C.** *Complete the sentence below. Then, write a short paragraph in which you connect this idea to the Big Question.*

An example of nonverbal communication in my life is _____

_____

_____

_____

_____

_____

_____

_____

Name _____   Date _____

**"Childhood and Poetry"** by Pablo Neruda

**"Alphabet"** by Naomi Shihab Nye

# Literary Analysis: Sensory Language

In literature, **sensory language** is writing that appeals to one or more of the five senses—sight, hearing, touch, taste, and smell. The use of sensory language creates clear word pictures, or **images,** for the reader. Look at these lines of poetry, for example.

> Crickets sing, curtains stir; / from the dog a gentle snore.

> Soft sheets, white moon; / Summer night is at my door.

The language in this word picture appeals to several senses. The crickets' song and the dog's snore appeal to the sense of hearing. The swaying curtains and white moon appeal to the sense of sight. The soft sheets appeal to the sense of touch. All together, these images bring a summer evening to life in the reader's mind.

**A. DIRECTIONS:** *Read each passage. On the lines below, first write words or phrases that appeal to one or more of the five senses, and then write the senses to which each word or phrase appeals.*

**from "Childhood and Poetry" by Pablo Neruda**

1. The sheep's wool was faded. Its wheels had escaped. All of this only made it more authentic. I had never seen such a wonderful sheep. I looked back through the hole but the boy had disappeared. I went into the house and brought out a treasure of my own: a pinecone, opened, full of odor and resin, which I adored. I set it down in the same spot and went off with the sheep.

| Sensory Language | Senses |
|---|---|
| | |
| | |

**from "Alphabet" by Naomi Shihab Nye**

2. One by one
   the old people
   of our neighborhood
   are going up
   into the air
   their yards
   still wear
   small white narcissus
   sweetening winter

| Sensory Language | Senses |
|---|---|
| | |
| | |

**"Childhood and Poetry"** by Pablo Neruda
**"Alphabet"** by Naomi Shihab Nye
# Vocabulary Builder

## Word List

furtively    glisten    persecution    phrasings    vaguely

**A. DIRECTIONS:** *On each line, write the letter of the phrase that could be substituted for the italicized word in each sentence.*

1. ___ I could *vaguely* make out the road          A. shine or sparkle
   signs.                                            B. cruel acts
2. ___ The thief entered the room *furtively*.       C. not clearly
3. ___ The rain did *glisten on* the sidewalk.       D. in a sneaky way
4. ___ Each language has its own                     E. ways of speaking
   *phrasings*.
5. ___ Stand up against *persecution*!

**B. DIRECTIONS:** *Decide whether each statement below is true or false. Explain your answers.*

1. If you *furtively* glance at someone, you do not want that person to know about it.

   _____

   _____

2. People enjoy *persecution*.

   _____

   _____

3. You can string *phrasings* together to make a necklace.

   _____

   _____

4. Melting icicles *glisten* in the sunlight.

   _____

   _____

5. If you *vaguely* remember someone, that person cannot be a good friend.

   _____

   _____

**"Childhood and Poetry"** by Pablo Neruda
**"Alphabet"** by Naomi Shihab Nye

# Support for Writing a Comparative Essay

Before you draft your essay comparing and contrasting the use of sensory language in these selections, complete the graphic organizers below. In the boxes, write examples of vivid images from each selection. Then, write down an idea that these images help the author express.

## "Childhood and Poetry"

| Image | Image | Image |
|---|---|---|
|  |  |  |

### What idea do the images help express?

## "Alphabet"

| Image | Image | Image |
|---|---|---|
|  |  |  |

### What idea do the images help express?

Now, use your notes to write an essay comparing and contrasting the use of sensory language in the essay and the poem. Be sure to tell which selection you believe uses stronger, more vivid sensory language.

**BQ Tunes**

## Who I Am, performed by Fake Gimms

It's easy to follow a pattern
And copy from the **trend.**
Let it shape my **appearance**
and how I'll look to them.
I feel their **expectations** weigh me down
Is this a **conscious** decision?
Or am I just blindly following the crowd?

I'm sucked in again
By your **reaction.**
I keep thinking over
Over, over and over just what you said.
But if I have **ideals**
And things that I believe
I'll know then just who I am.

So I **reflect,**
I think a little more.
Create a fresh **perspective**
On what I've seen before.
A **custom**, a tradition of my own.
It's not the same old story.
A **unique** way to show
I'm not blindly following the crowd.

I'm sucked in again
By your **reaction.**
I keep thinking over
Over and over just what you said.
But if I have **ideals**
And things that I believe
I'll know then just who I am.

*Continued*

How do I **respond**?

What do I say?

It's so **similar**

So very much the same.

I need **individuality** to break apart the norm,

**Diverse** and many different ways to show who I am,

My **personality**.


I'm sucked in again

By your **reaction**.

I keep thinking over

Over and over just what you said.

But if I have **ideals**

And things that I believe

I'll know then just who I am.

---

Song Title: **Who I Am**
Artist / Performed by Fake Gimms
Vocals & Guitar: Joe Pfeiffer
Guitar: Greg Kuter
Bass Guitar: Jared Duncan
Drums: Tom Morra
Lyrics by Joe Pfeiffer
Music composed by the Fake Gimms
Produced by Mike Pandolfo, Wonderful
Executive Producer: Keith London, Defined Mind

Name _____ Date _____

# Unit 5: Drama
# Big Question Vocabulary—1

 **The Big Question: How do we decide who we are?**

Part of who we are has to do with other people. Other people see us a certain way because of what we choose to show them.

**appearance:** the way someone looks to other people

**custom:** something shared by people of the same culture, like a ritual or ceremony

**diverse:** not similar; varied

**expectations:** what a person thinks or hopes will happen

**similar:** closely the same

**DIRECTIONS:** *Pick any group that you are a member of, such as your class at school, a youth group, a sports team, or a group of friends. Answer the following questions about how you fit into the community you chose. Use all five vocabulary words in your answers.*

| | | |
|---|---|---|
| **2.** How are you the same as others in the group? | | **3.** How are you different from others in the group? |
| | **1.** Describe the group: | |
| **4.** What kinds of things are you supposed to do as a group member? | | **5.** What does the group do together? |

# Unit 5: Drama
# Big Question Vocabulary—2

**The Big Question: How do we decide who we are?**

People are happiest when they can express who they are without worrying about what others will think.

**conscious:** awake; aware of what is going on

**individuality:** the quality that makes someone or something different from others

**perspective:** a personal way of thinking about something

**trend:** a way of doing something or thinking that is fashionable

**unique:** being without equal

**DIRECTIONS:** *Read the passage. Then, answer the question below. Use the vocabulary words in parentheses for your responses.*

"Nobody plays board games anymore!" Clifford said to Mark. Mark's room was full of board games. It was his favorite thing to do. Mark was not sure what to say. His thoughts were going in two different directions. Should he stand up for himself or pretend to agree with Clifford? What is Mark thinking?

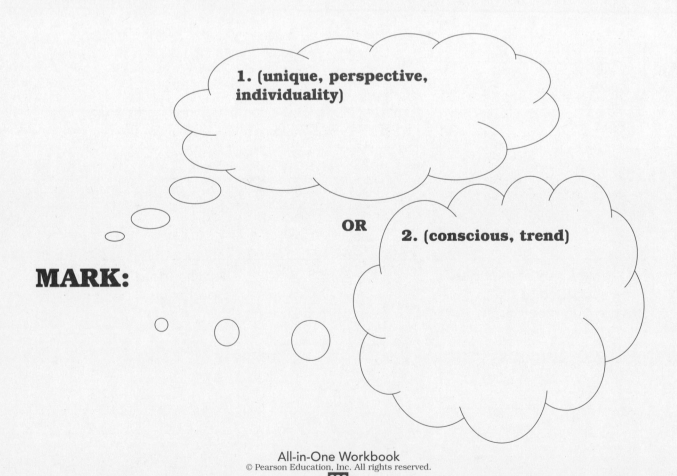

1. (unique, perspective, individuality)

OR

2. (conscious, trend)

**MARK:**

Name _____ Date _____

## Unit 5: Drama
## Big Question Vocabulary—3

**The Big Question: How do we decide who we are?**

Often you show your values and beliefs to others by the way you act, but sometimes your actions do not reveal your deeper feelings.

**ideals:** someone's ethics and beliefs

**personality:** a person's character, particularly the way he or she behaves toward others

**reaction:** action in response to an event or influence

**reflect:** to think back about something's value or importance

**respond:** to react positively to something that has been done or said

**DIRECTIONS:** *Fill in the boxes below to answer the questions. Use the vocabulary words in parentheses.*

**Who am I?**

1. How do I behave?

> **(personality)**

2. What do I believe?

> **(ideals)**

3. What do I think about?

> **(reflect)**

4. How do I act in difficult situations?

> **(react, respond)**

Name _____ Date _____

# Unit 5: Drama
# Applying the Big Question

**How do we decide who we are?**

**DIRECTIONS:** *Complete the chart below to apply what you have learned about how we decide who we are. One row has been completed for you.*

| Example | Event or situation | What it shows about a person or character | What the person or character learns about himself or herself | What I learned |
|---------|--------------------|-------------------------------------------|--------------------------------------------------------------|----------------|
| **From Literature** | In "The Phantom Tollbooth," Milo rescues Rhyme and Reason. | Milo is willing to take risks. | He learns that he is reliable and courageous. | Solving a difficult problem can reveal our strengths. |
| **From Literature** | | | | |
| **From Science** | | | | |
| **From Social Studies** | | | | |
| **From Real Life** | | | | |

Name _____ Date _____

**Joseph Bruchac**
# Listening and Viewing

## Segment 1: Meet Joseph Bruchac
- Why does Joseph Bruchac believe it is important to write stories from your ancestry and tradition? What stories would you like to tell about your ancestors?

_____

_____

_____

_____

## Segment 2: Drama
- How does Joseph Bruchac incorporate Abenaki tradition into his writing? Give specific examples.

_____

_____

_____

_____

## Segment 3: The Writing Process
- What is Joseph Bruchac's revision process? Why do you think revising is an important step in the writing process?

_____

_____

_____

_____

## Segment 4: The Rewards of Writing
- How is storytelling rewarding to Joseph Bruchac? Have you learned more about yourself or the world around you from a particular book or story you have read? Explain.

_____

_____

_____

_____

All-in-One Workbook
**235**

# Learning About Drama

A **drama,** or play, is a story that is written to be performed by actors. A drama includes **characters,** people who take part in the action. Sometimes, one of the characters is a **narrator,** or storyteller. A drama often also includes a **conflict,** a problem between two people or two forces. Most dramas include the following elements.

| Elements of Drama | Definitions |
|---|---|
| Acts and Scenes | **Acts** are the units of action in a drama. Acts are often divided into smaller parts called **scenes.** |
| Script | The **script** is the printed form of the drama. |
| Dialogue | **Dialogue** is what the characters say. Quotation marks do not appear in the script. Instead, the words each character says appear next to the character's name.<br>MAYA: What time does the train arrive? |
| Stage Directions | **Stage directions** are the sets of bracketed information that tell what the stage looks like and how the characters should move and speak.<br>MAYA: [looks concerned as she walks toward the ringing telephone] Maybe that's Gina calling. I hope she's not lost! |
| Set and Props | The **set** is the construction on stage that suggests the time and place of the action. The **props** are movable items that the actors use to make their actions seem realistic. |

**DIRECTIONS:** *Read the following excerpt from a drama. Then answer the questions.*

[A clearing in a dark forest. MARCO, a 15-year-old boy dressed for hiking, sits down slowly by a small campfire. His movements suggest that he is very tired.]

MARCO [speaks to himself, somewhat worried]: It's getting cold. I wish I could find that trail! I wonder where the others are.

TOM [enters from the right, running. He carries a lighted flashlight. His voice shows relief and happiness]. Marco? Man, we've been looking all over for you! Are you OK?

1. Describe the set. _____

2. What characters appear in this scene? _____

3. Give an example of a stage direction that tells how a character speaks.

_____

4. Give an example of a stage direction that tells how a character moves.

_____

5. What conflict does Marco face? _____

Name _____ Date _____

"**Gluskabe and Old Man Winter**" by Joseph Bruchac
# Model Selection: Drama

"Gluskabe and Old Man Winter" is a drama, a play that includes **characters,** people who take part in the action, and a **conflict,** a problem between two people or two forces. A drama can be a **comedy** or a **tragedy.** A comedy has a happy ending. The humor often comes out of the characters' dialogue and situations. In a tragedy, events lead to the downfall of the main character. This character is often a person of great significance, like a king or a heroic figure.

Other elements of drama are included in the chart below.

| Elements of Drama | Definitions |
|---|---|
| Dialogue | **Dialogue** is what the characters say. The words each character says appear next to the character's name. |
| Stage Directions | **Stage directions** are the lines of information that tell what the stage looks like and how the characters should move and speak. |
| Set | The **set** is the construction on stage that suggests the time and place of the action. |
| Props | The **props** are movable items that the actors use to make their actions seem realistic. |

**DIRECTIONS:** *Answer these questions about the elements of drama that appear in "Gluskabe and Old Man Winter."*

1. The set changes from scene to scene. Where does each scene take place? _____
_____

2. What characters appear in Scene I? _____

3. The main conflict develops in Scene II. Describe the conflict and tell what two char-acters, or forces, are involved in it. _____
_____

4. What props are used in Scene II? _____

5. At the beginning of Scene III, what actions are described by the stage directions? _____

6. What conflict develops in Scene III? How is the conflict resolved? _____
_____

7. How is the main conflict solved in Scene IV? _____
_____

Name _____ Date _____

**The Phantom Tollbooth, *Act I,*** based on the book by Norton Juster, by Susan Nanus
# Writing About the Big Question

**How do we decide who we are?**

## Big Question Vocabulary

| | | | | |
|---|---|---|---|---|
| appearance | conscious | custom | diverse | expectations |
| ideals | individuality | personality | perspective | reaction |
| reflect | respond | similar | trend | unique |

**A.** *Use one or more words from the list above to complete each sentence.*

1. You can get clues to help you decide who you are in many _____ ways.

2. How you _____ to others is one way.

3. Your _____ to different kinds of people tells a great deal about you.

4. Another clue to who you are is your _____ on important issues.

5. All the special qualities that make you different from others make up your _____ _____ .

**B.** *Follow the directions in responding to each of the items below.*

1. In two sentences, tell how you feel about two important issues in your school.

   _____

   _____

2. Write two sentences explaining why you feel the way you do about one of the preceding issues. Use at least two of the Big Question vocabulary words.

   _____

   _____

**C.** *In* The Phantom Tollbooth, *Act I, we meet Milo, a bored and unmotivated boy who receives an unexpected gift that leads him to take an amazing trip and to discover an adventurous side of himself. Complete the sentences below. Then, write a short paragraph in which you connect one of your answers to the Big Question.*

Boredom can often be overcome if there is a **conscious** _____

In order to discover our **individuality**, we can _____

_____

_____

_____

Name _____  Date _____

### The Phantom Tollbooth, *Act I,* based on the book by Norton Juster, by Susan Nanus
## Reading: Identify Main Events to Summarize

A **summary** of a piece of writing is a short statement that presents the main ideas and most important points. To summarize a drama, first **reread to identify main events.** Your summary should include only major events that move the story forward. Then, organize events in the order in which they happen.

**DIRECTIONS:** *As you read, use the road map below to record the major events in Act I of* The Phantom Tollbooth. *Write important information about the events in the signposts. Some of the signs have been filled in for you.*

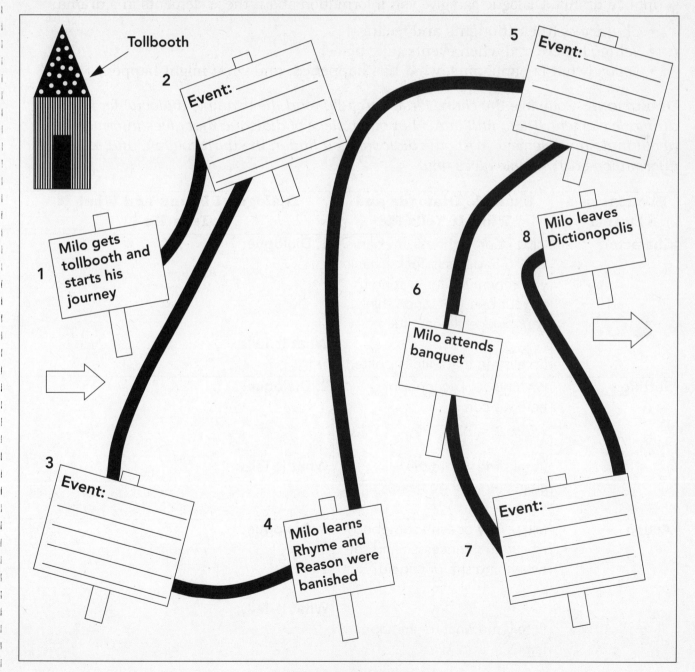

Tollbooth

2 Event: _____

1 Milo gets tollbooth and starts his journey

3 Event: _____

4 Milo learns Rhyme and Reason were banished

5 Event: _____

6 Milo attends banquet

8 Milo leaves Dictionopolis

7 Event: _____

**The Phantom Tollbooth, *Act I,*** based on the book by Norton Juster, by Susan Nanus
## Literary Analysis: Dialogue

A *drama* is a story that is written to be performed. Like short stories, dramas have characters, a setting, and a plot. In a drama, these elements are developed mainly through **dialogue,** the words spoken by the characters. When you read the script, or written form, of a drama, the characters' names appear before their dialogue.

MILO. I'm thinking as hard as I can.

WATCHDOG. Well, think just a little harder than that. Come on, you can do it.

Paying attention to what the characters say will help you understand and enjoy the script of a drama. Dialogue can give you information about these elements in a drama:

- *Characters* (their thoughts and feelings)
- *Setting* (where and when events take place)
- *Action* (what is happening, what has happened, and what might happen)

**DIRECTIONS:** *Complete the chart. First, carefully read the example dialogue for each dramatic element. Then, find in Act I another piece of dialogue that gives information about that same element. Write the dialogue you find in the third column, and tell what information each sample gives you.*

| Element of a Drama | Example Dialogue and What It Tells Me | Dialogue I Found and What It Tells Me |
|---|---|---|
| Character | MILO. Your Highness, my name is Milo and this is Tock. Thank you very much for inviting us to your banquet, and I think your palace is beautiful!<br><br>(It tells me that Milo is polite.) | 1. Dialogue:<br><br><br><br>What It Tells: |
| Setting | WATCHDOG. Dictionopolis, here we come.<br><br><br><br>(It tells me where the characters will go next.) | 2. Dialogue:<br><br><br><br>What It Tells: |
| Action | MILO. Why doesn't somebody rescue the Princesses and set everything straight again?<br><br><br><br>(It tells me what might happen later.) | 3. Dialogue<br><br><br><br>What It Tells: |

Name _____ Date _____

**The Phantom Tollbooth, *Act I,*** based on the book by Norman Juster, by Susan Nanus
# Vocabulary Builder

**Word List**

    ferocious    ignorance    misapprehension    precautionary    unabridged    unethical

**A. DIRECTIONS:** *For each item, write a sentence following the instructions given. Be sure that you use the underlined Word List word correctly and that your sentence expresses the meaning of the word.*

1. Use <u>precautionary</u> in a sentence about preparing for a big storm.

   _____

   _____

2. Use <u>ferocious</u> in a sentence about animals at a zoo.

   _____

   _____

3. Use <u>misapprehension</u> in a sentence about exercise.

   _____

   _____

4. Use <u>ignorance</u> in a sentence about a test.

   _____

   _____

5. Use <u>unabridged</u> in a sentence about a book.

   _____

   _____

6. Use <u>unethical</u> in a sentence about a thief.

   _____

   _____

**B. WORD STUDY:** The root *-eth-* means "character" or "custom." Answer each of the following questions using one of these words containing *-eth-*: *ethics, unethical.*

1. Why would someone study *ethics*?

   _____

2. What might be considered *unethical* behavior by a doctor?

   _____

**The Phantom Tollbooth,** *Act I,* based on the book by Norton Juster, by Susan Nanus
# Integrated Language Skills: Grammar

## Prepositions and Appositives

A **preposition** relates a noun or pronoun to another word in the sentence. Common prepositions include *on, with, by,* and *from.* A **prepositional phrase** begins with a preposition and includes a noun or pronoun called the **object of the preposition.**

An **appositive** is a noun or pronoun that identifies or explains another noun or pronoun in the sentence. An **appositive phrase** is a noun or pronoun with modifiers that identifies or explains another noun or pronoun in the sentence.

| *Preposition/* Prepositional Phrase | *Appositive/*Appositive Phrase |
|---|---|
| Milo begins his journey *to Dictionopolis.* [*Dictionopolis* is the object of the preposition.] | Milo, <u>a young *boy*</u>, takes time for granted. [The phrase explains *Milo.*] |
| He travels *with* brave Tock. [*Tock* is the object of the preposition.] | Tock, <u>a loyal *clock*</u>, helps him. [The phrase explains *Tock.*] |

**A. PRACTICE:** *Underline the prepositonal phrase in each sentence. Draw a circle around the object of the preposition.*

  1. Milo will face many dangers on his journey.

  2. Azaz gives Milo a box of letters.

**B. PRACTICE:** *Underline the appositive phrase in each sentence. Draw a circle around the noun or pronoun it identifies or explains.*

  1. The spelling bee, a large colorful bee, can spell anything.

  2. Humbug, a funny character, has trouble telling the truth.

**C. Writing Application:** *Write four sentences that tell about any of the events in* The Phantom Tollbooth, Act I. *For the first two sentences, use a prepositional phrase in each sentence. Underline each prepositional phrase that you use. For the last two sentences, use an appositive phrase in each sentence. Underline each appositive phrase that you use.*

  1. _____

  2. _____

  3. _____

  4. _____

Name _____ Date _____

**The Phantom Tollbooth,** *Act I,* based on the book by Norton Juster, by Susan Nanus
# Support for Writing a Summary

A **summary** should include only the most important events, characters, and ideas. Use this chart to prepare to write a summary of Act I of *The Phantom Tollbooth.* In the left-hand column, list the important events that you recorded on your earlier chart or your road map. Make sure you list the events in the order that they occurred. Then, in the right-hand column, add details about the events. For example, you might add that Rhyme and Reason are princesses who try to make peace by saying that words and numbers are equally important. Add words such as *first, then,* and *next* to make the order of events clear.

| Events in Order | Details |
|---|---|
| 1. | |
| 2. | |
| 3. | |
| 4. | |
| 5. | |
| 6. | |
| 7. | |
| 8. | |

Now, use the events and details you have listed to write your summary.

Name _____ Date _____

**The Phantom Tollbooth,** *Act II,* based on the book by Norman Juster, by Susan Nanus

# Writing About the Big Question

**How do we decide who we are?**

## Big Question Vocabulary

| | | | | |
|---|---|---|---|---|
| appearance | conscious | custom | diverse | expectations |
| individuality | personality | perspective | reaction | reflect |
| respond | similar | trend | unique | ideals |

**A.** *Use one or more words from the list above to complete each sentence.*

1. Ana and her friend Sarah are _____ in many ways.

2. For example, they both follow the latest fashion _____.

3. However, each girl is _____ in her own way.

4. Ana likes to take time to _____ before making a decision.

5. Sarah shows her _____ by making snap decisions without giving them a second thought.

**B.** *Follow the directions in responding to each of the items below.*

1. In two sentences, tell two ways that you are different from your friends.

   _____

   _____

2. Write two sentences explaining one of the differences above and what it tells about you. Use at least two of the Big Question vocabulary words.

   _____

   _____

**C.** *In* The Phantom Tollbooth, *Act II, Milo comes back from his adventure and finds that he is interested in all of the things in his room which bored him previously. Complete the sentences below. Then, write a short paragraph in which you connect one of your answers to the Big Question.*

New experiences can give us a new **perspective** on _____

_____

In **response** to a new experience, people can develop _____

_____

_____

_____

Name _____ Date _____

**The Phantom Tollbooth, *Act II*,** based on the book by Norman Juster, by Susan Nanus
# Reading: Picture the Action to Compare and Contrast

When you **compare** two things, you tell how they are alike. When you **contrast** two things, you tell how they are different. As you read drama, **picture the action** to compare and contrast characters, situations, and events in the play. To picture the action, pay attention to the dialogue and the descriptions of how characters speak and act.

**DIRECTIONS:** *Use details from Act II to compare and contrast the following pairs of characters.*

**DISCHORD**
1. Doctor of noise
2. _____
   _____
3. _____
   _____

**BOTH**
1. Are met outside Digitopolis
2. _____
3. _____
   _____

**DODECAHEDRON**
1. A shape with 12 faces
2. _____
   _____
3. _____
   _____

**AZAZ**
1. King of Dictionopolis
2. _____
   _____
3. _____
   _____

**BOTH**
1. Never agree
2. _____
   _____
3. _____
   _____

**MATHEMAGICIAN**
1. Owns a number mine
2. _____
   _____
3. _____
   _____

Name _____ Date _____

**The Phantom Tollbooth,** *Act II,* **based on the book by Norman Juster, by Susan Nanus**
# Literary Analysis: Stage Directions

**Stage directions** are the words in a drama that the characters do not say. They tell performers how to move and speak, and they help readers picture the action, sounds, costumes, props, lighting, setting, and scenery. Stage directions are usually printed in italics and set between brackets, as in this example.

MILO. [*Timidly.*] Are you a doctor?

DISCHORD. [VOICE.] I am KAKAFONOUS A. DISCHORD, DOCTOR OF DISSONANCE!

[*Several small explosions and a grinding crash are heard.*]

Stage directions tell the actor who plays Milo to speak as if he is frightened. The stage directions following Dischord's first speech reveal the meaning of *dissonance,* an unpleasant noise.

**DIRECTIONS:** *Read each piece of dialogue with stage directions in the left-hand column. Then, follow the instructions or answer the questions in the right-hand column.*

| Stage Direction | Information |
|---|---|
| DODECAHEDRON. We're here. This is the numbers mine. [*LIGHTS UP A LITTLE, revealing Little Men digging and chopping, shoveling and scraping.*] Right this way and watch your step. [*His voice echoes and reverberates. Iridescent and glittery numbers seem to sparkle from everywhere.*] | **1.** Underline the stage directions that make the numbers seem like jewels. **2.** The stage directions call for turning the lights up a little (from very dim light). What effect would this change have on the audience? _____ _____ |
| MILO. But . . . what bothers me is . . . well, why is it that even when things are correct, they don't really seem to be right? MATHEMAGICIAN. [*Grows sad and quiet.*] How true. It's been that way ever since Rhyme and Reason were banished. [*Sadness turns to fury.*] And all because of that stubborn wretch Azaz! It's all his fault. | **3.** What two different feelings does the Mathemagician show here? _____ _____ |
| MILO. Boy, I must have been gone for an awful long time. I wonder what time it is. [*Looks at clock.*] Five o'clock. I wonder what day it is. [*Looks at calendar.*] It's still today! I've been gone for an hour! [*He continues to look at calendar, and then begins to look at his books and toys and maps and chemistry set with great interest.*] | **4.** Circle the two most important props listed in these stage directions. **5.** What change in Milo do the stage directions reveal? _____ _____ _____ |

Name _____  Date _____

**The Phantom Tollbooth, *Act II,*** based on the book by Norman Juster, by Susan Nanus
# Vocabulary Builder

**Word List**

admonishing    deficiency    dissonance    iridescent    malicious    transfixed

**A. DIRECTIONS:** *Based on the instructions given, write sentences that use the Word List words correctly and express the meanings of both words.*

1. Write a sentence about a coach speaking to players who are not paying attention. Use *admonishing* and *deficiency.*

   _____

   _____

2. Write a sentence about the way a brightly colored but noisy bird looks and sounds. Use *iridescent* and *dissonance.*

   _____

   _____

3. Write a sentence about a snowball fight. Use *transfixed* and *malicious.*

   _____

   _____

**B. WORD STUDY:** The prefix *trans-* means "across" or "through." Answer each of the following questions using one of these words containing *trans-*: *transcends, transfixed, translation, transparent.*

1. What are two items that are *transparent*?

   _____

2. Why would you need a *translation* of a book?

   _____

3. What might cause a deer to be *transfixed*?

   _____

4. What kind of story *transcends* belief?

   _____

Name _____ Date _____

**The Phantom Tollbooth, *Act II,*** based on the book by Norton Juster, by Susan Nanus
# Integrated Language Skills: Grammar

## Gerunds and Gerund Phrases

A **gerund** is a verb form that ends in *-ing* and is used as a noun. A **gerund phrase** is a group of words containing a gerund and any modifiers or other words that relate to it.

| | | |
|---|---|---|
| **Gerund** | *Dancing* is fun. | I enjoy *skating.* |
| **Gerund phrase** | *Dancing with you* is fun. | I enjoy *skating in the park.* |

**A. DIRECTIONS:** *Underline the gerund or gerund phrase in each sentence.*

1. Please make that dog stop barking.

2. Training a puppy is hard work.

3. I have been working on my singing.

4. Running, walking, and swimming are good ways to exercise.

5. We listened to the howling of wolves in the distance.

**B. WRITING APPLICATION:** *Write about some of the things you do during summer vacation. Include and underline gerunds or gerund phrases in three of the sentences.*

_____

_____

_____

_____

_____

_____

_____

_____

_____

_____

_____

Name _____ Date _____

**The Phantom Tollbooth,** *Act II,* based on the book by Norman Juster, by Susan Nanus
# Support for Writing a Review

Use this page to make notes for your **review** of *The Phantom Tollbooth.* Remember that you are reviewing the entire play, not just Act II.

1. **Introduction** (state your overall opinion; be sure to include the title and author of the work):

_____
_____

2. **Parts I liked** (include reasons and supporting details):

_____
_____
_____

3. **Parts I disliked** (include reasons and supporting details):

_____
_____
_____

4. **Characters I liked most** (and why):

_____
_____
_____

5. **Characters I liked least** (and why):

_____
_____
_____

6. **Conclusion** (end with strong and interesting sentences that summarize your over-all opinion):

_____
_____
_____

Now, use the opinions and examples you have listed to write your review.

Name _____ Date _____

*from* **You're a Good Man, Charlie Brown** by Clark Gesner
**"Happiness Is a Charming Charlie Brown at Orlando Rep"** by Matthew MacDermid

# Writing About the Big Question

**How do we decide who we are?**

## Big Question Vocabulary

| | | | | |
|---|---|---|---|---|
| appearance | conscious | custom | diverse | expectations |
| ideals | individuality | personality | perspective | reaction |
| reflect | respond | similar | trend | unique |

**A.** *Use one or more words from the list above to complete each sentence.*

1. It is the _____ of some people to make snap judgments about others.

2. People cannot tell what you are really like by just looking at your outward _____
   _____ .

3. They should make a _____ effort to get to know what you are like on the inside.

4. In any case, you should not try to live up to others' _____
   of you.

5. Always be true to your own set of _____ .

**B.** *Follow the directions in responding to each of the items below.*

1. In two sentences, give two instances when your first impression of someone turned out to be wrong.

   _____

   _____

2. Write two sentences explaining one of the instances above and what it taught you. Use at least two of the Big Question vocabulary words.

   _____

   _____

   _____

**C.** *In the drama you will read, Lucy asks questions to find out more about herself. In the nonfiction article, the author discusses how the actors embody the characters they play. How does an actor decide who a character is? Complete the sentence below. Then, write a short paragraph in which you connect this idea to the Big Question.*

   To play a character successfully, an actor needs to understand certain things about the character, such as _____

   _____

#### from **You're a Good Man, Charlie Brown** by Clark Gesner
#### "Happiness Is a Charming Charlie Brown at Orlando Rep" by Matthew MacDermid
# Literary Analysis: Author's Purpose in Drama and Nonfiction

The **author's purpose** is the main reason the author writes a work. The types of details used in the work suggest the purpose. An author might have many different reasons for writing, such as

- to entertain
- to explain a process
- to persuade
- to inform
- to share an opinion

**A. DIRECTIONS:** *Read each passage, and answer the questions that follow.*

### from **You're a Good Man, Charlie Brown by Clark Gesner**

LUCY. Come on, Linus, answer the question.

LINUS. *(Getting up and facing LUCY)* Look, Lucy, I know very well that if I give any sort of honest answer to that question you're going to slug me.

LUCY. Linus. A survey that is not based on honest answers is like a house that is built on a foundation of sand. Would I be spending my time to conduct this survey if I didn't expect complete candor in all the responses? I promise not to slug you. Now what number would you give me as your crabbiness rating?

LINUS. *(After a few moments of interior struggle)* Ninety-five. *(LUCY sends a straight jab to his jaw which lays him out flat)*

LUCY. No decent person could be expected to keep her word with a rating over ninety. *(She stalks off, busily figuring away on her clipboard)*. . .

1. What type of details does the author use?

   _____

2. What is the author's purpose? _____

### from **"Happiness Is a Charming Charlie Brown at Orlando Rep" by Matthew MacDermid**

However, three performers take their characters to a higher level, stealing the spotlight with every opportunity and even chewing a bit of the scenery along the way. Shannon Bilo is a wonder as Lucy, with a clarion belt and expert comic timing that seem to go for days. Mark Catlett is outstanding as her kid brother Linus, sucking his thumb and doing the tango with his blanket, all the while exuding the mind-numbing intelligence of such a youngster. . . .

3. What type of details does the author use?

   _____

4. What is the author's purpose? _____

### from You're a Good Man, Charlie Brown by Clark Gesner
### "Happiness Is a Charming Charlie Brown at Orlando Rep" by Matthew MacDermid
## Vocabulary Builder

**Word List**

abundantly    civic    evoking    embody    objectionable    tentatively

**A. DIRECTIONS:** Provide an answer and an explanation for each question.

1. If you *tentatively* answer a question, how sure are you about your answer?

   _____

2. If someone is *objectionable* at a party, would the host be likely to invite that person to his next party?

   _____

3. If you find a lesson to be *abundantly* clear, how much help would you need to understand the material?

   _____

4. If a movie is *evoking* laughter, what kind of movie is it?

   _____

5. If you see objects that *embody* the ideas of an architect, what are you viewing?

   _____

6. If you have *civic* duties, can you be a recluse?

   _____

**B. DIRECTIONS:** *Circle the letter of the word that is most nearly opposite in meaning to the word in CAPITAL letters.*

____ 1. OBJECTIONABLE:
   A. cautious       B. clever       C. cruel       D. pleasant

____ 2. TENTATIVELY:
   A. kindly       B. boldly       C. finally       D. justly

____ 3. ABUNDANTLY:
   A. seriously       B. orderly       C. somewhat       D. readily

____ 4. CIVIC:
   A. private       B. biased       C. specific       D. illegal

*from* **You're a Good Man, Charlie Brown** by Clark Gesner
**"Happiness Is a Charming Charlie Brown at Orlando Rep"** by Matthew MacDermid
## Support for Writing a Comparative Essay

Before you draft your essay comparing and contrasting each writer's purpose for writing, complete the graphic organizers below.

| Story told by fictitious characters | Selection Title: |
|---|---|
| **Which details create humor?** | |
| **Which details suggest a lesson to be learned?** | |

| Contains writer's thoughts and feelings | Selection Title: |
|---|---|
| **What does he praise?** | |
| **What does he criticize?** | |
| **What is his overall point of view?** | |

Now use your notes to write an essay comparing and contrasting each writer's purpose for writing.

## Roots, performed by The Dave Pittinger Band

One **generation** passes to its children
The **values** and the things that they believe in
To **influence** and help them make decisions
In the hope that they'll have a better life

So please don't **isolate** yourself — let them in

One **belief** I've got
Is the confidence that we **support** and hold each other up
Our **community**, the people who surround us and
Make us who we are

Just like a bird is affected by the wind
Our **culture** and surroundings help to shape us
If there's a bond, a **connection** with those around us,
We have a better chance to grow

Together as a **group** we strengthen each other
By working toward the **common** goals we share
Our loved ones and our **families** all benefit from knowing that
We'll all make a better world

One **belief** I've got
Is the confidence that we **support** and hold each other up
Our **community**, are the people who surround us and
Make us who we are

**Roots,** *continued*

When we pitch in and get **involved**

When we join in and **participate**

**History** has shown that in the past

We've had a better chance, <u>a better chance</u>

One **belief** I've got

Is the confidence that we **support** and hold each other up

Our **community**, are the people who surround us and

Make us who we are

---

Song Title: **Roots**
Artist / Performed by The Dave Pittenger Band
Vocals & Guitar: Dave Pittenger
Bass Guitar: Jon Price
Drums: Josh Dion
Lyrics by Dave Pittenger
Music composed by Dave Pittenger
Produced by Mike Pandolfo, Wonderful
Executive Producer: Keith London, Defined Mind

# Unit 6: Themes in Folk Literature
# Big Question Vocabulary—1

### The Big Question: How much do our communities shape us?

For many people, family is their most important community. This may include extended family—grandparents, cousins, aunts, and uncles; just immediate family—parents and siblings; or any group of people that a person lives with and has close ties to.

**common:** shared by all

**family:** a group of people who are all related and usually live together

**generation:** a group of people who were all born around the same time

**influence:** to have an effect on the way someone or something develops, behaves, or thinks without using force

**support:** to agree with someone else and offer your help

**DIRECTIONS:** *Answer the following questions using the vocabulary words in parentheses.*

1. What are the names of the people you live with? **(family)**

   _____

   _____

2. What are the ages of people in your family? How many people in your extended family are in similar age groups? **(generation)**

   _____

   _____

3. What do you share with your family? **(common)**

   _____

   _____

4. How have you helped other members of your family and/or how have they helped you? **(support)**

   _____

   _____

5. What effect do other members of your family have on you? **(influence)**

   _____

   _____

# Unit 6: Themes in Folk Literature
## Big Question Vocabulary—2
### The Big Question: How much do our communities shape us?

Larger groups of people that we are associated with form our communities. They can be the people in our neighborhood, our school, a club that we belong to, or at the place where we work.

**belief:** the feeling that something is definitely true or definitely exists

**community:** a group of people who live in the same area or a group of people who share a common interest

**connection:** a situation where two or more people understand each other

**participation:** taking part in an activity or event

**values:** a person's principles about what is right and wrong and what is important in life.

Elana belongs to a youth group. She is making a brochure for new members, but she is having trouble finishing her sentences. Finish Elana's sentences for her. Include all of the above vocabulary words at least once.

**Webbville Youth Group (WYG)**
WYG is more than just a youth group. We are a (1) _____.
This is demonstrated by (2) _____ _____
_____.

The members of WYG share the (3) _____ that helping
one another and being there for one another is (4) _____
_____.

If you decide to join WYG, you won't regret it. Your (5) _____
_____
_____.

**WYG'S (6)** _____
Be kind.
Be supportive of your friends.
Be polite.
Help others.

# Unit 6: Themes in Folk Literature
## Unit 6 Big Question Vocabulary—3
### The Big Question: How much do our communities shape us?

People who share a similar background often understand each other more easily than people with diverse backgrounds. But through communication, people can learn about and feel comfortable with those from other backgrounds.

**culture:** ideas, beliefs, and customs that are shared by people in a society

**group:** several people or things that are related in some way.

**history:** everything that has happened in the past

**involve:** to include something as a necessary part

**isolate:** to stop something or someone from having contact with particular people or ideas

Brian just moved from a small town to a big city. He was feeling lonely. In his town he knew everybody. He also shared the same ideas, beliefs and customs as his small town friends. Here, he didn't understand the ideas, beliefs and customs.

Brian told his old friend Steve,

**1. (isolate, culture)**

Steve advised Brian to find others with similar interests so that he will meet people. He said

**2. (involve, group)**

Brian was grateful for Steve's advice. Brian understood him because they shared a similar past. He said

**3. (history)**

Name _____ Date _____

# Unit 6: Themes in Folk Literature
# Applying the Big Question

 How much do our communities shape us?

**DIRECTIONS:** *Complete the chart below to apply what you have learned about ways that communities shape the lives of their members. One row has been completed for you.*

| Example | Community | Description of this community | Problem or issue | Outcome of the problem or issue | What I learned |
|---|---|---|---|---|---|
| **From Literature** | animals in "He Lion, Bruh Bear, and Bruh Rabbit" | various large and small animals in a wilderness area | A loud, threatening lion scares the other animals. | community gets two wise members to teach the lion that he is not all-powerful | A community can use its resources to change the behavior of a member who is causing a problem. |
| **From Literature** | | | | | |
| **From Science** | | | | | |
| **From Social Studies** | | | | | |
| **From Real Life** | | | | | |

**Julius Lester**
# Listening and Viewing

### Segment 1: Meet Julius Lester
- What types of stories does Julius Lester write? Why do you think it is important to retell these stories?

_____

_____

_____

### Segment 2: Themes in Folk Literature
- Who was Bob Lemmons, and why did Julius Lester write a story about him? Why do you think details and vivid language are important when writing a story like the story of Bob Lemmons?

_____

_____

_____

### Segment 3: The Writing Process
- How is the process of writing an act of discovery for Julius Lester? What do you think he means by "writing is also an act of self-discovery"?

_____

_____

_____

### Segment 4: The Rewards of Writing
- How do Julius Lester's stories act as a bridge between the past and the present? How do you think reading can help you "make sense" of your own life?

_____

_____

_____

# Learning About the Oral Tradition

Passing along stories from one generation to the next is called the **oral tradition.** Here are some common characteristics:

| Characteristics of Stories in the Oral Tradition | Definitions and Examples |
|---|---|
| Universal theme | A **universal theme** is a message about life that can be understood by people of many cultures (the value of hard work). |
| Fantasy | **Fantasy** is writing that is highly imaginative and contains elements that are not found in real life (a man who can fly). |
| Figurative language | **Hyperbole** is exaggeration or overstatement. It is often used to create humor (a man as tall as a tree). **Personification** is the giving of human characteristics to a nonhuman subject (an animal that can talk). |
| Story types | **Folk tales** often deal with heroes, adventure, magic, or romance ("Jack and the Beanstalk"). Some folk tales are **tall tales**—stories that contain hyperbole (stories about Paul Bunyan or Pecos Bill). **Myths** are tales that explain the actions of gods and heroes (the Greek god Apollo) or explain things in nature (how the leopard got its spots). **Legends** are stories about the past. They are often based on facts, but storytellers have added imaginative details (George Washington cutting down the cherry tree). **Fables** are brief stories, usually with animal characters, that teach a moral or lesson (Aesop's fable "The Tortoise and the Hare," which has the moral *Slow and steady wins the race*). |

**DIRECTIONS:** *Underline the term in each pair that best describes each numbered item.*

1. Friendship is the most valuable gift of all.                universal theme        personification

2. The god Zeus hurls a bolt of thunder across the sky.        myth        folk tale

3. A fox learns that it is important to be loyal and honest.        tall tale        fable

4. Raindrops feel sorry for a hot traveler.        hyperbole        personification

5. An elf grants a hardworking farmer three magic wishes.        tall tale        folk tale

Name _____ Date _____

**"Black Cowboy, Wild Horses"** by Julius Lester
# Model Selection: The Oral Tradition

"Black Cowboy, Wild Horses" is an example of literature in the **oral tradition**. A story in the oral tradition was passed down from generation to generation by word of mouth long before it was written down. Stories in the oral tradition often contain a **universal theme,** a message about life. They also contain **fantastic details** that could not happen in real life and **personification,** figurative language that gives human characteristics to nonhuman subjects. **Hyperbole,** an exaggeration or an overstatement, is often found in these stories as well.

Stories written in the oral tradition may be **folk tales** told to entertain and to communicate the shared values of a culture. Folk tales often deal with heroes, adventure, magic, or romance. **Myths** explain the actions of gods and heroes or explain natural phenomena. **Legends** are stories that are widely told about the past. These stories are often based on fact and are a culture's familiar and traditional stories.

**A. DIRECTIONS:** *Answer the following items.*

1. In the opening paragraph, the author states that the land stretched out "as wide as love." What term is used to describe this type of exaggeration? _____

2. Find another example of this type of exaggeration._____

3. The author also states that at the edge of the world, "land and sky kissed." What term describes this type of figurative language? _____

4. Find another example of this type of figurative language. _____

5. In what ways is Bob similar to other cowboys? In what ways is he different?

   _____

   _____

   _____

**B. DIRECTIONS:** *Tell what type of story you think "Black Cowboy, Wild Horses" is. Explain what features of the story led to your answer.*

   _____

   _____

   _____

   _____

   _____

Name _____ Date _____

**"The Tiger Who Would Be King"** by James Thurber
**"The Ant and the Dove"** by Leo Tolstoy
# Writing About the Big Question

## How much do our communities shape us?

### Big Question Vocabulary

| | | | | |
|---|---|---|---|---|
| common | community | connection | culture | family |
| generation | group | history | influence | involve |
| isolate | participation | support | values | belief |

**A.** *Use one or more words from the list above to complete each sentence.*

1. Juan enjoyed going to the town picnic because it made him feel he was part of a _____.

2. Every time Elizabeth played a tennis match, she had a strong _____ that she would win.

3. David and Shauna discovered that being in the photography club had begun to _____ the kinds of photos they took, since they were learning from the other members.

4. Before Raj decided to work on the senator's re-election campaign, he checked into her _____, including her voting record and speeches.

**B.** *Follow the directions in responding to each of the items below.*

1. List two different times when being part of a group made you act in a certain way.
   _____
   _____

2. Write two sentences explaining one of the preceding experiences, and describe how it made you feel. Use at least two of the Big Question vocabulary words.
   _____
   _____
   _____

**C.** *Complete the sentence below. Then, write a short paragraph in which you connect this experience to the Big Question.*

Members of my community helped one another when _____
   _____
   _____
   _____
   _____

Name _____ Date _____

# Reading: Reread to Analyze Cause-and-Effect Relationships

A **cause** is an event, an action, or a feeling that produces a result. The result that is produced is called an **effect.** Sometimes an effect is the result of a number of different causes. To help you identify the relationships between an event and its causes, **reread** important passages in the work, looking for connections. In some stories, all the causes (the events) lead in one way or another to the effect (how the story turns out).

You can use a chart like the one below to record events and actions that work together to produce an effect. You may need to rearrange the lines and arrows for different works. This chart shows you how causes lead to two effects in "The Tiger Who Would Be King."

**DIRECTIONS:** *Fill in the missing causes and effect.*

**1. CAUSE:** The tiger wants to be king of beasts.

   **EFFECT A:** The tiger challenges the lion.

**2. CAUSE:** _____

**3. CAUSE:** The lion defends his crown.

**4. CAUSE:** _____ → **EFFECT B:** _____

**5. CAUSE:** _____

Name _____ Date _____

"The Tiger Who Would Be King" by James Thurber
"The Ant and the Dove" by Leo Tolstoy
## Literary Analysis: Fables and Folk Tales

**Fables** and **folk tales** are part of the oral tradition of passing songs, stories, and poems from generation to generation by word of mouth.

- **Fables** are brief stories that teach a lesson or moral. They often feature animal characters.
- **Folk tales** feature heroes, adventure, magic, and romance. These stories often entertain while teaching a lesson.

**DIRECTIONS:** *Read "The Tiger Who Would Be King" and "The Ant and the Dove." Answer the following items as you read.*

### "The Tiger Who Would Be King"

1. Who are the main characters in this fable? _____

_____

2. Which character, if any, is someone you can admire as a hero? _____

3. Give one reason for your answer to question 2. _____

_____

4. In your own words, what is the moral or lesson of the fable? _____

_____

_____


### "The Ant and the Dove"

5. Who are the main characters in this folk tale? _____

_____

6. Which character, if any, is someone you can admire as a hero? _____

7. Give one reason for your answer to question 6. _____

_____

8. What lesson about life does this folk tale teach? _____

_____

_____

**"The Tiger Who Would Be King"** by James Thurber
**"The Ant and the Dove"** by Leo Tolstoy
## Vocabulary Builder

**Word List**

inquired    monarch    prowled    repaid    repulse    startled

**A. DIRECTIONS:** *Write a* **synonym** *for each vocabulary word. Use a thesaurus if you need one. Write a sentence that includes the synonym. Be sure that your sentence makes the meaning of the word clear.*

Vocabulary word: defend

Synonym: protect

Sentence: The tigress fought to <u>protect</u> her cubs during the battle.

1. Vocabulary word: **startled**      Synonym: _____

   Sentence: _____

2. Vocabulary word: **prowled**      Synonym: _____

   Sentence: _____

3. Vocabulary word: **repulse**      Synonym: _____

   Sentence: _____

4. Vocabulary word: **inquired**      Synonym: _____

   Sentence: _____

5. Vocabulary word: **repaid**      Synonym: _____

   Sentence: _____

6. Vocabulary word: **monarch**      Synonym: _____

   Sentence: _____

**B. WORD STUDY:** The suffix *-ment* means "the act, art, or process of." Complete each of the following sentences about a word containing *-ment-*.

1. As *repayment* to a friend for a favor, you might

   _____

2. The *argument* between the two teams involved

   _____

3. The candidate gave a *statement* in which

   _____

**"The Lion and the Bulls"** by Aesop
**"A Crippled Boy"** by My-Van Tran
# Writing About the Big Question

## How much do our communities shape us?

## Big Question Vocabulary

| | | | | |
|---|---|---|---|---|
| common | community | connection | culture | family |
| generation | group | history | influence | involve |
| isolate | participation | support | values | |

**A.** *Use one or more words from the list above to complete each sentence.*

1. When Dariah broke her leg and had to quit the soccer team, she felt
_____ and alone, since she didn't see her teammates as often.

2. Gene feels stronger and happier about himself on days when he spends a little time
with his parents because his _____ encourages him to do well.

3. Teaching a youth church group was important to Will because it allowed him to
share some of his _____ with others.

4. Working on the block's garage sale was fun, and contributing to the
_____ good of her neighbors made Susannah feel productive.

**B.** *Follow the directions in responding to each of the items below.*

1. List two different times when you felt alone, like an outsider.

_____.

_____.

2. Write two sentences explaining one of the preceding experiences, and describe how
it made you feel. Use at least two of the Big Question vocabulary words.

_____

_____

_____

**C.** *Complete the sentence below. Then, write a short paragraph in which you connect this
experience to the Big Question.*

One time, someone asked me for help with _____ because

_____

_____

_____

_____

Name _____ Date _____

"The Lion and the Bulls" by Aesop
"A Crippled Boy" by My-Van Tran

# Reading: Reread to Analyze Cause-and-Effect Relationships

A **cause** is an event, an action, or a feeling that produces a result. The result that is produced is called an **effect.** Sometimes an effect is the result of a number of different causes. To help you identify the relationships between an event and its causes, **reread** important passages in the work, looking for connections. In some stories, all the causes (the events) lead in one way or another to the effect (how the story turns out).

You can use a chart like the one below to record events and actions that work together to produce an effect. You may need to rearrange the lines and arrows for different works. This chart shows you how causes lead to two effects in "The Lion and the Bulls."

**DIRECTIONS:** *Fill in the missing causes and effect.*

1. **CAUSE:** The lion tries to lure away a bull.

**EFFECT A:** The bulls are safe.

2. **CAUSE:** _____

3. **CAUSE:** The lion thinks of a plan.

4. **CAUSE:** _____ → **EFFECT B:** _____

5. **CAUSE:** _____

Name _____ Date _____

### "The Lion and the Bulls" by Aesop
### "A Crippled Boy" by My-Van Tran
# Literary Analysis: Fables and Folk Tales

**Fables** and **folk tales** are part of the oral tradition of passing songs, stories, and poems from generation to generation by word of mouth.

- **Fables** are brief stories that teach a lesson or moral. They often feature animal characters.
- **Folk tales** feature heroes, adventure, magic, and romance. These stories often entertain while teaching a lesson.

**DIRECTIONS:** *Reread "The Lion and the Bulls" and "A Crippled Boy." Answer the following items as you read.*

**"The Lion and the Bulls"**

1. Who are the main characters in this fable? _____
   _____

2. Which character, if any, is someone you can admire as a hero? _____

3. Give one reason for your answer in question 2. _____
   _____

4. In your own words, what is the moral or lesson of this fable? _____
   _____
   _____

**"A Crippled Boy"**

5. Who are the main characters in this folk tale? _____
   _____

6. Which character, if any, is someone you can admire as a hero? _____

7. Give one reason for your answer in question 6. _____
   _____

8. What lesson about life does this folk tale teach? _____
   _____
   _____

Name _____  Date _____

**"The Lion and the Bulls"** by Aesop
**"A Crippled Boy"** by My-Van Tran
# Vocabulary Builder

**Word List**

crippled    demonstrate    lure    official    provided    slanderous

**A. DIRECTIONS:** *Revise each sentence so that the underlined vocabulary word is used logically. Be sure to keep the vocabulary word in your revision.*

1. People enjoy hearing <u>slanderous</u> remarks about their friends.

   _____

2. In schools of the future, a cat may be <u>provided</u> to help students with homework.

   _____

3. To <u>demonstrate</u> the law of gravity, Tom read a book about falling rocks.

   _____

4. The rabbit with the <u>crippled</u> foot hopped away quickly.

   _____

5. The <u>official</u> Web site for the store says, "Our prices are too high!"

   _____

6. I tried to <u>lure</u> my cat to sit on my lap by growling like an angry dog.

   _____

**B. WORD STUDY:** The suffix *-ous* means "having, full of, or characterized by." Answer the following questions about these words containing *-ous: slanderous, humorous, laborious.*

1. How would a *slanderous* magazine article about someone you admire make you feel, and why? _____

2. What would you do if you heard a *humorous* story, and why?_____

   _____

3. If someone told you something is a *laborious* job, how would you feel about doing it, and why? _____

**"The Tiger Who Would Be King"** by James Thurber
**"The Ant and the Dove"** by Leo Tolstoy
**"The Lion and the Bulls"** by Aesop
**"A Crippled Boy"** by My-Van Tran

# Integrated Language Skills: Grammar

## Clauses: Independent and Subordinate

A **clause** is a group of words with its own subject and verb. An **independent clause** has a subject and a verb and can stand on its own as a complete sentence. A **subordinate clause** has a subject and a verb but cannot stand on its own as a complete sentence.

| | |
|---|---|
| **Independent clause:** | All winter we went to school. |
| **Subordinate clause:** | All winter after we went to school |

A subordinate clause depends on an independent clause to complete its meaning.

**Subordinate clause**       **Independent clause**

All winter after we went to school, we played in the snow.

**A. PRACTICE:** *Identify each of the following items as an independent or a subordinate clause.*

Example: Before the tiger left his den      underline{subordinate}

1. Most people fear tigers and lions _____
2. When you read a fable _____
3. He learned his lesson well _____
4. Before he got into trouble again _____

**B. Writing Application:** *Add to each subordinate clause to make a complete sentence. Write the complete sentence on the line following each subordinate clause.*

As we came to the end of the path,
As we came to the end of the path, we saw a cabin.

1. After we finished eating,

   _____

2. By the time we saw the bear,

   _____

3. Although we got away that time,

   _____

Name _____ Date _____

**"The Tiger Who Would Be King"** by James Thurber
**"The Ant and the Dove"** by Leo Tolstoy
**"The Lion and the Bulls"** by Aesop
**"A Crippled Boy"** by My-Van Tran

## Support for Writing a Fable

Before you write your fable, figure out the causes and effects that lead up to the lesson of your story. Begin by writing down your story ideas on the chart below.

| Lesson | |
|---|---|
| Animal characters | |
| Their situation or conflict | |

Next, decide on the action in your fable. Write one story event on each line. Use only as many lines as you need. Draw arrows between events to show causes and effects that are connected. Finally, write how your fable will end.

**Story events:**

_____

_____

_____

_____

**How my fable will end:**




Now, use your notes to draft a fable that teaches a lesson.

## "Arachne" by Olivia E. Coolidge
# Writing About the Big Question

### How much do our communities shape us?

### Big Question Vocabulary

| | | | | |
|---|---|---|---|---|
| common | community | connection | culture | family |
| generation | group | history | influence | involve |
| isolate | participation | support | values | belief |

**A.** *Use one or more words from the list above to complete each sentence.*

1. Diana's grandmother said that her parents had told her animal stories with lessons, as a way to pass wisdom on from one _____ to the next.

2. Sanjay enjoys reading myths from the Hindu tradition and is happy that his _____ has a strong tradition of old stories.

3. Stories like "Jack and the Beanstalk" and *To Kill a Mockingbird* _____ the idea that it is good to fight evil, no matter how small you are.

4. Len's dad told interesting stories about the odd jobs he did to pay for college as a way of passing onto his kids the _____ of education and hard work.

**B.** *Follow the directions in responding to each of the items below.*

1. List two different times when you learned a lesson from doing something wrong.

   _____.

   _____.

2. Write two sentences explaining one of the preceding experiences, and describe what you learned and how you felt about it. Use at least two of the Big Question vocabulary words.

   _____

   _____

**C.** *Complete the sentence below. Then, write a short paragraph in which you connect this experience to the Big Question.*

The story of _____ taught me that _____

_____

_____

_____

_____

Name _____     Date _____

# Reading: Ask Questions to Analyze Cause-and-Effect Relationships

A **cause** is an event, an action, or a feeling that makes something happen. An **effect** is what happens. Sometimes, an effect can become the cause of another event. For example, seeing an empty soda can on the sidewalk can cause you to pick it up. The good example you set can then cause someone else to pick up litter when he or she sees it. As you read, look for clue words such as *because, as a result, therefore,* and *so* to signal a cause-and-effect relationship. Then, **ask questions** such as "What happened?" and "Why did this happen?" to help you follow the cause-and-effect relationships in a literary work.

**DIRECTIONS:** *Look at the organizer below. Some of the causes and effects and the questions you might ask about them in the first half of "Arachne" have been listed for you. Fill in the missing causes, questions, and effects. Notice as you work that events may follow each other without one causing the next. Also, notice that an effect can become the cause of another event.*

| CAUSE | | EFFECT |
|---|---|---|
| **1.** Arachne becomes famous as a weaver. | **2.** What happened? → | **3.** People say Athene must have taught Arachne. |
| **4.** _____ _____ | **5.** _____ → | **6.** _____ _____ |
| **7.** _____ _____ | **8.** Why? → | **9.** The old woman shows herself to be Athene. |
| **10.** _____ _____ | **11.** _____ → | **12.** Arachne competes with Athene. |

Name _____ Date _____

"**Arachne**" by Olivia E. Coolidge
# Literary Analysis: Myths

**Myths** are fictional tales that describe the actions of gods or heroes. Every culture has its own collection of myths. A myth can do one or more of the following:

- tell how the universe or a culture began
- explain something in nature, such as the return of spring after winter
- teach a lesson
- express a value, such as courage or honor

**DIRECTIONS:** *As you read "Arachne," look for examples of each characteristic of a myth. Use the examples to fill in the chart below. If you do not find an example of a particular characteristic, write "None" in the second column.*

| A Myth Can . . . | How "Arachne" Shows This |
|---|---|
| **1.** Describe the actions of gods or heroes | |
| **2.** Tell how the universe or a culture began | |
| **3.** Explain something in nature | |
| **4.** Teach a lesson | |
| **5.** Express values and traditions that are important to the culture | |

**All-in-One Workbook**

Name _____ Date _____

"**Arachne**" by Olivia E. Coolidge
# Vocabulary Builder

**Word List**

humble    indignantly    mortal    obscure    obstinacy    strive

**A. DIRECTIONS:** *Complete each sentence below. Use examples or details from the story to show that you understand the meaning of the underlined vocabulary word. You may write additional sentences if necessary.*

Example:  Some of Arachne's visitors were *nymphs,* _____.
Some of Arachne's visitors were nymphs, minor nature goddesses.

1. Arachne lived in an <u>obscure</u> village, a place that was _____

   _____

2. Someone who is <u>mortal</u> must eventually _____

   _____

3. Arachne showed her <u>obstinacy</u> when she _____

   _____

4. Far from being <u>humble</u>, Arachne was actually _____

   _____

5. The goddess spoke <u>indignantly</u>, because _____

   _____

6. When we <u>strive</u> for a goal, we _____

   _____

**B. WORD STUDY:** The Latin root *-mort-* means death. Each of the following statements contains a word based on *-mort-*. Correct each statement to make it more logical.

1. His speed record seemed *immortal,* since it lasted about a week.

   _____

2. The young woman was a *mortal,* and so she was equal to the mythological gods.

   _____

Name _____ Date _____

### Prologue *from* **The Whale Rider** by Witi Ihimaera
# Writing About the Big Question

**How much do our communities shape us?**

## Big Question Vocabulary

| | | | | |
|---|---|---|---|---|
| common | community | connection | culture | family |
| generation | group | history | influence | involve |
| isolate | participation | support | values | belief |

**A.** *Use one or more words from the list above to complete each sentence.*

1. Meg loves to _____ her sisters in her musical projects, since they are talented and fun to work with, and they always improve on her ideas.

2. _____ in a nature walk is one of our Thanksgiving Day traditions, as we collect leaves and pinecones to decorate the table and wait for dinner to finish cooking.

3. Jorge's favorite season is the spring, when the new plant life and warmer weather _____ him to be more hopeful and think about new projects for himself.

4. Kendra has done research into her grandparents and great-grandparents in order to create a _____ tree as an anniversary present for her parents.

**B.** *Follow the directions in responding to each of the items below.*

1. List two different experiences when you felt a strong link with nature.

_____.

_____.

2. Write two sentences explaining one of the preceding experiences, and describe what you learned and how you felt about it.  Use at least two of the Big Question vocabulary words.

_____

_____

**C.** *Complete the sentence below. Then, write a short paragraph in which you connect this experience to the Big Question.*

If I could be an animal for one day, I would be a _____ because I would be able to _____

_____

_____

_____

Name _____ Date _____

# Reading: Ask Questions to Analyze Cause-and-Effect Relationships

A **cause** is an event, an action, or a feeling that makes something happen. An **effect** is what happens. Sometimes, an effect can become the cause of another event. For example, seeing litter in the park can cause you to pick it up. The good example you set might then cause someone else to help keep the park clean. As you read, look for clue words such as *because, as a result, therefore,* and *so* to signal a cause-and-effect relationship. Then, **ask questions** such as "What happened?" and "Why did this happen?" to help you follow the cause-and-effect relationships in a literary work.

**DIRECTIONS:** *Look at the organizer below. Some of the causes and effects and the questions you might ask about them in the Prologue have been listed for you. Fill in the missing causes, questions, and effects. Notice as you work that events may follow each other without one causing the next. Also, notice that an effect can become the cause of another event.*

| CAUSE | | EFFECT |
|---|---|---|
| **1.** Land and sea feel a great emptiness. | **2.** Why? | **3.** They are waiting for the gift of mankind. |
| **4.** _____ _____ | **5.** _____ | **6.** _____ _____ |
| **7.** A man rides high on the back of a gigantic whale. | **8.** What happened? | **9.** _____ _____ |
| **10.** _____ _____ | **11.** _____ | **12.** The spears turn into living creatures. |

Name _____ Date _____

**Prologue *from* The Whale Rider** by Witi Ihimaera
# Literary Analysis: Myths

**Myths** are fictional tales that describe the actions of gods or heroes. Every culture has its collection of myths. A myth can do one or more of the following:

- tell how the universe or a culture began
- explain something in nature, such as the return of spring after winter
- teach a lesson
- express a value, such as courage or honor

**DIRECTIONS:** *As you read the Prologue from* The Whale Rider, *look for examples of each characteristic of a myth. Use the examples to fill in the chart below. If you do not find an example of a particular characteristic, write "None" in the second column.*

| A Myth Can . . . | How Prologue from *The Whale Rider* Shows This |
|---|---|
| **1.** Describe the actions of gods or heroes | |
| **2.** Tell how the universe or a culture began | |
| **3.** Explain something in nature | |
| **4.** Teach a lesson | |
| **5.** Express values and traditions that are important to the culture | |

Name _____ Date _____

**Prologue *from* The Whale Rider** by Witi Ihimaera
# Vocabulary Builder

**Word List**

  apex   clatter   reluctant   splendor   teemed   yearning

**A. DIRECTIONS:** *Complete each sentence below. Use examples or details from the story to show that you understand the meaning of the underlined vocabulary word. You may write additional sentences if necessary.*

  **Example:** The lizard was a *sentinel* that _____
  The lizard was a sentinel that watched, guarded, and waited for what might happen.

1. The forest was filled with <u>clatter</u> as _____

   _____

2. The fairy people were <u>reluctant</u> to welcome people because _____

   _____

3. The flying fish saw <u>splendor</u> in the whale rider's _____

   _____

4. His political career reached its <u>apex</u> when he _____

   _____

5. Adele's <u>yearning</u> for her old home was finally satisfied when _____

   _____

6. Yesterday the music store <u>teemed</u> with autograph seekers because _____

   _____

**B. WORD STUDY:** The Latin root *-splend-* means "to shine." Answer each of the following questions using one of these words containing *-splend-*.

1. If a house is noted for its <u>splendor</u>, what would you expect to find in it?

   _____

2. What might cause a sky to be described as *resplendent*? _____

   _____

Name _____  Date _____

"Arachne" by Olivia E. Coolidge
Prologue *from* The Whale Rider by Witi Ihimaera

# Integrated Language Skills: Grammar

**Sentences: Simple, Compound, and Complex Sentence Structure**

Sentences can be classified according to the number and kinds of their **clauses**—groups of words with their own subjects and verbs.

- A **simple sentence** has one independent clause.

  The sun came out. Sam and Al raced. Priya stayed inside and played.

- A **compound sentence** has two or more independent clauses. Independent clauses are usually joined by a comma and a conjunction such as *and, but, or, nor,* or *yet.*

  We packed our bags, Mom made lunch, and Dad put gas in the car.

- A **complex sentence** has one independent clause and one or more subordinate clauses. Some words that begin subordinate clauses are *after, because, before, if, when, where,* and *who.*

  I have a cousin who is a performer.

**A. PRACTICE:** *Identify each sentence below. Write* **S** *if it is a simple sentence,* **CP** *if it is a compound sentence, or* **CX** *if it is a complex sentence.*

____ 1. Nobody knows who first made up myths and folk tales.

____ 2. Myths, folk tales, and fables are usually stories from oral tradition.

____ 3. In some myths, when humans are too proud, they are punished by the gods.

____ 4. Good behavior is rewarded, and bad behavior has serious consequences.

**B. Writing Application:** *Imagine that you are at an amusement park with friends. Write a paragraph about the things you might see and do there. Use at least one of each type of sentence in your paragraph.*

_____

_____

_____

_____

_____

_____

_____

_____

_____

_____

Name _____ Date _____

"**Arachne**" by Olivia E. Coolidge
**Prologue** *from* **The Whale Rider** by Witi Ihimaera
## Support for Writing a Compare-and-Contrast Essay

**Writing: "Arachne"**

Use the following chart to take notes for your **compare-and-contrast essay**. In the first column, write down lessons learned from "Arachne." In the second column, write down lessons learned from your own experience.

| Lessons learned from "Arachne" | Lessons learned from my own experience |
| --- | --- |
| | |
| | |
| | |

Now, use your notes to draft your essay. As you write, remember to compare the difference between learning lessons from a myth and learning lessons from your own experience.

**Writing: Prologue *from* The Whale Rider**

Use the following chart to take notes for your **compare-and-contrast essay**. In the first column, write down the feelings expressed in Prologue. In the second column, write down your own experience of waiting for something exciting to happen.

| Feelings the myth expresses | Your feeling of yearning for something |
| --- | --- |
| | |
| | |
| | |

Now, use your notes to draft your essay. As you write, focus on the difference between the feelings expressed in the Prologue and your real-life feelings.

Name _____ Date _____

**"Mowgli's Brothers"** by Rudyard Kipling
*from* **James and the Giant Peach** by Roald Dahl
# Writing About the Big Question

## How much do our communities shape us?

**Big Question Vocabulary**

| | | | | |
|---|---|---|---|---|
| common | community | connection | culture | family |
| generation | group | history | influence | involve |
| isolate | participation | support | values | belief |

**A.** *Use one or more words from the list above to complete each sentence.*

1. When his family moved to the United States from India, Siddhartha was a little nervous about living in a place with such a different _____ from his own, but he settled in very quickly.

2. LeeAnn loved watching the life going on in her ant farm, in which individuals worked together for the _____ good.

3. Jen's favorite fantasy is to time-travel to a different period in _____; her favorite time-travel destination would be Elizabethan England, where she could meet William Shakespeare.

4. Jaime is fascinated with the social behavior of wolves, especially the way they recognize different levels of status within their _____.

**B.** *Follow the directions in responding to each of the items below.*

1. List two different times when you were in a very unusual environment.

_____.

_____.

2. Write two sentences describing one of the preceding experiences. Tell what it was like and how you felt about it. Use at least two of the Big Question vocabulary words.

_____

_____

**C.** *Complete the sentence below. Then, write a short paragraph in which you connect this experience to the Big Question.*

If I could spend time in any other place in the universe, I would like to go to _____ because _____

_____

_____

Name _____ Date _____

## "Mowgli's Brothers" by Rudyard Kipling
### *from* James and the Giant Peach by Roald Dahl
## Literary Analysis: Elements of Fantasy

**Fantasy** is imaginative writing that contains elements not found in real life. Stories about talking animals, books that come to life, or time travel are all examples of fantasy. Many fantastic stories, however, contain **realistic elements**—characters, events, or situations that are true to life. In a fantastic story about a talking cat, for example, the cat might do many things that real cats do. She might purr, stretch, and flex her claws, all of which are real-life cat behaviors.

**DIRECTIONS:** *Read each passage below and answer the questions.*

### from "Mowgli's Brothers" by Rudyard Kipling

It was the jackal—Tabaqui the Dishlicker—and the wolves of India despise Tabaqui because he runs about making mischief, and telling tales, and eating rags and pieces of leather from the village rubbish-heaps. . . .

"Enter, then, and look," said Father Wolf, stiffly, "but there is no food here."

"For a wolf, no," said Tabaqui, "but for so mean a person as myself a dry bone is a good feast. Who are we, the Gidur-log [the jackal-people], to pick and choose?" He scuttled to the back of the cave, where he found the bone of a buck with some meat on it, and sat cracking the end merrily.

1. List two details that are not found in real life.

   _____

2. List two details that are true to life.

   _____

### from *James and the Giant Peach* by Roald Dahl

"Is that a Glow-worm?" asked James, staring at the light. "It doesn't look like a worm of any sort to me."

"Of course it's a Glow-worm," the Centipede answered. "At least that's what she calls herself. Although actually you are quite right. She isn't really a worm at all. Glow-worms are never worms. They are simply lady fireflies without wings. Wake up, you lazy beast!"

But the Glow-worm didn't stir, so the Centipede reached out of his hammock and picked up one of his boots from the floor. "Put out that wretched light!" he shouted, hurling the boot up at the ceiling.

3. List two details that are not found in real life.

   _____

4. List two details that are true to life.

   _____

### "Mowgli's Brothers" by Rudyard Kipling
### *from* James and the Giant Peach by Roald Dahl
## Vocabulary Builder

**Word List**

colossal    dispute    fostering    intently    monotonous    quarry

**A. DIRECTIONS:** *Each sentence below features a word from the Word List. If the sentence makes sense, explain why. If it does not make sense, write a new sentence using the word correctly.*

1. I watched the *colossal* specks of dust drift through the ray of sun.

   _____

2. "Please stop *fostering* me!" Ella said to her little brother.

   _____

3. We ended our *dispute* by shaking hands and agreeing to disagree.

   _____

4. If you read the book *intently*, you will probably miss some important details.

   _____

5. The leopard eyed his *quarry* from a low tree branch and prepared to pounce.

   _____

6. True, the adventure movie was long, but it was also exciting and *monotonous*!

   _____

**B. DIRECTIONS:** *Use a word from the Word List to complete each analogy. Your choice should create a word pair whose relationship matches the relationship between the first two words given.*

1. *Run* is to *quickly* as *work* is to _____.
2. *Elf* is to *small* as *giant* is to _____.
3. *Idea* is to *thought* as *disagreement* is to _____.
4. *Detective* is to *clue* as *hunter* is to _____.

Name _____ Date _____

### "Mowgli's Brothers" by Rudyard Kipling
### *from* James and the Giant Peach by Roald Dahl
# Writing to Compare Literary Works

Before you draft your essay comparing and contrasting each story's fantastic and realistic elements, complete the graphic organizers below. For each graphic organizer, decide which story best fits each sentence.

| Animals |
| --- |
| The animals in _____ seem more realistic because _____ _____. |
| In contrast, the animals in _____ do more fantastic things such as _____. |

| Human Character |
| --- |
| The boy in _____ is more fantastic because he _____ _____. |
| In contrast, the boy in _____ does more realistic things such as ___ _____. |

| Setting |
| --- |
| The setting in _____ seems more realistic because _____ _____. |
| In contrast, the setting in _____ seems more fantastic because ____ _____. |

| Situation |
| --- |
| The situation in _____ *might* really happen because _____ _____. |
| In contrast, the situation in _____ could never happen because ____ _____. |

Now, use your notes to write an essay comparing and contrasting the authors' use of fantastic and realistic elements in these two stories. Begin your essay by stating which story contains more fantastic elements overall.

© Pearson Education, Inc. All rights reserved.

Name _____ Date _____

**"Why the Tortoise's Shell Is Not Smooth"** by Chinua Achebe

# Writing About the Big Question

## How much do our communities shape us?

### Big Question Vocabulary

| | | | | |
|---|---|---|---|---|
| common | community | connection | culture | family |
| generation | group | history | influence | involve |
| isolate | participation | support | values | belief |

**A.** *Use one or more words from the list above to complete each sentence.*

1. Rob plays funny tricks, but his tricks tend to _____ him a little because we don't trust him completely.

2. Because she had been on the wrong end of some practical jokes, Marina identified with stories that _____ the idea that playing tricks is wrong.

3. In a popular story, a _____ ignores a boy's genuine cries for help because he had tricked everyone before by crying "wolf" when there was no wolf.

4. Glenna learned the hard way that playing tricks, even harmless ones, could break an important _____ between her and her best friends.

**B.** *Follow the directions in responding to each of the items below.*

1. List two different times when someone played a trick on you.

   _____.

   _____.

2. Write two sentences explaining one of the preceding experiences, and describe what happened and how you felt about it. Use at least two of the Big Question vocabulary words.

   _____

   _____

**C.** *Complete the sentence below. Then, write a short paragraph in which you connect this experience to the Big Question.*

   I played a trick on _____ when I _____

   _____

   _____

   _____

   _____

**"Why the Tortoise's Shell Is Not Smooth"** by Chinua Achebe
# Reading: Preview the Text to Set a Purpose for Reading

Your **purpose** for reading is the reason you read a text. Sometimes, you may choose a text based on a purpose you already have. Other times, you may set a purpose based on the kind of text you have in front of you. **Setting a purpose** helps you focus your reading. You might set a purpose to learn about a subject, to gain understanding, to take an action, or simply to read for enjoyment.

**Preview the text** before you begin to read. Look at the title, the pictures, and the beginnings of paragraphs to get an idea about the literary work. This will help you set a purpose or decide if the text will fit a purpose you already have.

**DIRECTIONS:** *Answer the following questions as you preview "Why the Tortoise's Shell Is Not Smooth." You can use questions like these as you preview any text.*

1. Look at the title. What ideas or feelings do you have about the title? _____
   _____

2. Who is the author? What do you know about this author? _____
   _____

3. Look at any photographs, drawings, or artwork in the text. How does the artwork help you set a purpose for reading? _____
   _____

4. Read the beginning of several paragraphs in the text. What kind of text does this seem to be? _____
   _____

5. Think about the clues you picked up during your preview. What purpose will you set to help you focus your reading of this text? _____
   _____

**All-in-One Workbook**
**288**

Name _____  Date _____

**"Why the Tortoise's Shell Is Not Smooth"** by Chinua Achebe
# Literary Analysis: Personification

**Personification** is the representation of an animal or an object as if it had a human personality, intelligence, or emotions. In folk literature, personification is often used to give human qualities to animal characters. The actions of these animal characters can show human qualities, behavior, and problems in a humorous way.

**DIRECTIONS:** *As you read, think about the human and animal qualities shown by the tortoise, the birds, and the parrot in the story. Next to each name below, write two of that character's animal qualities on the lines at the left and two of that character's human qualities on the lines at the right. Treat the group of birds as one character.*

**Animal Qualities**                                                    **Human Qualities**

_____                          _____

_____     ( 1. Tortoise )      _____


_____                          _____

_____     ( 2. the birds )     _____


_____                          _____

_____     ( 3. Parrot )        _____

Name _____  Date _____

**"Why the Tortoise's Shell Is Not Smooth"** by Chinua Achebe
# Vocabulary Builder

**Word List**

compound    cunning    custom    eloquent    famine    orator

**A. DIRECTIONS:** *Write your answer in a complete sentence using a Word List word.*

1. What might happen to people who live in a place where there is a *famine*?

   _____

2. What kind of job might require someone to be a skilled *orator*? Why?

   _____

3. Imagine that you have been asked to write an *eloquent* article for the paper. What will you write about?

   _____

4. Why is being <u>cunning</u> helpful in a competition?

   _____

5. How could a single house be turned into a <u>compound</u>?

   _____

6. What is your favorite family <u>custom</u>?

   _____

**B. DIRECTIONS:** *Choose the word or words that mean almost the same as the bold vocabulary word. Write the letter for your answer choice on the line.*

_____ 1. When Tortoise spoke at the party, his speech was **eloquent.**
   A. humorous                        C. long
   B. expressive                      D. illogical

_____ 2. The rains ended the drought that had caused years of **famine.**
   A. food abundance                  C. food shortage
   B. flooding                        D. rebellion

_____ 3. A child whose mother is a famous storyteller might want to be a great **orator.**
   A. doctor                          C. writer
   B. leader                          D. speaker

**C. WORD STUDY:** The suffix -*ary* means "related to or connected with." Change each of the italicized words in parentheses to a word that ends in -*ary*.

1. It is a *(custom)* _____ practice in many societies to celebrate an adolescent's passage to manhood or womanhood.

2. A sensitive child might have an *(imagine)* _____ friend.

3. My mother was given the *(honor)* _____ title of professor emeritus.

Name _____  Date _____

**"He Lion, Bruh Bear, and Bruh Rabbit"** by Virginia Hamilton
# Writing About the Big Question
**How much do our communities shape us?**

**Big Question Vocabulary**

| | | | | |
|---|---|---|---|---|
| common | community | connection | culture | family |
| generation | group | history | influence | involve |
| isolate | participation | support | values | belief |

**A.** *Use one or more words from the list above to complete each sentence.*

1. Because Sandra had very good judgment but didn't talk very much, whatever she did say always had a lot of _____ among her friends.

2. Stefan was the oldest and hardest-working of six brothers, and all the members of his _____ knew they could always count on him.

3. My Aunt Charlotte became prominent in her _____ when she organized a food drive, and later on she was elected to the school board.

4. Rachel often became the second-in-command in any organization she joined because she preferred not to be the one in charge, but she did like to _____ other people's ideas.

**B.** *Follow the directions in responding to each of the items below.*

1. List two times when you asked for advice.

   _____.

   _____.

2. Write two sentences describing one of the preceding experiences. Tell what happened, what you learned, and how you felt about it. Use at least two of the Big Question vocabulary words.

   _____

   _____

**C.** *Complete the sentence below. Then, write a short paragraph in which you connect this experience to the Big Question.*

If I had to classify myself as a leader or a follower, I would say that I am a
_____ because _____

_____

_____

_____

Name _____ Date _____

# Reading: Preview the Text to Set a Purpose for Reading

Your **purpose** for reading is the reason you read a text. Sometimes, you may choose a text based on a purpose you already have. Other times, you may set a purpose based on the kind of text you have in front of you. **Setting a purpose** helps you focus your reading. You might set a purpose to learn about a subject, to gain understanding, to take an action, or simply to read for enjoyment.

**Preview the text** before you begin to read. Look at the title, the pictures, and the beginnings of paragraphs to get an idea about the literary work. This will help you set a purpose or decide if the text will fit a purpose you already have.

**DIRECTIONS:** *Answer the following questions as you preview "He Lion, Bruh Bear, and Bruh Rabbit." You can use questions like these as you preview any text.*

1. Look at the title. What ideas or feelings do you have about the title? _____

    _____

2. Who is the author? What do you know about this author? _____

    _____

3. Look at any photographs, drawings, or artwork in the text. How does the artwork help you set a purpose for reading? _____

    _____

4. Read the beginning of several paragraphs in the text. What kind of text does this seem to be? _____

    _____

5. Think about the clues you picked up during your preview. What purpose will you set to help you focus your reading of this text? _____

    _____

Name _____ Date _____

# Literary Analysis: Personification

**Personification** is the representation of an animal or an object as if it had a human personality, intelligence, or emotions. In folk literature, personification is often used to give human qualities to animal characters. The actions of these animal characters can show human qualities, behavior, and problems in a humorous way.

**DIRECTIONS:** *As you read, think about the human and animal qualities shown by the lion, the bear, and the rabbit in the story. Next to each name below, write two of that character's animal qualities on the lines at the left and two of that character's human qualities on the lines at the right.*

**Animal Qualities**                                              **Human Qualities**

_____              ( **1. He Lion** )              _____

_____                                             _____


_____              ( **2. Bruh Bear** )            _____

_____                                             _____


_____              ( **3. Bruh Rabbit** )          _____

_____                                             _____

Name _____ Date _____

"He Lion, Bruh Bear, and Bruh Rabbit" by Virginia Hamilton
# Vocabulary Builder

**Word List**

cordial    lair    olden    peaceable    scrawny    thicket

**A. DIRECTIONS:** *Write your answer on the lines following each item. Use complete sentences for each answer.*

1. Give an example of a *cordial* comment you might make to someone.

_____

_____

2. What is one creature you might find in a *lair*?

_____

3. How would someone who is <u>peaceable</u> act during an argument?

_____

4. Why would a <u>thicket</u> be a good place to hide?

_____

5. How could a <u>scrawny</u> person change his appearance?

_____

6. What are people's memories of <u>olden</u> times like?

_____

**B. DIRECTIONS:** *Think about the meaning of the italicized vocabulary words and answer the questions. Use the vocabulary word in your answer.*

1. Imagine that you are walking in the woods and you find a *lair*. What would you do?

_____

_____

2. Imagine that you are camping in the woods. There is a bear outside your tent. How *cordial* would you be in greeting the bear? Why? What would you do?

_____

_____

_____

**C. WORD STUDY:** The suffix *-en-* means "to become, to cause to be, or to be made of." Change each of the italicized words in parentheses to a word that ends in *-en*.

1. As I heard the words of praise, I felt my face *(red)* _____

2. As they grew tired, their efforts started to *(weak)* _____

3. Movies set in graveyards always *(fright)* me. _____

**"He Lion, Bruh Bear, and Bruh Rabbit"** by Virginia Hamilton
**"Why the Tortoise's Shell Is Not Smooth"** by Chinua Achebe
# Integrated Language Skills: Grammar

## Punctuation: Commas

A **comma** is a punctuation mark used to separate words or groups of words. Commas signal readers when to pause. They also help prevent confusion in meaning. One important use for commas is to separate items in a series—three or more items written one after the other.

| | |
|---|---|
| Words in a series: | In February we saw sparrows, blue jays, and cardinals in the garden. |
| Phrases in a series: | Before I leave for school, I have to feed the cats, take the dog for a walk, put birdseed out for the birds, and take the garbage to the garbage can. |

**A. PRACTICE:** *Insert commas where they belong in the following sentences.*

1. Bears rabbits wild pigs and foxes are all creatures of the forest.

2. They came out of the woods crept closer to the farmhouse and scared away the cat.

3. We drove to the park the river my school and the store before we came home.

**B. WRITING APPLICATION:** *Write three sentences that tell about things you do on the weekend. In every sentence, use correctly punctuated words or phrases in a series.*

_____

_____

_____

_____

_____

_____

_____

_____

_____

_____

_____

_____

_____

**"Why the Tortoise's Shell Is Not Smooth"** by Chinua Achebe
**"He Lion, Bruh Bear, and Bruh Rabbit"** by Virginia Hamilton
# Support for Writing an Invitation

Use the graphic organizer below to record details for an invitation to a gathering described in one of these stories. Review the story to find details you can use. Begin your invitation with a paragraph that describes the purpose of the gathering. Make up additional details, such as time and date, that are not provided in the story. You may also want to add artwork that you can copy when you create your invitation.

**Come to** _____

**Purpose:** _____

_____

_____

_____

**Place:** _____

**Date:** _____

**Time:** _____

Now create your invitation.

Name _____    Date _____

**"The Three Wishes"** by Ricardo E. Alegría

# Writing About the Big Question

### How much do our communities shape us?

## Big Question Vocabulary

| | | | | |
|---|---|---|---|---|
| common | community | connection | culture | family |
| generation | group | history | influence | involve |
| isolate | participation | support | values | belief |

**A.** *Use one or more words from the list above to complete each sentence.*

1. Meredith wanted to live in a less competitive society, in which people tended to _____ one another rather than compete with one another.

2. When Lonnie compared his age group to his parents' _____, he was surprised to see how many similarities there were.

3. T.J. liked literature courses that gave points for class _____, since he really enjoyed discussing the readings with other students.

4. When she planned her school's arts festival, Maggi displayed the exhibits to emphasize whenever there was a _____ between two artists' points of view.

**B.** *Follow the directions in responding to each of the items below.*

1. List two different times when you wished for something.

_____

_____

2. Write two sentences describing one of the preceding experiences. Tell whether you got your wish, what you learned, and how you felt about it. Use at least two of the Big Question vocabulary words.

_____

_____

**C.** *Complete the sentence below. Then, write a short paragraph in which you connect this experience to the Big Question.*

If I could make sure everyone knew one particular old story, it would be the story of _____ because _____

_____

_____

_____

_____

Name _____  Date _____

**"The Three Wishes"** by Ricardo E. Alegría

# Reading: Adjust Your Reading Rate

Once you have set your purpose for reading, **adjust your reading rate** to help you accomplish that purpose. Specifically, you should adjust your reading rate by doing the following:

- When reading to remember information, your reading rate should be slow and careful. Pause now and then to think about what you have read, and read difficult pages over again until you understand them. Descriptive passages with much detail should also be read slowly.
- When reading for enjoyment, you may read more quickly. Reading dialogue quickly imitates the flow of a conversation.

**DIRECTIONS:** *As you read "The Three Wishes," think about how you should adjust your reading rate for different sections of the folk tale. Complete the graphic organizer below by filling in passages that you read slowly, moderately, and quickly.*

| **Slowly** | **Moderately** | **Quickly** |
|---|---|---|
| passage | passage | passage |
| passage | passage | passage |

Name _____ Date _____

### "The Three Wishes" by Ricardo E. Alegría
## Literary Analysis: Universal Theme

The theme of a literary work is its central idea or message about life or human nature. A **universal theme** is a message about life that is expressed regularly in many different cultures and time periods. Examples of universal themes include the importance of honesty, the power of love, and the danger of selfishness.

Look for a universal theme in a literary work by focusing on the story's main character, conflicts the character faces, changes he or she undergoes, and the effects of these changes. You can use a graphic organizer like the one shown to help you determine the universal theme.

**DIRECTIONS:** *Fill in the boxes with details from "The Three Wishes." What universal theme do the details of the story lead to?*

┌──────────────────────────────────────────────────┐
| **1. Main Character** |
| _____ |
| _____ |
└──────────────────────────────────────────────────┘
▼
┌──────────────────────────────────────────────────┐
| **2. Conflicts Character Faces** |
| _____ |
| _____ |
└──────────────────────────────────────────────────┘
▼
┌──────────────────────────────────────────────────┐
| **3. How Character Changes** |
| _____ |
| _____ |
└──────────────────────────────────────────────────┘
▼
┌──────────────────────────────────────────────────┐
| **4. Effects or Meaning of Change** |
| _____ |
| _____ |
└──────────────────────────────────────────────────┘
▼
┌──────────────────────────────────────────────────┐
| **5. Universal Theme** |
| _____ |
| _____ |
└──────────────────────────────────────────────────┘

"The Three Wishes" by Ricardo E. Alegría
# Vocabulary Builder

## Word List

covetousness    embraced    greed    repentance    scarcely

**A. Directions:** *Write a* **synonym** *for each vocabulary word. Use a thesaurus if you need one. Write a sentence that includes the synonym. Be sure that your sentence makes the meaning of the word clear.*

Vocabulary word: gratitude

Synonym: thankfulness

Sentence: We expressed our thankfulness to those who had helped us during the fire.

1. Vocabulary word: **embraced**    Synonym: _____

   Sentence: _____

2. Vocabulary word: **greed**    Synonym: _____

   Sentence: _____

3. Vocabulary word: **covetousness**    Synonym: _____

   Sentence: _____

4. Vocabulary word: **scarcely**    Synonym: _____

   Sentence: _____

5. Vocabulary word: **repentance**    Synonym: _____

   Sentence: _____

**B. Word Study:** The Latin root *-pen-* means pain or punishment. Rewrite each of the following statements containing a word based on this root to make it more logical.

1. I felt *repentant* because I had done something to help my friend.

   _____

2. The team cheered when the referee gave their star player a *penalty*.

   _____

3. The prisoner was given a longer sentence because he expressed *penitence* for his crime.

   _____

Name _____ Date _____

"The Stone" by Lloyd Alexander
# Writing About the Big Question

## How much do our communities shape us?

### Big Question Vocabulary

| | | | | |
|---|---|---|---|---|
| common | community | connection | culture | family |
| generation | group | history | influence | involve |
| isolate | participation | support | values | belief |

**A.** *Use one or more words from the list above to complete each sentence.*

1. Emilio's father wanted to move to a new town to shorten his commute, but he worried about the effect of the move on his wife and children, who had strong ties to the _____.

2. When Raina tried out for her school's sketch-comedy team, she didn't think about how her new activity would _____ her from her old friends.

3. When Josh wrote an offbeat, funny story for his class, he had no idea that his story would _____ his classmates to see him as a comic genius.

4. Dania finally saw a _____ between her reading and her choice of friends when she realized that she was drawn to people who reminded her of certain characters.

**B.** *Follow the directions in responding to each of the items below.*

1. List two different times when a goal of yours conflicted with what someone else wanted.

   _____.

   _____.

2. Write two sentences describing one of the preceding experiences. Tell whether you got your wish, what you learned, and how you felt about it. Use at least two of the Big Question vocabulary words.

   _____

   _____

**C.** *Complete the sentence below. Then, write a short paragraph in which you connect this experience to the Big Question.*

   If I could make one wish come true for my life, I would want _____ because _____

   _____

   _____

   _____.

**"The Stone"** by Lloyd Alexander
# Reading: Adjust Your Reading Rate

Once you have set your purpose for reading, **adjust your reading rate** to help you accomplish that purpose. Specially, you should adjust your reading rate by doing the following:

- When reading to remember information, your reading rate should be slow and careful. Pause now and then to think about what you have read, and read difficult pages over again until you understand them. Descriptive passages with much detail should also be read slowly.
- When reading for enjoyment, you may read more quickly. Reading dialogue quickly imitates the flow of a conversation.

**DIRECTIONS:** *As you read "The Stone," think about how you should adjust your reading rate for different sections of the folk tale. Complete the graphic organizer below by filling in passages that you read slowly, moderately, and quickly.*

| **Slowly** | **Moderately** | **Quickly** |
|---|---|---|
| passage | passage | passage |
| passage | passage | passage |

Name _____ Date _____

## "The Stone" by Lloyd Alexander
# Literary Analysis: Universal Theme

The theme of a literary work is its central idea or message about life or human nature. A **universal theme** is a message about life that is expressed regularly in many different cultures and time periods. Examples of universal themes include the importance of honesty, the power of love, and the danger of selfishness.

Look for a universal theme in a literary work by focusing on the story's main character, conflicts the character faces, changes he or she undergoes, and the effects of these changes. You can use a graphic organizer like the one shown to help you determine the universal theme.

**DIRECTIONS:** *Fill in the boxes with details from "The Stone." What universal theme do the details of the story lead to?*

**Main Character**
_____

↓

**Conflicts Character Faces**
_____
_____

↓

**How Character Changes**
_____
_____

↓

**Effects or Meaning of Change**
_____
_____

↓

**Universal Theme**
_____
_____

Name _____  Date _____

"The Stone" by Lloyd Alexander
# Vocabulary Builder

**Word List**

    feeble    jubilation    plight    rue    sown    vanished

**A. DIRECTIONS:** *Write a **synonym** for each vocabulary word. Use a thesaurus if you need one. Write a sentence that includes the synonym. Be sure that your sentence makes the meaning of the word clear.*

    Vocabulary word: heartening

    Synonym: encouraging

    Sentence: The sales rep found the good response to the product very encouraging.

1. Vocabulary word: **plight**      Synonym: _____

   Sentence: _____

2. Vocabulary word: **feeble**      Synonym: _____

   Sentence: _____

3. Vocabulary word: **sown**      Synonym: _____

   Sentence: _____

4. Vocabulary word: **vanished**      Synonym: _____

   Sentence: _____

5. Vocabulary word: **jubilation**      Synonym: _____

   Sentence: _____

6. Vocabulary word: **rue**      Synonym: _____

   Sentence: _____

**B. WORD STUDY:** The Latin root *-van-* means "empty." Answer each of the following questions using one of these words containing *-van-: vanish, evanescent, vain*

1. What is a good way to make a rumor *vanish*?

   _____

2. Why would morning ground mist become *evanescent* as the day goes on?

   _____

3. How do you feel when your hard work has been in *vain*?

   _____

Name _____ Date _____

"**The Three Wishes**" by Ricardo E. Alegría
"**The Stone**" by Lloyd Alexander
# Integrated Language Skills: Grammar

## Punctuation: Semicolons and Colons

A **semicolon** connects two independent clauses that are closely connected in meaning.
(Remember that an independent clause can stand alone as a sentence.) A semicolon is
also used to separate items in a series if those items have commas within them.

> Alice had never been given three wishes before; she was amazed at how the wishes might
> change her future.

> We visited some interesting places on our vacation, including New Bedford, Massachusetts;
> Providence, Rhode Island; and Danbury, Connecticut.

A **colon** is used after an independent clause to introduce a list of items, to show time, in
the salutation of a business letter, and on warnings and labels.

> This is what he wished for: eternal youth, a new car, and an end to poverty in the world.

> Warning: Be careful what you wish for.

**A. DIRECTIONS:** *Rewrite each item below, inserting a colon or a semicolon wherever one
is needed.*

1. We discussed three figures of speech simile, metaphor, and personification.

   _____

   _____

2. Warning No skateboarding here after 400 P.M.

   _____

   _____

3. My sister and I share a bedroom sometimes that room seems very small.

   _____

   _____

4. The train stops in Dallas, Texas St. Louis, Missouri and Chicago, Illinois.

   _____

   _____

**B. Writing Application:** *Imagine that you have three wishes, guaranteed to come true.
Write three sentences about what you might wish for. Use at least one semicolon or one
colon in each sentence.*

   _____

   _____

   _____

Name _____ Date _____

# Integrated Language Skills: Support for Writing a Plot Proposal

A plot proposal is a plan of story events. Use this page to take notes for your plot proposal that illustrates a universal theme.

Universal theme: _____

_____

Conflict or situation that could be used to demonstrate that theme: _____

_____

Events that lead to the theme:

_____

_____

_____

_____

_____

_____

_____

_____

_____

_____

_____

_____

_____

_____

_____

_____

_____

_____

_____

Now use your notes to write your plot proposal.

Name _____ Date _____

"Lob's Girl" by Joan Aiken
"Jeremiah's Song" by Walter Dean Myers
## Writing About the Big Question

How much do our communities shape us?

### Big Question Vocabulary

| | | | | |
|---|---|---|---|---|
| common | community | connection | culture | family |
| generation | group | history | Influence | involve |
| isolate | participation | support | values | belief |

**A.** *Use one or more words from the list above to complete each sentence.*

1. For her school project, Zoe started an online tutoring network, so that students could help and _____ one another.

2. Mikel found that his _____ in a service club helped him make new friends and feel good—without hurting his studies.

3. When Marilinda joined her neighbors in preparing for a hurricane, the experience _____ her to take a free class in disaster preparedness.

4. Last winter's bad weather taught TJ that a _____ can work together, when one of his neighbors organized teams to check on elderly neighbors shut in after each storm.

**B.** *Follow the directions in responding to each of the items below.*

1. List two different times when someone helped you through a difficult experience.

_____.

_____.

2. Write two sentences explaining one of the preceding experiences, and describe how it made you feel. Use at least two of the Big Question vocabulary words.

_____

_____

_____

**C.** *Complete the sentence below. Then, write a short paragraph in which you connect this experience to the Big Question.*

One time, our neighbors helped _____ when _____

_____

_____

_____

_____

**"Lob's Girl"** by Joan Aiken
**"Jeremiah's Song"** by Walter Dean Myers
# Literary Analysis: Plot Techniques

Writers can use a range of **plot techniques** to help them tell the events in a story. Two common plot techniques are foreshadowing and flashback.

- **Foreshadowing** is the author's use of clues to hint at what might happen later in the story. For example, a story's narrator might describe a sign that reads *Danger* hanging on a fence. This detail might suggest that something dangerous will happen later in the story. It also helps the author build suspense, the quality that keeps you wondering what will happen next.
- A **flashback** is a scene that interrupts a story to describe an earlier event. Flashback is often used to show something about a character's past. For example, a flashback about the loss of a special pet might explain why a character dislikes the new family dog.

**DIRECTIONS:** *Read each of the following passages from "Lob's Girl" and "Jeremiah's Song." Then, complete the sentence that follows.*

1. **from "Lob's Girl"**

   A. [Aunt Rebecca] found the family with white shocked faces; Bert and Jean were about to drive off to the hospital where Sandy had been taken, and the twins were crying bitterly. <u>Lob was nowhere to be seen.</u>

   The underlined detail foreshadows _____ .

   B. The twins were miserably unhappy. They forgot that they had sometimes called their elder sister bossy and only remembered how often she had shared her pocket money with them, how she read to them and took them for picnics and helped with their homework.

   From the flashback in this paragraph, you learn that _____
   _____ .

2. **from "Jeremiah's Song"**

   A. Grandpa Jeremiah had been feeling poorly from that stroke, and one of his legs got a little drag to it. Just about the time Ellie come from school the next summer he was real sick.

   This description of Grandpa foreshadows _____ .

   B. When the work for the day was finished and the sows fed, Grandpa would kind of ease into one of his stories and Macon, he would sit and listen to them and be real interested.

   This flashback about Macon tells the reader that _____
   _____ .

**"Lob's Girl"** by Joan Aiken
**"Jeremiah's Song"** by Walter Dean Myers
## Vocabulary Builder

**Word List**

decisively    diagnosis    melancholy    resolutions

**A. DIRECTIONS:** *Revise each sentence so that the underlined vocabulary word is used logically. Be sure to keep the vocabulary word in your revision.*

Sentence:    After I told her every detail, Mom thanked me for the <u>summary</u>.

Revision:    Mom thanked me for the brief <u>summary</u> of what had happened.

1. Unsure what to do with the ball, Aaron threw it <u>decisively</u> to first base.

_____

_____

2. Our club could not decide what to do, so we were able to make good <u>resolutions</u> for the coming year.

_____

_____

3. The story's funny, happy ending made Li feel <u>melancholy</u>.

_____

_____

4. After the vet's clear <u>diagnosis</u>, we still didn't know what was wrong with Spot.

_____

_____

**B. DIRECTIONS:** *Write the letter of the word that means the same or almost the same as the vocabulary word.*

____ 1. melancholy
   A. depressed
   B. peaceful
   C. sweet
   D. mean

____ 2. diagnosis
   A. speech
   B. measurement
   C. disease
   D. conclusion

____ 3. resolutions
   A. apologies
   B. guesses
   C. promises
   D. chores

"Lob's Girl" by Joan Aiken
"Jeremiah's Song" by Walter Dean Myers
# Writing to Compare Literary Works

Before you draft your essay comparing and contrasting the authors' use of foreshadowing and flashback in these stories, complete the graphic organizers below.

| Foreshadowing | |
|---|---|
| **Examples from "Lob's Girl"** | **Examples from "Jeremiah's Song"** |
| | |
| **Which story's foreshadowing creates greater suspense? Why?** | |

| Flashback | |
|---|---|
| **Examples from "Lob's Girl"** | **Examples from "Jeremiah's Song"** |
| | |
| **Which story's flashbacks reveal more about its characters? How?** | |

Now, use your notes to write an essay comparing and contrasting the authors' use of foreshadowing and flashback in these two stories. Remember to tell which story you enjoyed more and why.

Name _____ Date _____

# Tips for Improving Your Reading Fluency

You've probably heard the expression "Practice makes perfect." Through your own experiences, you know that practice improves all types of skills. If you play a guitar, you know that practicing has made you a better player. The same is true for sports, for crafts, and for reading. The following tips will help you to practice skills that will lead to reading **fluency**—the ability to read easily, smoothly, and expressively.

- **Choose your practice materials carefully.**

  Make reading fun! Make a list of subjects that interest you. Then, search for reading materials—books, magazines, newspapers, reliable Web sites. As you learn more about your interests, you will also be practicing your reading skills.

- **Choose your practice space and time carefully.**

  Help your concentration skills. Find a quiet, comfortable place to read—away from the television and other distractions. Get in the habit of treating yourself to an hour of pleasure reading every day—apart from homework and other tasks. Reading about interesting topics in a quiet, comfortable place will provide both pleasure and relaxation.

- **Practice prereading strategies.**

  A movie preview gives viewers a good idea about what the movie will be about. Before you read, create your own preview of what you plan to read. Look at pictures and captions, subheads, and diagrams. As you scan, look for unfamiliar words. Find out what those words mean before you start reading.

- **Use punctuation marks.**

  Think of punctuation marks as stop signs. For example, the period at the end of a sentence signals the end of a complete thought. From time to time in your reading, stop at that stop sign. Reread the sentence. Summarize the complete thought in your own words.

- **Read aloud.**

  Use your voice and your ears as well as your eyes. Read phrases and sentences expressively. Pause at commas and periods. Show emphasis in your voice when you come to an exclamation point. Let your voice naturally rise at the end of a question. If possible, record your reading. Then listen to the recording, noting your pacing and expression.

- **Pause to ask questions.**

Stop reading after a short amount of time (for example, five minutes) or at the end of a meaty paragraph. Look away from the text. Ask yourself questions—What are the main ideas? What message does the author want me to get? What might happen next? If the answers seem unclear, reread—either silently or aloud. Find the answers!

- **Use what you know.**

As you read an informational article, think about what you already know about the topic. Use your knowledge and ideas as background information. Doing so will help you to understand new ideas. As you read fiction or a personal narrative, think about your own experiences. If you have been in a situation that is similar to that of a fictional character, you will be better able to understand his or her feelings, actions, and goals.

- **Talk about it.**

Ask a friend or family member to read what you have read. Take turns reading aloud together, listening to both content and expression. Then discuss what you read. Share, compare, and contrast your ideas. Doing so will reinforce your knowledge of the content of what you read, and may provide new and interesting perspectives about the topic.

# Reading Fluency Assessment Passage 1

It seemed as if every time Angela began to feel at home in a new place, it was time to pick up and move again.

"Do we really have to move?" she asked, fearful that the question might upset her father.

"We can't stay here without a job," her father[50] replied. He was a husky man, but he looked weak now as he slouched sadly in his favorite chair.

Angela clasped her hands tightly together and held them under her chin, thinking. She was not looking forward to the prospect of starting over again as the new kid in some[100] unfamiliar city. She decided to explore her options thoroughly.

"Couldn't you find a job around here?" she asked. "My friend's father is a foreman at the factory . . . "

"They're not hiring at the factory right now," her father interrupted, and Angela could detect the frustration in his[150] voice. "Anyway, you know I can't stand the drone of machinery. The endless rattling gives me a headache."

That settled it, then—they would be moving. Without thinking, as if by instinct, Angela smiled and leaned over to kiss her father's cheek. She knew this move was important to him.[200]

"Where are we moving this time?" she asked.

"Back to California," he said. "Actually, our new apartment isn't far from where we used to live."

"Really?" said Angela. Suddenly the future looked a lot happier, as she imagined them loading up the car and setting out for sunny California. As[250] much as she liked it here, Angela had to admit that she loved California's warm weather and beaches even more. And it *would* be awfully nice to hang out with her old friends again.

Maybe this move wouldn't be so bad after all![293]

830L

## Check Your Understanding

1. Angela finally feels happier about moving.

   **True / False?** Explain:

   _____

   _____

2. Describe the feelings Angela has when she raises the question about moving with her father.

   _____

   _____

   _____

# Reading Fluency Assessment Passage 2

Christopher did not like his next-door neighbor very much. In fact, Christopher thought that old Mr. Milligan was the biggest grouch on the planet.

When Christopher and his friends played baseball, they dreaded hitting the ball into Mr. Milligan's backyard. Hearing them climb over the rickety fence to retrieve the[50] ball, the old man would suddenly appear at the window, wearing what seemed to be a permanent frown. The boys always hurried away once they retrieved their baseball. "If he doesn't want neighbors," Christopher often said, "he should install barbed wire around his house. Then every-one would keep their distance!"[100]

Christopher's mother attempted to explain that the old man was lonely. He lived by himself, and he had never had any children. She said that probably Mr. Milligan just wasn't used to being around kids. Christopher was not convinced.

One day, against his wishes, Christopher's mother assigned him the job[150] of taking freshly baked cinnamon bread next door. She coaxed Christopher by saying that Mr. Milligan would probably really appreciate the treat. "I doubt it," Christopher grumbled. "He probably loves eating old, stale bread. It would suit him and his false teeth just fine."

When Christopher knocked on Mr. Milligan's[200] door, there was no response. Then, when Christopher heard what sounded like a cry for help, he pushed open the door. The old man was doubled up in pain. "It's my stomach," he groaned. With shaking hands, Christopher dialed 911 for an ambulance.

Mr. Milligan had appendicitis. When Christopher and[250] his mother visited him in the hospital, Mr. Milligan said, "You saved my life, son. Please take this gift." It was an antique silver dollar. That was the beginning of a new friendship between them. And Mr. Milligan never frowned again when the boys came into his yard.[298]

860L

## Check Your Understanding

1. Christopher and his friends did not like Mr. Milligan because _____

   a. he had false teeth.

   b. he wore a permanent frown.

   c. he put barbed wire around his yard.

2. What did Christopher do for Mr. Milligan?

   _____

   _____

3. What did Mr. Milligan do in return?

   _____

All-in-One Workbook: Reading Fluency Assessment
**314**

# Reading Fluency Assessment Passage 3

Like most baby animals, a newborn wolf is nearly helpless at first. The baby wolf, called a pup, is born in a den. The den shelters the pup from the weather, and also protects it from predators.

The wolf's mother will have built the den a few weeks before. She[50] may have dug it out of the ground, or she may have stumbled upon a den already constructed by another animal.

In this den, the wolf pup begins its life. It squints its eyes, although it cannot yet see. Once it can open its eyes completely, light will be blinding.[100] The pup whimpers softly as it begins to sense a presence nearby, a brother or sister pup. Mother wolves give birth to multiple pups at a time. The average size of the group is five.

The pup is small, weighing just about a pound. It is hungry, though, and it[150] gulps down its mother's milk. It will grow bigger with help. This pup belongs to a pack, and pack members will hunt to retrieve food for the baby, as well as its nursing mother.

In time, the pup will grow to weigh a hundred pounds or more. It will become[200] fast and strong, with long legs and powerful leg muscles. It will be able to run at speeds of up to 35 miles an hour for short periods. Often, these bursts of speed occur during the hunt, which ends the moment that the wolf lunges after its prey. Wolves feed[250] on the flesh of other animals such as deer, elk, and caribou.

The pup will remain with the pack until it is a young adult. Then it may leave, find a new pack, or even start its own.[288]

870L

## Check Your Understanding

1. Wolf pups are born _____

   a. along with other pups in the clan.

   b. alone.

2. Name two things the wolf pup will be able to do as it grows.

   _____

   _____

# Reading Fluency Assessment Passage 4

Today, most fourteen-year-olds go to school, but during the Civil War, fourteen-year-old Susie King Taylor *taught* school to soldiers. To understand this remarkable story, go back to 1848. That year, Susie King Taylor was born into slavery on an island off the Georgia coast. When Taylor was about six, she[50] went to live with her grandmother in Savannah, Georgia.

Slaves were not allowed to learn to read and write. However, taking considerable risk, Taylor's grandmother had a neighbor teach these skills to Taylor and other slave children. Every day the children secretly went to the neighbor's house. Each of them[100] had a strong desire to escape slavery and a fierce ambition to learn.

Just after the war began, Taylor escaped from Savannah and fled to an island that was under the control of the Northern troops. There, she set up a school for African American children and adults. The following[150] year, at fourteen, she married Sergeant Edward King, an African American soldier. She began to teach her husband's soldiers and do their laundry, too.

She also began to nurse wounded soldiers. For a time, she worked with Clara Barton, founder of the American Red Cross. There was very little medicine,[200] and many soldiers suffered from terrible wounds. Taylor tried to help them through their pain and suffering. She also tried to find them food.

In 1902, Susie King Taylor wrote a book about those war years. She wrote: "It seems strange ... how we are able to see the most sickening sights....[250] Instead of turning away, how we hurry to ... bind up their wounds, and press the cool water to their parched lips, with feelings only of sympathy and pity."[277]

880L

## Check Your Understanding

1. It was risky for Susie's grandmother to ask a neighbor to teach Susie to read because

   a. the Civil War was raging.

   b. the neighbor was cruel.

   c. slaves were not allowed to read and write.

2. Name two things that Susie did do to help the soldiers and their families?

   _____

   _____

# Reading Fluency Assessment Passage 5

Natalie decided to volunteer at the Hillsborough Avenue Retirement Home. She thought she had many interesting activities to share with the residents. After all, she figured, most of them were elderly and probably most of them were bored. Learning new skills and information might perk them up.

On her first[50] Saturday, she brought some books about gardens and flowering trees. She gathered a group of residents in the recreation room and began to read to them. But Natalie became discouraged when some residents fell asleep in their chairs and others drifted out of the room.

On the next Saturday, Natalie[100] decided to organize an art class, so she brought paper, brushes, and pots of paint. She thought people would enjoy making colorful murals to brighten their rooms. But only a few residents seemed interested in her project.

Natalie was late arriving there the following Saturday. She had spent the morning[150] at the library, doing research for her report on the attack on Pearl Harbor, which led to the United States entering World War II. Dashing into the recreation room, she dropped her book bag, and out spilled a book entitled *Pearl Harbor: Horror at Dawn*. An elderly man stooped down[200] to help Natalie retrieve her books. "Ah, Pearl Harbor!" he said. "That was the most terrible morning of my life."

Natalie gasped. "You were at Pearl Harbor?" she asked.

"Yes, I was, and so was Albert, who's sitting over there, in the back of the room. My friend Mrs. Henderson[250] wasn't at Pearl, but her brother Charlie was badly wounded there. Oh, yes—we have a lot of memories of that day, my dear."

Grabbing a notebook and pencil, Natalie said, "Please tell me about it. I'm sure that you all have many interesting things to share with me."[299]

880L

## Check Your Understanding

1. At first, Natalie wanted to work at the retirement home because
   a. she was interested in learning stories about Pearl Harbor.
   b. she wanted to share her interests with the residents.
   c. she knew many of the residents there.

2. What lesson do you think Natalie learned?

Explain

_____
_____
_____

# Reading Fluency Assessment Passage 6

When the Spanish-American War ended in 1898, the island of Puerto Rico became a United States territory. In 1899, the United States Army formed the first battalion of Puerto Ricans. These soldiers were responsible for helping to defend their island home.

In 1917, Puerto Ricans were given American citizen-ship. With[50] this right, adults could vote in United States elections. Also, Puerto Rican men could be drafted for service in World War I. In all, 18,000 Puerto Ricans served in this war. Many worked together to guard the Panama Canal against an enemy attack.

During World War II, 65,000 Puerto Ricans[100] served in the military. More than one-third of them signed up as vol-unteers. However, it was during the Korean War that Puerto Rican service became most obvious. In this conflict, 756 Puerto Ricans lost their lives. One Puerto Rican soldier received the Congressional Medal of Honor during the Korean War.[150] His name was Fernando Luis García, and he gave the greatest sacrifice of all for his country. García died in a heroic effort that allowed his fellow soldiers to live.

The proud military traditions of Puerto Ricans have continued. Island soldiers have served in every major conflict since the Korean[200] War. Art, music, and poetry celebrate the soldiers' heroism. Throughout the island country, young people who have recently graduated from high school join elderly war veterans, some in wheelchairs, at coffee shops and other local places. They discuss courage, loyalty, and determination in the defense of democratic ideas. Puerto Rico[250] does not want its children to grow up unaware, or ignorant, of the sacrifices that have been made. Truly, there have been many. As one army general has stated: "Puerto Rico has done for this nation more than its share."[290]

900L

## Check Your Understanding

1. Puerto Rico became a United States territory at the close of World War I.

   **True / False?** Explain:

   _____

   _____

2. Which answer best describes the wars in which Puerto Ricans have served?
   a. the Korean War
   b. World Wars I and II and every other war since the Korean War
   c. only the Korean War and conflicts that followed

# Reading Fluency Assessment Passage 7

Training for a marathon can be a very lonely pursuit. The runner must spend many hours all alone, putting one foot in front of the other for long distances. Whether training on hills or in lowlands, the runner faces a tiresome process.

Many people think that the greatest challenge for[50] a marathon runner is to make it to the *finish* line. After all, 26 miles and 385 yards is a very long run! Others say that the greatest challenge for the marathon runner is to make it to the *starting* line. Training errors often result in injuries that may prevent[100] runners from ever getting to enter a race.

A training runner might make any of a number of errors. For example, some runners follow the "more is better" line of thought. They build up their mileage too quickly. Soon, they suffer breakdown and injury.

Another common training error is not[150] being consistent. Some runners miss several workouts in a row. Then, recognizing that they are behind in their training, they run too much in an effort to catch up.

If you want to train as a marathon runner, follow good sense. Do not become a slave to your training schedule.[200] Pay attention to what your legs are communicating to you. Suppose you usually run five or six easy miles during the middle of the week. However, on one particular Wednesday, your muscles feel fatigued or sore. Your intuition should tell you to take an extra day off and save your[250] legs for the long weekend run. Also, remember to incorporate rest days into your training schedule prior to hard workouts such as a long run or a race.

Follow tips like these, and you just may find yourself at the marathon finish line, showing off your gold medal![298]

910L

## Check Your Understanding

1. Some marathon runners never enter a race because they
   a. are not fast enough.
   b. get injuries due to training errors.
   c. do not have enough endurance.

2. Name two reasons that training to be a marathon runner is difficult.

   _____
   _____

# Reading Fluency Assessment Passage 8

*Fiddler on the Roof* is a famous musical play and movie, based on a humorous short story. This important work was introduced to the Broadway stage in 1964. It later became a movie. *Fiddler on the Roof* is one of the first musicals to show serious issues, such as persecution[50] and poverty.

The story is set in 1905, in a small Jewish village in Russia. The main character is a poor dairy farmer named Tevye. During the action of the story, each of Tevye's daughters comes to him. Each asks him[100] to allow her to break with strong traditional values by marrying the man she loves. The story is both humorous and sad. It deals with Tevye's struggle to hang on to traditions in the face of a changing world.

At the time the story takes place, there were difficult events[150] facing Russian Jews. Persecution, poverty, and violence were common. The conditions that Tevye must deal with reflect those difficult times.

In one scene, Tevye tends to the many details of caring for the barn animals. When he is done, he is huddled among the bales of hay, daydreaming of how[200] different things would be if he were rich. He then performs the song "If I Were a Rich Man."

In another scene, the Jewish tradition of lighting holy candles and saying prayers is beautifully portrayed. Music and flickering candlelight playing on the faces of the children create a beautiful scene.[250]

At the end of the story, Tevye's family and his entire village face a crisis. Tevye realizes that his family and friends are in serious trouble. They must pack a few belongings and flee. Although their traditions still live in them, the life they have known has vanished.[299]

920L

## Check Your Understanding

1. The play *Fiddler on the Roof* is set in a Russian village.
   a. True
   b. False

2. Name two traditions portrayed in one scene of the play.

   _____

   _____

# Reading Fluency Assessment Passage 9

Angel Island is located in San Francisco Bay. Throughout history, people have used it for different purposes. New settlers sailing into the bay often stopped there before proceeding to their new homes on the mainland. It also served as a shelter for people with contagious diseases, such[50] as tuberculosis.

A tribe of Native Americans were the first to enjoy the beauty and resources of Angel Island. They crossed the bay by boat to hunt and fish there. The Native Americans never lived there permanently, but they built protective shelters. They would visit the island in good weather,[100] staying as long as they wanted.[100] Then they would return to their small villages on the mainland.

Like all early peoples who lived by hunting and gathering, these Native Americans had varying levels of success. The rich resources on the island helped them fight off hunger and remain in good[150] physical condition. It also provided them with a peaceful, beautiful place to enjoy nature.

If you visit Angel Island today, you will still be able to enjoy its natural beauty. You will also share some of the experiences the Native Americans had when they paddled out there so many years[200] ago. You can hike the hilly trails. You can admire the many beautiful plants and trees. As you stand high up on the island, you can still feel the salty ocean breezes as you look out to sea. You might even get to watch sea lions sunning themselves on the[250] rocks and playing on the waves. And, if you are really lucky, you might even hear the sounds of the Native Americans' drums and flutes carried across time on the fresh ocean breezes.[283]

930L

## Check Your Understanding

1. The earliest people to enjoy the beauty of Angel Island were
   a. settlers on their way to the mainland of San Francisco.
   b. people suffering from contagious diseases.
   c. the Miwok, who came to hunt and fish.

2. Name two sights that modern visitors to Angel Island might see today.

   _____

   _____

# Reading Fluency Assessment Passage 10

Alexander Graham Bell (1847–1922) was a distinguished scientist and educator. Today, he is best known for inventing the telephone.

Growing up in Scotland, Bell showed a great talent for music. His intention, however, was to follow in his father's footsteps and become a teacher of the deaf. Bell began working[50] with his father while still in his teens. In 1870, the family moved to Canada. The following year, Bell was offered a job in Boston teaching deaf children to speak. Before long, he became a professor at Boston University and opened his own school for the deaf.

With the help[100] of his partner, Thomas Watson, Bell began to work on an electrical device that would transmit sound over telegraph wires. The two men struggled vainly for years trying to get the device to work. Then, one day in 1876, Bell and Watson were working on their invention in separate rooms.[150] Bell spilled some acid on himself. Agitated by the accident, he said, "Mr. Watson, come here. I want you!" To the astonishment of both men, Watson heard Bell's voice through the device on his workbench.

Bell's telephone had become a reality!

Bell and Watson began demonstrating their amazing invention. Soon,[200] the first telephone company was established. Bell and then set sail for England to introduce the telephone to the people of Europe. When the French government awarded him a prize for his important work, Bell used the money to set up a laboratory devoted to helping the deaf. He lived[250] more than 45 years after inventing the telephone and continued to make many important contributions to science throughout his life.

A witty observation that was often repeated in Bell's later years was that the great inventor disliked the telephone because callers were constantly interrupting his experiments.[296]

930L

## Check Your Understanding

1. Although he is best known for his invention of the telephone, Alexander Graham Bell's primary goal was to
   a. be a scientist.
   b. educate the deaf.
   c. establish the first telephone company.

2. In his later years, why did Bell dislike the telephone?
   _____
   _____

# Reading Fluency Assessment Passage 11

You'll read about dragons in stories and novels. You'll watch dragons in cartoons, coming out of their lairs, or homes, to breathe fire. In movies, you'll see princes and warriors slicing off dragons' heads, but you'll hardly ever see one in real life.  In fact, you'll never see one, because[50] dragons don't really exist. Although they have always been the most feared animals in literature, they are merely make-believe. In ancient times, great European dragons, such as the *Gargler*, haunted popular legends. Author J.R.R. Tolkien's tales feature dragons that are closely based on those in legendary Europe, but no dragons[100] have ever been found.

Many other creatures exist only in legends and fairy tales. The mermaid, a lovely maiden of the sea, is half woman and half fish. She has a woman's head and body but a fish's scaly tail instead of legs. In some stories, the mermaid sings a[150] siren song that enchants sailors and leads them to walk off their boats and drown in the sea. In the real world, many people have labored hard to find a real mermaid, but without any luck. Half-women, half-fish creatures simply don't exist.

Another famous make-believe creature is the unicorn, an[200] animal that looks something like a beautiful white horse. What makes a unicorn special is that it has a long, pointed horn on its forehead. In stories, poems, and pictures, it sometimes has a billy-goat beard, a lion's tail, and cloven hooves. It often appears in paintings from the Middle[250] Ages. Like the dragon, the unicorn was thought to be real by people of earlier times. However, no unicorn has ever strolled on Earth.[274]

950L

## Check Your Understanding

1. Ancient Europeans found real dragons.

   **True / False?** Explain:

   _____

   _____

2. Name two legendary creatures other than dragons.

   _____

   _____

**323**

# Reading Fluency Assessment Passage 12

At the dawn of the twentieth century, few people believed  that human beings would ever be able to fly. Yet, Orville and Wilbur Wright were about to make that dream come true.

The Wright brothers had never been afraid of a challenge. Together, as young men, they opened a bicycle[50] shop in Dayton, Ohio. Their business was a commercial success, but simply making money was not enough to satisfy them. Soon, they developed an interest in flying and built a series of gliders. Then, fearing that the gliders would be unable to withstand strong winds, they built a sturdier airplane.[100] It was powered by a lightweight gasoline engine. They took their new airplane to Kitty Hawk, North Carolina, to test it out.

On December 17, 1903, the brothers tossed a coin to see who would go up first. Orville won. He flew for 12 seconds and traveled 120 feet. Although[150] the plane flew only 825 feet that first day, the brothers were rightfully proud of their extraordinary aerial feat. They knew they had begun a great chapter of aviation history.

The Wright brothers soon began making better and better airplanes. When they offered their invention to the United States government,[200] officials showed no interest. What practical use could there be for a flying machine? It didn't take very long, however, for people around the world to realize that the Wright brothers' invention could change the course of history.

Wilbur died shortly before the airplane was used during World War I.[250] Orville, however, lived long enough to see air travel become a reality for ordinary people.

Today, the original airplane flown by the Wright brothers at Kitty Hawk is on display at the National Air and Space Museum in Washington, D.C.[290]

970L

## Check Your Understanding

1. Orville Wright was the first brother to fly because

   a. He won the coin toss.
   b. He was more adventurous than Wilbur.
   c. He worked at the Air and Space Museum.

2. Name two abilities or traits that led the Wright brothers to be successful.

   _____

   _____

Name _____  Date _____

# Screening Test

**Directions:** Read the following passages. Then read the questions. On the answer sheet, fill in the bubble for the answer that you think is correct.

**1 The chapter that gives information about water and weather begins on what page?**
A 1
B 4
C 25
D 58

**2 What topic is covered on page 77?**
F Ocean Life
G Ocean Adventures
H Sea Monsters
J Swimming with Dolphins

Hundreds of years ago, the Incas of South America produced cloth unlike any the world has seen since. The Incas carefully bred animals called alpacas to get the finest, softest wool possible. Using the alpaca wool, the Incas wove colorful, silky cloth that was used for clothing, decorations, and even as money. When the Spaniards conquered the Incas, the secret to breeding the alpacas was lost.

**3 What is the main idea of this paragraph?**
A The Incas made a special kind of cloth.
B The Incas discovered how to breed alpacas.
C The Incas were conquered by the Spaniards.
D The Incas used colorful cloth as money.

Most of the world has been thoroughly explored, but scientists are still discovering large mammals. In 1993, scientists in Vietnam found the giant muntjac, a type of deer. The Chacoan peccary, a South American pig, was not identified until 1972. These discoveries give hope to people who believe that the forests of the world still hide unknown animals.

**4 This paragraph is *mostly* about —**
F the giant muntjac and other rare species
G the continuing discoveries of large mammals
H the exploration of South America and Vietnam
J the habitat and food of the Chacoan peccary

Jill looked at the clock and groaned. It was only eight o'clock on a Saturday morning. What was that awful hammering sound? She crawled out of bed and peeked outside. Seeing nothing, she closed the window with a thud. Then she snuggled back under the covers and tried to go back to sleep.

**5 What causes Jill to close the window?**
**A** Her room has gotten too cold.
**B** The sun is shining in her eyes.
**C** She is bothered by a noise outside.
**D** The traffic outside is too loud.

Max asked his mother if he could run with her in the morning. Max's mother was eager for a running partner, so she said yes. Max was surprised when his mother said they had to do some warm-up stretches first. She explained that their leg muscles might get sore if they didn't do the stretches. After they stretched, Max said his legs felt looser and he would be able to run better.

**6 What is the effect of stretching?**
**F** Both Max and his mother are able to run farther.
**G** Max's mother has a sore leg.
**H** Both Max and his mother run faster.
**J** Max's legs feel looser.

1 Animation was first used with toys in the 1800s. One of these toys was called the zoetrope, or wheel of life. A long paper strip covered with drawings was placed into the zoetrope's viewing tube. The user then peered through slots, twirled the tube, and watched the drawings move. This toy led to the first animated films.
2 In the 1920s, the Russians made animation with puppets. The Germans created animated films using dark shapes. Other countries experimented with frame-by-frame photographs of clay figures.
3 In the late 1920s, Walt Disney came on the scene. Disney created some of the best-loved animated movies of all time with characters such as Mickey Mouse, Donald Duck, Goofy, and Pluto.

**7 Which of these is a *fact* about the zoetrope?**
**A** It was the first animated film.
**B** It wasn't very much fun to watch.
**C** It was a toy that led to animation.
**D** It had a strange name.

**8 Which of the following is an *opinion* from the passage?**
**F** The Russians used puppets for their animation.
**G** The Germans created animated films using dark shapes.
**H** Other countries experimented with clay figures.
**J** Disney created the best-loved animated movies.

1 Sitting on a small triangle of land at the corner of Fifth Avenue and Broadway is one of the most interesting buildings in New York City. It is called the Flatiron Building.

2 The first thing people notice about the Flatiron Building is that it is built in a wedge shape. It looks like a tall piece of pie. It is only six feet wide at its round, narrow end. The building got its name from this shape. When it was built in 1902, it was called the Fuller Building. Its shape reminded people of an old-fashioned clothes iron. They started calling it the Flatiron Building, and the name stuck.

3 In 1902, there were very few tall buildings in New York City. The Flatiron Building was one of the first skyscrapers in the city. It is 285 feet high and has about 22 stories. At the time, that was huge. New Yorkers were afraid that a good gust of wind would blow this tall building over. That never happened, however. Today, the Flatiron Building looks tiny next to the huge skyscrapers in New York City. Even so, it is now the oldest skyscraper still standing in New York.

**9 What do you learn in Paragraph 2 of this passage?**

A where the Flatiron Building is located

B the shape of the Flatiron Building

C the height of the Flatiron Building

D how the Flatiron Building compares with other skyscrapers

**10 Which words from the passage give the *best* description of the Flatiron Building?**

F At the time, that was huge.

G It looks like a tall piece of pie.

H It is called the Flatiron Building.

J They started calling it the Flatiron Building, and the name stuck.

MOTHER: Harry, did you clean up your room?

HARRY: I guess it depends on what you mean by clean.

FATHER: Harry, would you please answer your mother?

**11 What form of literature is this?**

A play

B poem

C fiction

D nonfiction

**12 Which of these is an example of fiction?**

F the story of the first woman to fly a plane

G a book about how the Brooklyn Bridge was built

H a made-up story about animals that talk

J a book that tells you how to play soccer better

Name _____ Date _____

**Directions:** Read the following passages. Then read the questions. On the answer sheet, fill in the bubble for the answer that you think is correct.

---

1   The Celts were an ancient people who lived in Europe. During their reign, the Celts were feared and respected by the rest of the world.

2   Women in Celtic civilization had great freedom. Some Celtic women became important warriors and queens. The most famous Celtic queen was Boudicca. She led a rebellion against Roman rule.

3   At first, Boudicca and the Celts won many battles. They even destroyed the city of London, which was a Roman fortress then. Finally, however, the Romans defeated Boudicca and the Celts. No one knows exactly what happened to Boudicca. No matter what, she remains a symbol of Celtic power and freedom.

---

**13 What is this story *mostly* about?**
   **A** ancient people who lived in Europe long ago
   **B** a Celtic queen who battled the Romans
   **C** why some Celtic women were warriors
   **D** why London became a Roman fortress

**14 The Romans defeated the Celts —**
   **F** after Boudicca was stripped of power
   **G** after Boudicca and the Celts won many battles
   **H** before Boudicca led a rebellion against Roman rule
   **J** before Boudicca came to power

---

Corinne loved to play basketball, so she and her dad planned to build a basketball court. Corinne held the ladder steady, while her dad fastened a hoop and backboard to their garage. Then, they carefully measured and painted a free-throw line on the driveway. Corinne's dad smiled and said, "Well, champ, want to go one-on-one?"

---

**15 Based on this paragraph, why does Corinne's dad help her with the basketball court?**
   **A** He wants to encourage Corinne to play basketball.
   **B** He is tired of taking Corinne to basketball practice.
   **C** He enjoys playing basketball with his friends.
   **D** He thought it would be fun to do a project with Corinne.

---

There was once a scientist who believed that, if he studied the stars carefully enough, he could predict the future. The scientist went for long walks at night with his eyes fixed on the heavens. Refusing to take his eyes off the stars, the scientist tripped and fell into a deep, muddy hole. His cries for help attracted the villagers, who rescued him. One of them said, "You seek to read the future in the stars, but you fail to see what is at your feet!"

---

**16 What lesson can be learned from this story?**
   **F** The wise do not let themselves be tricked twice.
   **G** Do not count your chickens before they hatch.
   **H** Hurry in the present, and regret it in the future.
   **J** Do not let dreams of the future spoil the present.

Favian Mercado thought it would be neat to run for student-body president, so he did. When the votes were counted, and Favian had won the election, he met with the vice principal to go over his new duties. Afterwards, Favian felt overwhelmed. He had no idea he would have to attend school-board meetings, write monthly reports, and organize the annual fundraiser. If he had known being president would be so much work, he might not have run.

**17 The person telling this story is —**
A Favian Mercado
B an outside narrator
C the current student-body president
D none of the above

**18 The moral of this story is —**
F nothing is worth more than freedom
G with greatness comes responsibility
H misfortune is the test of friendship
J common sense is a valuable treasure

**Directions:** Read each sentence. Choose the word that has the opposite meaning of the underlined word in the sentence. On the answer sheet, fill in the bubble for the answer that you think is correct.

**19 My sister is always <u>alert</u> just before she plays in her soccer games.**
A hungry
B dazed
C talkative
D nervous

**20 Alex imagined what it would be like to live in a stone <u>mansion</u> with high ceilings and big windows.**
F hut
G pasture
H cave
J castle

**Directions:** Read each sentence. Choose the word that has the same meaning as the underlined word in the sentence. On the answer sheet, fill in the bubble for the answer that you think is correct.

**21 Victoria thought that it was <u>absurd</u> to have only one week to complete the term paper.**
A intelligent
B ridiculous
C timely
D busy

**22 Henri decided to <u>combine</u> all the ingredients for the brownies at the same time instead of adding the eggs last.**
F sift
G purchase
H separate
J mix

**Directions:** Look at this section of a dictionary on the right. Use this information to answer the questions below. On the answer sheet, fill in the bubble for the answer you think is correct.

**23 According to the dictionary, the term "free and easy" means —**
A without
B not under control of another
C release from bondage
D informal

**24 The letters -ie in the word <u>freebie</u> are pronounced like the same letters in which of these words?**
F diet
G lie
H either
J sieve

---

**free** (frē) **adj. fre•er, fre•est** [OE, *freo*]
**1.** not under the control or power of another, having liberty, independent **2.** having civil liberties **3.** able to move in any direction; loose **4.** not burdened by obligations, discomforts, constraints, etc. **5.** not confined to the usual rules [*free* verse] **6.** not exact [a *free* translation] **7.** generous, profuse [*free* spending] **8.** with no charge or cost **9.** exempt from taxes, duties, etc. **10.** clear of obstructions [a *free* road] **11.** frank, straightforward **12.** open to all [a *free* port] **13.** not fastened **—adv.**
**1.** without cost **2.** in a free manner **—vt. freed, free•ing** to make free; specif., *a*) to release from bondage, arbitrary power, obligation, etc. *b*) to clear of obstruction, etc. **—free and easy** informal **—free from** (or **of**) without **—make free** wish to use freely **—set free** to release; liberate **—freely adv.**
**free•bie, free•by** (frē´ bē) **n. pl. –bies** [Slang] something given or gotten free of charge

---

**Directions:** Read the words below. Then look for mistakes in spelling. Fill in the bubble on the answer sheet that has the same letter as the mistake. If there is no mistake, fill in the last answer choice.

**25 A** anger
**B** trailer
**C** tracter
**D** *(No mistakes)*

**26 F** abuse
**G** spruce
**H** announce
**J** *(No mistakes)*

**Directions:** Read the sentences below. Then look for mistakes in capitalization. Fill in the bubble on the answer sheet that has the same letter as the mistake. If there is no mistake, fill in the last answer choice.

**27 A** Sarah and Carolyn
**B** want to attend Humphry
**C** College in september.
**D** *(No mistakes)*

**28 F** Michael picked
**G** out a new Book
**H** to read to his students.
**J** *(No mistakes)*

Name _____  Date _____

# Practice Test 1

*Answer the questions that follow.*

1. Which of these is an example of simile?
   - A. The children were exhausted.
   - B. Her eyes were like jewels.
   - C. The cymbals crashed noisily.
   - D. He jumped into the icy lake.

2. Find the meaning of the underlined word in the sentence below.

   Most of the class considered Mr. Carter to be <u>dreamy</u>.
   - A. attractive and wonderful
   - B. tired and boring
   - C. thoughtful and bright
   - D. sleepy and withdrawn

*Read the following selection. Then answer the questions that follow.*

### The Kitten

Margo and Fallon went to the old barn for the third day in a row. Quietly they slipped in through a hole on the side of the barn. There in the middle of the barn was a tiny ball of matted fur, lapping up milk from the bowl sitting in front of him.

"He's drinking it up!" Margo whispered with delight. The girls slowly moved forward. The kitten started. He looked up, saw the girls, and bolted up into the hayloft.

"He's too scared. Hell never trust us to take care of him," Margo said.

"I have one more idea. You wait here," said Fallon. She came back in a few minutes with a can of tuna. They took little pieces of tuna and made a path from the hayloft ladder to where they were standing. The kitten slowly began to follow the tuna trail. Finally he came cautiously near the girls. He sniffed and picked at each bite of tuna until he was eating out of their hands.

3. What is the setting of this story?
   - A. a mountain cabin
   - B. an old barn
   - C. a seaside shack
   - D. a haunted mansion

4. Why did the girls make a trail of tuna for the kitten?
   - A. The kitten was supposed to be outside.
   - B. They wanted the kitten to trust them.
   - C. They wanted to see if the kitten liked tuna.
   - D. They kitten was hungry and needed food.

*Read the selection. Then answer the question that follows.*

### The New Girl

Students buzzed happily on their way to class, but Nina was alone. It was her first day at Comstock, and she wished it were her last.

All-in-One Workbook: Standardized Test Practice
© Pearson Education, Inc. All rights reserved.

**331**

In homeroom, Nina sat near a girl with red hair. The girl leaned over and whispered, "Hey, aren't you new?"

Nina nodded. The red-haired girl smiled and extended her hand. "I'm practically new. We moved here from Virginia two months ago."

The girl's name was Kaila, and by the time homeroom was over, a friendship had begun, and Nina felt much better about her new school.

5. What is the theme of this story?
   A. Feeling lonely is sometimes good.
   B. There is comfort in friendship.
   C. There is no friendship in a crowd.
   D. Real friends never let each other down.

*Answer the questions that follow.*

6. Which of these sentences **probably** came from a fairy tale?
   A. Atlantis was said to have existed long ago and to have been the site of an advanced civilization.
   B. Ulysses S. Grant had been unsuccessful at almost everything he tried.
   C. Flying across the ocean along was an enormous challenge that had cost several people their lives.
   D. The great troll stood up, sniffed the air, and then turned and walked into the forest.

7. What feeling is created in this line from a poem?

   Surrounded by fluffy, white clouds

   A. jealousy
   B. peacefulness
   C. anger
   D. anxiety

8. What type of image is created in these lines from a poem by Herman Melville?

   When ocean-clouds over inland hills

   Sweep storming in late autumn brown

   A. dismal
   B. cheerful
   C. scary
   D. busy

*Read the following selection. Then answer the questions that follow.*

### Something Special for Mom

Isaac wanted to do something special for his mother, so he decided to make lasagna, her favorite dish. Laying out all the ingredients, Isaac checked to make sure he had everything the recipe called for.

"Oh no!" Isaac said to himself. He thought for a moment and then grabbed a small bowl and dashed out the front door. Within minutes he was back from Mrs. Arnold's house and carefully setting the bowl of eggs on the counter.

9. Why did Isaac go to Mrs. Arnold's house?
   A. He needed to borrow eggs for the lasagna.
   B. He asked her for a recipe for lasagna.
   C. Mrs. Arnold showed him how to cook the pasta.
   D. Mrs. Arnold made some lasagna for Isaac.

10. Which of the following is an effect of Isaac wanting to do something special for his mother?
   A. Isaac realized that he did not have eggs.
   B. Isaac decided to make lasagna.
   C. Isaac went to Mrs. Arnold's house.
   D. Isaac grabbed a small bowl.

*Read the following selection. Then answer the questions that follow.*

### Owning a Pet

Owning a pet teaches responsibility. Pets require regular feeding, grooming, and sometimes walking and playing. Some pets live in cages. Their cages must be cleaned and the cage lining must be replaced. Certain animals need special care. Horses wear shoes that must be cared for. Fish must have clean water to swim in. Some fish even need to live in water that stays at a certain temperature. When pet owners go on trips, they must plan for the care of their pets while they are gone. A person can learn a lot from owning a pet.

11. Which of the following is the **best** summary of the selection?
   A. Some pets have cages that must be cleaned.
   B. Horses wear shoes that must be cared for.
   C. People must take their pets with them on trips.
   D. The various tasks involved in pet ownership teach people responsibility.

12. Which of the following conclusions can you draw from this selection?
   A. Dogs are easier to care for than fish.
   B. People who own horses are the most responsible pet owners.
   C. Caring for a pet can be hard work.
   D. Animals that live in cages don't make good pets.

*Read the following selection. Then answer the questions that follow.*

### Lessons Learned

For years, the huge old Andrews place has sat empty in a weedy lot. It had once been a grand home, but now it was a wreck. The Main Street Historical Society wanted to turn the house into a museum. The members held bake sales and flea markets to raise money, but still there wasn't enough. The society wrote to the newspaper for help.

The next meeting of the Historical Society was packed with people. Maddie Rose, the society's president, was surprised. The room was filled with kids! Most of the group's members were older, and many of them were grandparents. They had never seen kids at their meetings before.

When the meeting started, a smiling young girl stood up. "My name is Sarah Wilson, and these are my friends," she said. "We are in the sixth grade and saw your letter in the newspaper. We've been studying city history in class. We'd like to help you fix the Andrews House."

Many society members were against the idea. They didn't believe that a bunch of kids could be of any help. One member, Fred Thompson, was especially against the idea. Over his objections, the society agreed to let the kids help.

The next day, Saturday, was clean-up day at the Andrews House. Maddie arrived early. The place was swarming with kids and society members. Together, they were pulling out the weeds, raking the yard, and hauling away trash. The place buzzed with activity, and everyone seemed to be having a good time.

Fred saw Maddie and walked over to her. He said sheepishly, "I never would have believed that kids could do this much good."

Maddie smiled. She knew better. "Now what do you think of letting kids help out?"

13. From the information in the selection, what can you infer about Sarah?
    A. She was against the idea of helping at first.
    B. She probably helped organize the students.
    C. She never helped out like this before.
    D. She really didn't like Fred Thompson.

14. How do Maddie's and Fred's attitudes toward the kids differ before the end of the selection?
    A. Fred thinks the kids will be a big help to the society.
    B. Maddie thinks the kids may try to steal things from the Andrews House.
    C. Maddie doesn't think that the kids will work hard enough.
    D. Fred doesn't think that the kids would be much of a help to the society.

15. What assumption about kids does the author of this selection make?
    A. Kids are always ready to help out for a good cause.
    B. Kids are only good for cleaning up messes.
    C. Kids don't read newspapers often enough.
    D. Kids work harder than anyone else.

*Read the following selection. Then answer the questions that follow.*

### The Forbidden City

The Forbidden City in Beijing, China, is the largest palace complex in the world. Set in the middle of Beijing, it covers and area of 720,000 square meters and even has a moat around the outside for protection.

For almost 500 years the Forbidden City housed the emperors of China. The buildings of the city were home to the emperor's family and were also the area from which the emperor and his officials ruled the country. The city was closed to all but the highest government and military officials. Today, the city has been renamed the Palace museum and is open to the public.

It took 15 years to complete the palace, which was started during the Ming Dynasty. According to Chinese records, over one million workers were needed to build the city. It was made from wood and brick. The main color used in all the buildings was yellow, even though the official name of the city was the Purple Forbidden City. Yellow is the color most closely linked to emperors, and in the Forbidden City, all but one building has a yellow tile roof.

The Forbidden City now consists of more than ten different museums for the art within the palace and the records are held there. The city is China's largest museum, housing about one million objects, many of which are one of a kind. Although the palace is no longer the ruling center of China, it still has an impact on the many people who visit every day.

16. What is the purpose of this selection?
   A. to persuade readers to visit China
   B. to describe what life was like for an ancient Chinese emperor
   C. to inform readers about the Forbidden City in Beijing, China
   D. to entertain readers with an amusing story about life in Beijing, China

17. What question is left unanswered by the third paragraph?
   A. What was used to build the palace?
   B. How long did it take to build the palace?
   C. What was the main color used in the Forbidden City?
   D. Why was the city named the Purple Forbidden City?

18. Why was the palace complex known as the Forbidden City?
   A. People, except for important officials, were not allowed to enter the city.
   B. People were not allowed to speak while inside the city.
   C. The emperor's family was not allowed to leave the city.
   D. People were not allowed to bring weapons into the city.

*Read the following selection. Then answer the questions that follow.*

### Who Invented Band-Aids®?

Although many people don't even know his name, Earle Dickson was responsible for creating one of today's most common household items. Dickson was the genius behind Band-Aids®.

In 1917, Dickson was a newly married man a cotton buyer for a successful bandage company in New Jersey called Johnson & Johnson. As the story goes, Dickson's wife, Frances, was accident-prone. She often cut herself or nicked her fingers doing various household tasks. The regular bandages were too big and clumsy for Frances, so Dickson devised something better.

He folded pads of cotton gauze and place them on long strings of surgical tape. He covered this with a material called *crinoline*. This prevented the tape from sticking to itself when it was rolled back together. Frances could unroll the bandage and cut off as much as she needed.

One day, Dickson mentioned his creation to a friend at work. Soon, Dickson was before the Johnsons, showing them what he had come up with. The Johnsons were especially impressed by the fact that you could put the new bandage on yourself. Up to that point, bandages had been difficult to apply without help.

Johnson & Johnson began producing Band-Aids®, but the bandages didn't take off until the mid-1920s when the company gave thousands of samples to the Boy Scouts. After that, Band-Aids® were a hit. Dickson was made vice president of Johnson & Johnson, and when he died in 1961, the company was selling $30,000,000 dollars' worth of Band-Aids® a year.

19. How did bandages differ before and after the creation of Band-Aids®?
   A. Regular bandages were much less expensive than Band-Aids®.
   B. Regular bandages were difficult to apply without help, unlike Band-Aids®.
   C. Regular bandages were smaller and less clumsy than Band-Aids®.
   D. Regular bandages were only given out by doctors, but Band-Aids® were sold in stores.

20. If you were writing a comparison-and-contrast essay about how bandages differed before and after the creation of Band-Aids®, which of the following would be the **best** pre-writing plan method?
   A. Venn diagram
   B. word web
   C. story map
   D. character-image map

21. If you were taking notes about this passage, which of the following would belong?
   A. Dickson invented crinoline.
   B. Band-Aids® were popular right away.
   C. Early bandages were easy to apply.
   D. Dickson worked for Johnson & Johnson.

22. Which of the following sentences from the passage shows the author's bias toward Dickson?
   A. One day, Dickson mentioned his creation to a friend at work.
   B. Up to that point, bandages had been difficult to apply without help.
   C. Dickson was the genius behind Band-Aids®.
   D. He covered this with a material called *crinoline*.

*Read the following article written by a student about a recent change in school policy. Then answer the questions that follow.*

**Requirement is Unfair to Athletes**

At its meeting last week, the school board decided to require student athletes to attend Physical Education (P.E.) classes. As an athlete, I feel this requirement is unfair.

Playing a team sport at school requires the same type of activity (physical exercise) as a P.E. course. Athletes may exhaust or injure themselves if they take part in both activities. In addition, the time spent in P.E. courses can be put to use by coaches as training time. That way, athletes would not have to spend so much time training after school and would have more time to study. This is especially important for athletes because they are not usually good students. Finally, as I understand it, P.E. courses are supposed to develop an interest in athletics. Students who take part in team sports already have this interest. For athletes, P.E. is unnecessary, and it might even be harmful—both physically and academically.

I hope our school district will consider the time and effort student athletes put into their teams and reconsider its decision.

**23.** Why was this article written?
   A. to complain about athletic teams
   B. to persuade the school board to change its decision
   C. to explain why the school board made its decision
   D. to describe the school's physical education program

**24.** What does the writer mean when she says that P.E. classes would be academically harmful for athletes?
   A. P.E. classes would be difficult for athletes and they might fail.
   B. P.E. classes take up time athletes could use to study for their other classes.
   C. Athletes who take P.E. classes would have to drop out of one of their other courses.
   D. P.E. classes would create too much homework for athletes.

**25.** Which of the following statements from the article is an example of stereotype?
   A. This is especially important for athletes because they are not usually good students.
   B. As an athlete, I feel this requirement is unfair.
   C. Athletes may exhaust or injure themselves if they take part in both activities.
   D. I hope our school district will consider the time and effort student athletes put into their teams and reconsider its decision.

# Practice Test 2

*Read the following passages. Then answer the questions that follow.*

## Encyclopedia Entry

The word *sabotage* comes from the French word *sabot*. A sabot is a wooden shoe. The commonly accepted origin, or history, of this word is as follows: During the Industrial Revolution, French factory workers became concerned about their future. They were worried about the possibility of losing their jobs because of new automated machinery. To avoid this possibility, the workers threw their wooden shoes into their machines so that the machines would break down. To throw a wooden shoe into a machine became known as sabotage, or the act of destroying property or plans on purpose. A saboteur is someone who causes sabotage.

## Dictionary Entry

sab-o-tage (sab' täzh) *n.* 1. any interference with production work in a plant or factory, especially by enemy agents or employees during a work dispute  2. any undermining of a cause *v.* to injure or attack by sabotage

## History Book

Sabotage is considered by many to be one of the most terrible crimes. The act of sabotage is sneaky at best. At worst, it makes the person committing the crime a traitor. Although it was given its name during the Industrial Revolution, sabotage has been around for thousands of years. It is likely that enslaved workers in Roman and Egyptian times used sabotage at least occasionally. In more modern times, sabotage has been a tool of warfare. It is hated by the side against whom the sabotage is committed. The side that causes the sabotage, however, sees it as a noble act.

1. Which information source gives the most complete information about sabotage?
   A. the encyclopedia entry
   B. the dictionary entry
   C. the history book
   D. They all give the same information.

2. If you were writing a report about the history of sabotage, which of the following could you use as a primary source?
   A. an encyclopedia entry about sabotage
   B. a journal entry from a 19<sup>th</sup> century saboteur
   C. a section from a social studies textbook about sabotage
   D. a movie about sabotage in a metal factory

*Read the following selection. Then answer the questions that follow.*

The Sahara is the largest desert in the world. __1__ in northern Africa, it covers more than three million square miles. It is one of the most difficult places on Earth in which to live. Despite this, __2__ consider it one of the most beautiful places on Earth.

3. Choose the word that belongs in space (1).
   A. Locater
   B. Locating
   C. Located
   D. Was located

**4.** Choose the word that belongs in space (2).

    **A.** some                              **C.** anybody

    **B.** somebody                         **D.** both

*Answer the questions that follow.*

**5.** Choose the word that best completes the following sentence:

    The carpenter's carving of the bear was done _____.

    **A.** skill                                **C.** skillful

    **B.** skillfulness                     **D.** skillfully

**6.** Which of the following words is spelled correctly?

    **A.** ceiling                              **C.** ceeling

    **B.** cieling                            **D.** cealing

*Read the following selection. Then answer the questions that follow.*

### Franklin Delano Roosevelt

(1) Historians believe that Franklin Delano Roosevelt was among the greatest american presidents. (2) During his terms in office, Roosevelt successfully faced two enormous challenges. (3) The Great Depression and World War II. (4) Their ability to deal with these events was recognized by the voters. (5) He one the presidency four times, a feat that no previous president had ever accomplished.

**7.** Which change should be made to correct sentence 1?

    **A.** change ***american*** to ***American***       **C.** change ***presidents*** to ***president***

    **B.** change ***Roosevelt*** to ***Roosevelt,***     **D.** change ***believe*** to ***believes***

**8.** Which of the following is a fragment?

    **A.** (1) Historians believe that Franklin Delano Roosevelt was among the greatest American presidents.

    **B.** (3) The Great Depression and World War II.

    **C.** (4) Their ability to deal with these events was recognized by the voters.

    **D.** (5) He one the presidency four times, a feat that no previous president had ever accomplished.

**9.** Which change should be made to correct sentence 4?

    **A.** change ***Their*** to ***His***               **C.** change ***was*** to ***were***

    **B.** change ***ability*** to ***abilities***       **D.** change ***events*** to ***events,***

**10.** Which change should be made to correct sentence 5?

    **A.** change ***He*** to ***Him***

    **B.** change ***one*** to ***won***

    **C.** change ***accomplished.*** to ***accomplished?***

    **D.** change ***had*** to ***has***

Name _____ Date _____

*Read the following sentences. Then answer the question that follows.*

(1) On calm days, cooking is a breeze.

(2) Jake as an unusual job.

(3) People always ask what it's like to cook at sea.

(4) But when the seas become violent, and the boat is tossed up and down and side to side, cooking can be a challenge.

(5) Jake says that it depends on the weather.

(6) He is a cook for a crew of five on a tugboat.

**11.** Which of the following reflects the **best** organization for the sentences above?

    **A.** 3, 5, 6, 1, 2, 4           **C.** 2, 6, 3, 5, 1, 4

    **B.** 1, 2, 5, 4, 3, 6           **D.** 6, 4, 2, 1, 3, 5


*Answer the questions that follow.*

**12.** Which of the following is the *best* way to revise this sentence?

Believing that poets are just like everyone else, William Wordsworth also thought that they are a little more sensitive to their surroundings.

    **A.** William Wordsworth believed that poets are just like everyone else, except that they are a little more sensitive to their surroundings.

    **B.** William Wordsworth believed that everyone else is sensitive like poets.

    **C.** William Wordsworth believed that poets were like everyone else, sensitive to their surroundings.

    **D.** William Wordsworth believed that everyone else was insensitive, while poets were more sensitive.

**13.** Which of the following sentences *best* demonstrates the relationship between ideas?

    **A.** Alex wanted to go to the farmer's market, and it was closed on Thursdays.

    **B.** Alex wanted to go to the farmer's market, or it was closed on Thursdays.

    **C.** Alex wanted to go to the farmer's market, but it was closed on Thursdays.

    **D.** Alex wanted to go to the farmer's market, so it was closed on Thursdays.

Suppose that you and several of your classmates must work in a small group to create an oral presentation convincing classmates about the importance of eating nutritious foods. Each group member must participate. Answer the questions that follow.

**14.** In your oral presentation, which of the following would you *most* likely include?

    **A.** figurative language           **C.** persuasive language

    **B.** a friend's opinion            **D.** complex technical language

15. Which of the following would be an inappropriate comment during a discussion about nutrition?
   A. My favorite nutritious snack is fruit.
   B. Many people don't have the time to cook nutritious foods.
   C. I think it's important to eat healthful foods.
   D. Nutrition is stupid.

16. Which of the following would be the best way to approach the presentation?
   A. complete the research, write the presentation, create the visual aids
   B. write the presentation, complete the research, create the visual aids
   C. create the visual aids, write the presentation, complete the research
   D. create the visual aids, complete the research, write the presentation

17. Which of the following behaviors would be the most appropriate while participating in a group activity?
   A. ignoring other group members
   B. arguing with the group leader
   C. listening to the other group members
   D. making fun of the other group members' opinions

The following two viewpoints were presented during a debate. Read the passages. Then answer the questions that follow.

Soccer is the most physically challenging sport one can play. In order to play soccer well, one must be in top condition.

Unlike soccer, tennis involves both the upper and lower body, giving the participant a total physical workout. Tennis requires strength, balance, coordination, and endurance. In addition, it requires mental focus and knowledge of strategy. That is why some of the best athletes in the world are tennis players.

18. Which of the following is a *fact* from the debate?
   A. Tennis involves both the upper and lower body.
   B. In order to pay soccer well, one must be in top condition.
   C. Some of the best athletes in the world are tennis players.
   D. Soccer is the most physically challenging sport one can play.

19. Of the two viewpoints above, which is the more convincing?
   A. the first viewpoint
   B. the second viewpoint
   C. Neither viewpoint is convincing.
   D. Both viewpoints are equally convincing.

Name _____  Date _____

*Answer the following questions.*

20. Which of the following is the *most* appropriate way to paraphrase information given in an oral presentation?
    A. copy the speaker's presentation word for word
    B. restate the information in your own words
    C. quote the speaker directly
    D. borrow language from the speaker

21. Which type of language would be the *least* appropriate to use in a formal presentation?
    A. technical                    C. scientific
    B. persuasive                   D. casual


*Read the following speech. Then answer the questions that follow.*

   The Park Action Committee (PAC) was started in 1979 to make sure that parks and wildlife would be protected. Many parks were in danger of becoming littered beyond help, and local wildlife was eating plastic bags and aluminum foil left behind by park guests. PAC has improved the national parks and kept animals safe for over 20 years. We ask the state of Montana to consider giving us money so that we can keep doing the job we do. Help PAC to help you by funding out projects this year.


22. If you were giving this speech, which of the following statements would be the best addition to help convince the state of Montana to give PAC money?
    A. Give PAC more money now!
    B. Without PAC's help, Montana's parks will not receive as many visitors, and its wildlife will not thrive.
    C. If all of its wildlife dies, it will be the state of Montana's fault, not PAC's.
    D. If Montana doesn't give PAC money, something really bad could happen.

23. Which is the *best* summary of the speech above?
    A. The Park Action Committee (PAC) needs funding from the state of Montana to continue its dedication to cleaning national parks and protecting wildlife.
    B. The Park Action Committee (PAC) needs help from the state of Montana to pick up litter.
    C. The Park Action Committee (PAC) wants to create more parks for Montana's wildlife.
    D. The Park Action Committee (PAC) wants wildlife to stop eating aluminum foil.

*Answer the following questions.*

24. Suppose you need to include sensory details in a story that you are writing. Which of the following sentences should you choose?

    A. The school cafeteria line a busy, happy place at lunchtime.

    B. Students shrieked with laughter and shouted happily as they snaked through the cafeteria line.

    C. It was loud in the cafeteria, and there were lots and lots of students in line.

    D. We all talked and laughed as we went through the cafeteria line.

25. Read the dictionary entry below. Other than *-s*, what ending would you add to make *tableau* plural?

    tab•leau *n, pl* tab•leaux *also* tableaus

    [origin: F, fr. MF *tablel*] 1: a graphic description or representation

    A. -ion

    B. -x

    C. -el

    D. -ses

Name _____     Date _____

# Practice Test 3

# Career Connections: Athletic Coaches

1) Squeaky is the fastest runner in her neighborhood, and she makes a real effort to train herself for her races. She might be an even faster runner, however, if she had a track coach to guide her training.

2) Athletic coaches can help make the difference between a good athlete and a great one. They teach beginners the fundamentals of a sport, lead athletes through a season, and help world champions sharpen their skills. Coaches and instructors also help amateurs who simply want to increase their personal enjoyment of a sport or improve their exercise routine.

3) Coaches can be found guiding teams and individuals at the professional and Olympic levels, at schools and colleges, and even at local fitness centers, ice rinks, and swimming pools. The nature of the work of all athletic coaches is to teach. As a result, they must be knowledgeable in their respective sports, keep up with the latest procedures and techniques, and develop an effective teaching method to share the information with their athletes.

4) Coaches at all levels must also be concerned with safety, ensuring that each athlete knows the proper methods of using equipment and maximizing performance without causing injury.

5) Athletic coaches at public and private schools are usually required to have a bachelor's degree from an accredited college or university. Sports instructors may not have a college or university degree, but they are usually skillful players of a particular sport.

6) If you are considering a career as an athletic coach or instructor, a great way to start preparing is to participate in sports now.

1. Which of the following is best supported by the selection?
   A. Coaches must continue to teach.
   B. Coaches must be professional athletes.
   C. Coaches must continually study their sport to be effective.
   D. Coaches must be in peak condition to be effective teachers.

2. Why do coaches need to be concerned with safety?
   A. to keep their licenses
   B. to keep good jobs
   C. to protect their schools and colleges
   D. to protect the athletes they are coaching

3. Why are some coaches required to have a college degree?
   A. because they are teachers
   B. because they have to play college sports
   C. because they have to be smart
   D. because they will be better coaches

4. Which of the following relationship is most similar to the relationship below?
   **coaches : athletes**
   A. mothers: fathers
   B. teachers : students
   C. students : teachers
   D. fathers : mothers

Name _____ Date _____

## A Noiseless Patient Spider
### By Walt Whitman

A noiseless patient spider,
I marked where on a promontory, it stood, isolated,
Marked how, to explore the vacant, vast surroundings,
It launched forth filament, filament, filament out of itself,
Ever unreeling them, ever tirelessly speeding them.

And you O my soul where you stand,
Surrounded, detached, in measureless oceans of space,
Ceaselessly musing, venturing, throwing, seeking the spheres to connect them,
Till the bridge you will need be formed—Till the ductile anchor hold,
Till the gossamer thread you fling catch somewhere, O my soul.

5. Based on the context of the poem, what is the meaning of *marked*?
   A. pushed
   B. watched
   C. listened
   D. moved

6. What was the spider doing in stanza 1?
   A. climbing a wall
   B. catching a bug
   C. building a web
   D. exploring a space

7. In stanza 2, the author compares the spider's web to which of the following?
   A. bridges
   B. his soul
   C. his thoughts
   D. thread

8. What is the main idea of the poem?
   A. Spiders and people are a lot alike.
   B. Spiders work very hard when building a large web.
   C. People are lonely like spiders.
   D. People must keep trying to understand themselves.

9. Which of the following relationships is most like the relationship below?
   **filaments : threads**
   A. thoughts : ideas
   B. teachers : students
   C. books : school
   D. religions : beliefs

# Natural Disasters

Nature can be an incredibly powerful force. Our relationship with nature must be treated with respect. When natural disasters strike unexpectedly, what can we do to defend ourselves?

Today's technology can help to predict hurricanes, blizzards, tornadoes, and earthquakes. Sometimes disasters arrive so fast, however, that we hardly have time to think. Wildfires, too, have the speed and strength to destroy everything in their path.

All of these natural disasters have lasting effects on the environment. They remind us that we are mortal and that life is fragile. We are fortunate that trained experts and volunteers are able to help a community recover from natural disasters. How do disaster professionals and communities work together to rebuild what has been destroyed? What is important to know when disasters strike? Let's find out.

## Hurricanes and Floods

Trees bend and snap in roaring winds. Rain pelts roofs and windows. Water is rising in the street. Electrical power is out. A serious storm is approaching.

A hurricane, also known as a tropical cyclone, is a very frightening and severe kind of storm. It forms over warm ocean water. Hurricane winds can exceed up to 74 miles an hour. A really fierce storm may have winds that are twice that high.

Winds, moving counterclockwise, gain force and speed. A hurricane can be up to 300 miles across. At the center is its eye. This clear, calm area is between 20 to 40 miles across. The most powerful winds surround the eye.

Hurricanes can unexpectedly strike the coasts of the Atlantic Ocean and the Gulf of Mexico anytime from June through November. The season reaches its peak from mid-August to late October.

The National Weather Service tracks hurricanes. It uses satellites, ships, planes, observing stations, and radar to follow storms. Even with all of these resources, it is still hard to predict when the next storm will hit. The National Weather Service tracks wind gusts, how fast a storm moves, and where a storm makes landfall. High winds and heavy rain can cause severe flooding. A storm surge—a large dome of water along the coast—can ruin lives as well as property.

One cause of a flood is a river overflowing its bank. The Red River of the North runs between the cities of Fargo, North Dakota and Moorhead, Minnesota. In April 1997, 2001, and 2006, local residents had to deal with serious flooding and destruction.

The spring thaw moved north with the flow of the river. Ice jams blocked the flow. The river was in a shallow valley across a flat plain. The slope of the river decreased north of Fargo, forming a huge, shallow lake. The result was a massive flood.

The type of aid required after such flooding is similar to what is needed after a hurricane. The main difference is that there is no wind damage. People's homes and belongings are often ruined beyond repair. They have to start from the ground up, rebuilding their lives. Fires, health issues, and accidents often add to residents' plight.

How does a community prepare for such a terrible storm? Many local, state, and national agencies have emergency plans. They provide detailed instructions to help people prepare for a hurricane. Their level of involvement depends on how severe the storm it. Often, people must rely on helping one another.

Name _____    Date _____

Lee County, Florida, provides a set of procedures to follow when a hurricane is coming. The first thing to do is to notify other people in the immediate area of the storm and decide who will be evacuating and when. People still in the area should take shelter in designated places.

Distributing resources should be based on such things as who may be injured, age, or individual needs until emergency teams are able to assist. Once the storm has passed, what gets rebuilt is based upon the amount of damage the storm caused.

In August 2005, Hurricane Katrina struck in and around New Orleans, Louisiana. It posed special problems for search and rescue teams. Many people who could have helped had already evacuated the area. Others were stranded on rooftops, bridges, or in the Superdome. Life became a matter of staying dry and free of the filthy water. People had to find food, water, and shelter. They tried to confirm the safety of loved ones.

The plight of Katrina's victims tugged at the heartstrings of the global community. Outreach efforts came in from all over the world. People sent money. Volunteers from all over the country came to New Orleans. Stories of life-or-death missions made headlines. When they succeeded in saving people or reuniting families, heartbreak changed to jubilation. Once the floodwaters dried up, the long, difficult process of rebuilding began. Many people have never returned home.

### Conclusion

Natural disasters can strike at any time. It is important to know what to do when one occurs in your area. Safety and evacuation procedures set up by local rescue organizations should be followed with care.

Technology, rescue professionals, government agencies, and volunteers cooperate in order to assist those in need, and to help rebuild communities. Positive responses to the aftermath of Hurricane Katrina are examples of the good that can come from combined efforts.

As long as people work together in communities, the damage caused by natural disasters can be overcome.

**10.** Based on the context of the passage, why *most likely* is tracking hurricanes useful?
  A. to estimate the property damage which may occur
  B. to determine patterns of future storms
  C. to predict when the next storm might hit
  D. to figure out the dollar amount of the property loss

**11.** Floods and hurricanes cause some of the same problems. Which of the following would *not* be a typical problem in the aftermath of a flood?
  A. People's homes and belongings are often ruined beyond repair.
  B. Wind damage occurs.
  C. Health issues are a concern.
  D. Safety is a large concern.

**12.** According to the text, "Fire, health issues, and accidents often add to residents' plight." Based on the context of the sentence, what is the meaning of the word *plight*?
  A. worry
  B. costs
  C. sad or dangerous situation
  D. insurance bills

**13.** According to the text, what is one reason Hurricane Katrina posed special problems for search and rescue teams?
  A. shortage of money
  B. lack of resources
  C. many people who could have helped had already evacuated the area
  D. lack of communication

**14.** Distributing resources during a disaster is based on many factors. What is *not* a factor that should be used?
  A. injuries
  B. financial position
  C. age
  D. individual needs

**15.** What is a lasting effect that a natural disaster may have on a community?
  A. property damage
  B. death
  C. communities destroyed
  D. all of the above

**16.** What is the main idea of the selection?
  A. There are procedures to follow if a hurricane is sighted.
  B. Many victims of Hurricane Katrina have not returned to their homes.
  C. Natural disasters can have lasting effects on the environment and the community.
  D. The Natural Weather Service can predict every storm.

Name _____  Date _____

## Let's Make a Piñata

*Most people think of children's parties in Mexico when they hear the word piñata, but according to legend, the piñata was actually introduced to the West by Marco Polo, who learned of them in China. Piñata's are hollow paper shapes usually formed to look like animals. They are filled with candy and trinkets. The fun starts when children are given a small bat which is used to bash the shape until is crumbles and all the goodies fall to the floor. The following is a recipe for making your own piñata. It is easy and fun.*

**Needed Materials:**
1 round balloon
Plenty of newspaper
Water
Flour
Glue
Scissors
Crêpe paper

**Steps:**

1)    Inflate your balloon. It will form the body of your piñata, so inflate it to the size you want your piñata to be.

2)    Cover the floor with newspaper to prevent a big mess.

3)    Fill a large bowl ¾ full of flour, and then add water until you have a thick mixture the consistency of wallpaper paste.

4)    Tear newspaper into strips that are about 2 inches wide. Dip the newspaper strips into the mixture. You have just made paper mâché! Make sure that the newspaper is totally saturated, but not dripping, and begin to lay the strips over the balloon. Continue until the balloon is covered in a thick layer of paper mâché.

5)    Let the balloon dry until it is stiff and no longer sticky. This may take overnight.

6)    When the paper mâché shape if dry glue colorful crepe paper to the outside and decorate your piñata in a creative way.

7)    This step is best done with the help of an adult! Using a serrated knife, cut a rectangular flap in one side of the piñata. Fill the cavity with candy, confetti, and (if you want) small toys. Then tape the flap shut. You can add more crêpe paper to cover the flap.

**Tips:**

*    Punch two small holes in the top of your Piñata and pass a string through the holes so that you can hang it.

*    If you want your piñata to have a traditional look you should attach paper streamers to each side.

*    Remember that this is your creation. You don't have to limit your decorations to crêpe paper. You can add glitter, feathers, fake flowers…whatever you like.

*    It is best to use wrapped candy. Remember that all the goodies will be falling to the floor.

*    A piñata adds fun to any party or family occasion. You could make an Easter egg or a jack-o-lantern or a fat reindeer. Use your imagination.

**17.** Why is it necessary to spread newspaper on the floor before you begin the project?
A. You can't make the piñata without newspaper.
B. Newspaper makes the best piñatas.
C. It will make it easier to clean up.
D. It is the only way to complete the project.

**18.** Why is it necessary to inflate the balloon?
A. You have to create a cavity.
B. You could pop the balloon.
C. The balloon is too large.
D. The balloon will not come out.

**19.** Why *most likely* would you want the piñata to have a sturdy string?
A. A weak string looks bad.
B. A weak string will break too easily.
C. Children will be hitting the piñata with a bat.
D. Children will cut the string.

**20.** Why *most likely* do most people think piñata's started in Mexico?
A. Because they have read it in books.
B. Because they are seen most often at Mexican parties.
C. Because they are Mexican.
D. Because all Mexican children have piñatas.

**21.** Why *most likely* do the directions tell you to use your imagination?
A. Because it is an art project.
B. Because no two should look alike.
C. Because you should not copy other people.
D. Because it is more fun.

**22.** What is paper mâché?
A. a Mexican tool
B. a serrated knife
C. newspaper and paste
D. a Mexican glue

# Ain't I a Woman?

## Sojourner Truth

*Sojourner Truth was born Isabella Baumfree in New York state in 1797. As a slave she was sold several times and endured many hardships. In 1828, New York abolished slavery and as a free woman Isabella changed her name. She traveled on foot through New York and Connecticut preaching emancipation and women's rights. She never had the benefit of an education; however, she was a powerful speaker. She died in 1883, but her ideas have lived on.*

1) Well, children, where there is so much racket there must be something out of kilter. I think that 'twixt the Negroes of the South and the women at the North, all talking about rights, the white men will be in a fix pretty soon. But what's all this here talking about?

2) That man over there says that women need to be helped into carriages, and lifted over ditches, and to have the best place everywhere. Nobody ever helps me into carriages, or over mud-puddles, or gives me any best place! And ain't I a woman?

3) Look at me! Look at my arm! I have ploughed and planted, and gathered into barns, and no man could head me! And ain't I a woman? I could work as much and eat as much as a man—when I could get it—and bear the lash as well! And ain't I a woman?

4) I have borne thirteen children, and seen them most all sold off to slavery, and when I cried out with my mother's grief, none but Jesus heard me! And ain't I a woman?

5) Then they talk about this thing in the head; what's this they call it? [Intellect, someone whispers.] That's it, honey. What's that got to do with women's rights or Negro's rights? If my cup won't hold but a pint, and yours holds a quart, wouldn't you be mean not to let me have my little half-measure full?

6) Then that little man in black there, he says women can't have as much rights as men, 'cause Christ wasn't a woman! Where did your Christ come from? Where did your Christ come from? From God and a woman! Man had nothing to do with Him. If the first woman God ever made was strong enough to turn the world upside down all alone, these women together ought to be able to turn it back, and get it right side up again!

7) And now they is asking to do it, the men better let them. Obliged to you for hearing me, and now old Sojourner ain't got nothing more to say.

23. Based on the context of paragraph 1, what is the meaning of 'twixt?
    A. beside
    B. according
    C. between
    D. available

24. Why *most likely* did the author repeat the words, "Ain't I a woman?"
    A. to make her work rhyme
    B. to show she was a woman
    C. to protect women's rights
    D. to point out injustice

25. Who *most likely* is the little man in black in paragraph 6?
    A. a politician
    B. a policeman
    C. a minister
    D. a soldier

26. Why *most likely* was the word intellect not in Sojourners vocabulary?
    A. She forgot the word.
    B. She could not read.
    C. She had never heard the word.
    D. She was not an educated person.

27. Why *most likely* was Sojourner concerned about women's rights?
    A. Her life had been very hard.
    B. She had been a slave.
    C. She had traveled through the North.
    D. Her family had been sold into slavery

28. What *most likely* was Truth referencing with her figurative language in paragraph 5?
    A. black versus. white
    B. men versus women
    C. ability to speak
    D. ability to learn

29. Which of the following relationships is most similar to the relationship below?
    **Truth : women's rights**
    A. ministers: men
    B. King : civil rights
    C. women : parents
    D. Lincoln : Civil War

30. What is the main idea of the selection?
    A. All black women should be free.
    B. All men should give women their rights.
    C. Women should have equal rights with men.
    D. All blacks should be free.

31. Why *most likely* does the selection contain Southern dialect?
    A. to make it more interesting
    B. to let the reader know how Truth spoke
    C. to make the selection funny
    D. to show that Truth had very little schooling

Name _____     Date _____

# *from* What Makes Us Dream?

As long as history has been recorded, we know that people have wondered about the nature of dreams. Where do they come from? Why do we have them? What do they mean?

In ancient days, the focus was on how to interpret dreams. In modern times much scientific study has been done to try to figure out *why* we dream. Researchers also look at what happens to our minds and bodies when we do.

Ancient dream interpreters and most modern scientists have this in common. They both believe that dreams are a way for our brain to communicate with us. They tell us about what we experience in our waking lives.

Science has not found all the answers about dreams and their purposes. Much of the dreaming process remains a mystery. Let's take a look at what we *do* know.

## What Are Dreams?

People who think we dream only in black and white are mistaken. Most dreams are in color. They often rely on sensory images made up of our memory of sights, sounds, smells, touch, and taste. They also draw on common emotions, such as fear, pleasure, worry, or sadness.

Dreams can be realistic or wildly fantastic. They can weave the events of the day into a crazy story that's hard to follow. Characters and settings range from the familiar to the farfetched. Have you ever dreamed about a family member suddenly turning into an animal? Have you ever dreamed that you walked into your house, only it wasn't your house at all? Instead, it was a huge castle with a hundred rooms?

Guess what! You're not alone. Most people's dreams don't make a lot of sense, at least not on the surface. Studies have shown that people all over the world actually share certain types of dreams. Here's a list of some of the most common dreams:

**Being chased or attacked.** Have you ever dreamed that you were walking through the woods and a wild animal started chasing you?

**Messing up a performance.** How about a dream where you had studied hard for a test, but when you sat down to take it, your brain was a complete blank? Or you try to write something, but your hand won't respond?

**Falling or drowning.** Have you ever had a dream where you are falling off a cliff? Did you grab the bed and wake yourself up?

**Flying.** One of the most fun things to dream is that you're flying through the air. You're sailing above the people and buildings below, your very own superhero!

**Being in public wearing very little.** For some reason, this has got to be one of the worst dream feelings you can come up with. You feel total embarrassment as you stand in front of a crowd and suddenly realize you're wearing nothing but your underwear!

**Being lost or trapped.** You dream you are completely lost. You find yourself trying to make your way through a dense jungle. Or maybe it's an unfamiliar house with long halls and locked doors.

People all over the world report having dreamed about these topics at least once. See, it isn't just you.

## What Do Dreams Mean?

Dreams seem to distort reality. They provide us with images of things that could never happen. But people all over the world share certain dream images, no matter what language they speak. This suggests that there is a connection between our dreams and common human experiences.

Of course, dreams can also be very personal. They draw on the things that happen to us in our daily life. The verbal expressions people use in dreams may not make sense. However, the subjects discussed can represent what our brains are trying to work through. The nonsense dialogue of our dreams may be a way of expressing feelings we aren't able to express when we are awake. The strange nonverbal images of our dreams can represent things that we have encountered during the day. A crazy gesture made by an alien figure may have meaning beyond what it seems to be in the dream.

## How Do Dreams Help Us?

In the past, some researchers felt that dreams were just the brain's "dumping ground." It was as if dreams were our way of taking out the mental trash of the day. In recent years, though, studies have suggested that dreams are very important to our physical and mental health. They may even help us learn to do certain tasks. They can also help us understand things that confuse us when we are awake.

Some scientists also believe that dreams can help us solve problems. Have you ever gone to sleep, worried about a problem? Then you woke up and felt as if you knew how to solve it? Maybe someone did something, and you took offense. You got angry and said something. When you went to bed, you were upset. You couldn't figure out how to make things better. By the morning, though, you were no longer upset. Maybe you had a dream that helped you work out the way to make things better with that person.

Rosalind Cartwright of Rush University Medical Center is a sleep disorders specialist. She did a study that found that the earlier in the sleep cycle a person was awakened, the less pleasant the dream was. Later in the cycle the dreams become more pleasant. The contrast was strong. That led her to believe that one reason we dream is to work out our problems. What was bothering us in the beginning of our sleep cycle may have been worked out through our dreams.

Dreams are also thought to help us tap into our creativity. Some painters say that they get some of their ideas from their dreams. You'd be amazed at the number of paintings called "The Dream"! Songs are written about dreams, poems describe dreams, and novels are based on some idea that came to a writer during a dream. Maybe, like helping us solve problems, dreams help us see things in a way that we aren't able to when we are awake.

32. According to the text, "Dreams seem to distort reality." Based on this context, what is the meaning of *distort*?
    A. connect
    B. hide
    C. change
    D. represent clearly

33. What is the main idea of the section "What Are Dreams"?
    A. We do not only dream in black and white.
    B. The "being chased" dream is the most common dream.
    C. Most people's dreams don't make a lot of sense, and many people share the same dreams.
    D. All dreams fall into the 6 categories discussed in this section.

34. What *most likely* is the reason for nonsense dialogue in our dreams?
    A. It is found in dreams about early childhood.
    B. It is a way to express feelings we can not express when awake.
    C. We are remembering languages learned in previous lifetimes.
    D. This dialogue is needed to start the dream process.

35. Reread the second paragraph of the section, "How Do Dreams Help Us." Based on the context of the passage, what is the meaning of the phrase "took offense"?
    A. broke the law
    B. felt hurt
    C. provoked an attack
    D. forgave someone

36. Based on the selection, what do current researchers believe is the purpose of dreams?
    A. to act as a "dumping ground" for our troubles
    B. to help us maintain good mental and physical health
    C. to entertain as we sleep
    D. to dispose of our mental trash

37. What evidence convinced Rosalind Cartwright that we dream to work out our problems?
    A. Her study found that early in the sleep cycle dreams are less pleasant than later in the cycle.
    B. She often went to bed with problems that she was able to solve the next day.
    C. If you are awakened several times during sleep, you are more likely to solve your problems.
    D. A scan of the brain revealed more active brain waves when dreaming takes place.

38. Which of the following is probably *not* what our dreams are designed to do?
    A. help us predict the future
    B. help us tap into our creativity
    C. help us see things in a new way
    D. help us learn to do certain tasks

39. Which of the following relationships is *most similar* to the relationship below?
    sleep : dream
    A. water : ice
    B. eat : food
    C. study : learn
    D. feet : dance

## from "Samuel Morse's Dream?"
## from *Born to the Land: An American Portrait* by Brent Ashabranner

**Passage 1:**

### Telegraph to Telephone

1)    As for Morse's dream of finding an effective way of improving communication, it had finally come true. The telegraph transformed the world. Cables stretched across the oceans, linking the Americas, Europe, and Asia. News and information sped from one city or country to the next.

2)    Telegraph operators soon learned to recognize Morse code by ear. All they had to do was listen to the long and short taps of the telegraph keys. A good operator could send 50 words a minute!

3)    The telegraph also led directly to the invention of the telephone. The first telegraph could send only one message at a time. Scientists and engineers worked to build a machine that could send several messages at the same time in both directions. Two of these scientists were the Americans Elisha Gray and Alexander Graham Bell. Both men, working independently, realized that a single wire could be made to carry different tones. From this they derived the idea of a new invention—the telephone.

### The Information Age

4)    Alexander Graham Bell patented the telephone in 1876. Radio would follow in the 1920s, then television, and today, of course, the Internet. With cell phones and satellites, there is no place so remote that information can't reach it.

5)    News, stock prices, business deals, military orders, and personal messages—all can now speed across continents in seconds where it used to take days or weeks. None of these inventions overshadows the dramatic impact that the telegraph had on modern communication, however. The telegraph marked the end of one era of communications and the start of another. The telegraph was truly the start of the Information Age. And Morse's simple code? It's still used today.

**Passage 2:**

*In the following passage, Frank, a farmer, is speaking with the author and a photographer about the history of his land and his family while giving them a tour of his farm.*

1)    He showed us some of his equipment. "That tractor cost $18.000 when I bought it in '77," he said, pointing it his International Harvester. "Now it's about $50,000. You can't keep up with that. I buy all my equipment secondhand. There's lots of equipment being auctioned off these days by fellows going out of business."

2)    Frank admits that he keeps his father's tractor partly for sentimental reasons, but he has no such feelings about the 1971 pickup he drives. he keeps it running because it saves him the price of a new one. "I don't need the smell of new paint'" he says.

3)    On the subject of equipment again Frank said, "Years ago all the neighbors around here would throw in and help each other. One would have a thrasher, another bean cutter. But after the war, families became independent and went their separate ways. Now we're reverting to our old ways because we can't afford all equipment need. It's kind of nice."

**40.** How did telegraph operators learn to recognize Morse code?
A. by studying the code for long hours
B. by listening to the long and short taps of telegraph keys
C. by memorizing the code carefully
D. by reading the Morse code self-study book

**41.** What is the meaning of *remote* in paragraph 4?
A. unreachable
B. unpopulated
C. technical
D. near

**42.** In what sense did the telegraph transform the world?
A. It improved communication.
B. It allowed news and information to travel from one city to the next.
C. It led to the invention of the telephone.
D. all of the above

**43.** Which of the following relationships is *most similar* to the relationship below?
**Alexander Graham Bell : scientist**
A. student : teacher
B. novel : book
C. author : writer
D. telephone : internet

**44.** Which of the following best describes Frank in part 2?
A. A farmer that did not work before the war.
B. A farmer that does not like his truck.
C. A farmer that does not like new tools.
D. A farmer who likes the idea of sharing.

**45.** Why does Frank buy his equipment second hand?
A. He is a good mechanic
B. New equipment is too expensive.
C. He likes old things.
D. New equipment cost $18,000

**46.** Based on the context of part 2, what is a *thrasher*?
A. a new tractor
B. an old tractor
C. farm equipment
D. old equipment

**47.** Which of the following relationships is *most similar* to the relationship below?
**Frank : farmer**
A. student : teacher
B. horse : rider
C. author : writer
D. novel : book

*from* "Cave Paintings" *from* Discoveries: Sharing Meaning

# Cave Paintings

1    Cave paintings left behind by early people are found in many parts of the world. Some date back to prehistoric times, a time before *written* history. Yet, art is a kind of nonverbal message. We see these paintings and try to understand what these people were *saying*. There are many theories, but no sure answers. Still, there is no doubt that these paintings convey a powerful message from the past.

2    Prehistoric cave paintings have been discovered throughout Europe, Africa, India, and Australia. The most numerous paintings are found on the walls and caves in southwest France and northern Spain. The contrast between our lives and the lives of the people who painted the caves could hardly be greater. Yet these paintings *speak* to us. They capture our imagination. Scientists may disagree about what the paintings represent, but they all agree that the paintings give us a look into our own distant past.

### Discovery! The Cave of Altamira, Spain

3    In 1879, an archeologist was searching a cave for objects left behind by ancient ancestors. Suddenly his young daughter called out, "Papa, look up. Bulls!" She was pointing to vivid paintings of life-sized bison racing across the five-foot high ceiling.

4    The girl's father, an archeologist, had been collecting stone tools and spear points from the cave floor. When he saw the cave painting on the ceiling, he was astonished.  Fifteen huge bison bounded across the ceiling, along with a horse and several other animals. Most of the animals, including wild boars and deer, were five to six feet long. The bison were not like any animal in Spain at the time.

The deer and horses were painted in red, brown, yellow, and black. They looked like animals that roamed the earth 11,000–19,000 years ago, during the Stone Age!

5    The girl and her father returned day after day to analyze the paintings. They saw that the animal shapes had been cut into the rock with a sharp tool. They were outlined in black and then filled in with color. Sometimes, part of an animal was painted on a bulge in the rock. This gave the feeling of the rounded form of the animal. The animal looked three-dimensional. Who would have believed prehistoric people could make such art?

## The Importance of Altamira

6    The archeologist knew his daughter's discovery was the first of its kind. He wrote an article about the cave. In it he claimed that the paintings were the works of Stone Age artists. The term "Stone Age" does not mean a certain time in Earth's history, or a certain number of years ago. It refers to people who made and used stone tools -- people who had not yet found out how to use metal tools.

7    The archeologist' article invited other scientists to visit and help him interpret the cave paintings. But the scientific community did not respond. They thought the paintings were part of a great hoax. Experts of the time believed the paintings were too advanced to be the work of "cave men." Their attitude illustrated once again how hard it can be to introduce new discoveries to the scientific community.

8    Then, in 1902, similar cave paintings were discovered in France. At last, the experts began to understand the importance of the Altamira paintings. By this time, the archeologist had died, but his daughter had the satisfaction of knowing that their discovery had been authentic.

**48.** Based on the context of the selection, what is the main reason that cave paintings are important today?

    **A.** They tell us exactly what was happening when the painting was created.

    **B.** They tell the date on which the painting was created.

    **C.** They give us a look into our own distant past.

    **D.** They teach us about modern history.

**49.** Why *most likely* did the archeologist and his daughter return to the cave everyday?

    **A.** They are experts on the Stone Age.

    **B.** They wanted to put the paintings in a museum.

    **C.** They wanted to hear the animals speak.

    **D.** They were fascinated by the paintings and wanted to learn more.

**50.** Based on the context of paragraph 8, what does *hoax* mean?

    **A.** truth

    **B.** importance

    **C.** trap

    **D.** joke

**51.** How *most likely* were these cave paintings created?

    **A.** They were cut into the rock and then filled with color.

    **B.** Scenes were drawn on a primitive paper.

    **C.** Figures were drawn on the skins of wild boars and deer.

    **D.** Nothing is known about the process.

**52.** What is the main idea of this selection?

    **A.** Most cave paintings are pictures of wild boars and deer.

    **B.** Scientists ignored the invitation to see the cave paintings.

    **C.** The cave paintings are an important discovery.

    **D.** The term Stone Age refers to a time before metal tools were used.

**53.** Why were scientists skeptical about the cave paintings at first?

    **A.** They did not understand what the paintings meant.

    **B.** They believed the paintings were too advanced to be the work of "cave men."

    **C.** They were not open to new discoveries.

    **D.** The paintings were very difficult to interpret.

**54.** Based on the context of paragraph 7, what does the word *illustrated* mean?

    **A.** showed

    **B.** painted

    **C.** persuaded

    **D.** improved

**55.** Which of the following relationships is *most similar* to the relationship below?

**artist : painting**

    **A.** yellow : brush

    **B.** ice skater : skates

    **C.** baker : bread

    **D.** student : teacher

# Writing Prompts

## Prompt 1

You are a teacher.  For several weeks you have been noticing that someone has been writing on desks and other pieces of classroom property, but you do not know who it is. You are determined to put a stop to the vandalism in your classroom but you are concerned that a false accusation might alienate your students.

Write a response in which you think of a solution to your problem.  Explain what you would do to stop the damage to classroom property.

As you write your response, remember to:

- Focus on the problem that you face, and propose a solution for what to do about the classroom vandalism.

- Consider the purpose, audience, and context of your response.

- Organize your ideas effectively.

- Include specific details that develop your writing.

- Edit your writing for standard grammar and language usage.

## Prompt 2

You are out shopping with your best friend at a popular clothing store near your house.  As you are getting ready to leave you realize that your friend is preparing to take an item from the rack out of the store without paying for it.  Your friend does not know that you have seen the shoplift attempt and you are not sure what to do.

Write an essay in which you think of a solution to your problem.  Explain what you would do if you were confronted with this situation and why.

As you write your essay, remember to:

- Focus on the problem that you face, and propose a solution for what to do about the classroom vandalism.

- Consider the purpose, audience, and context of your essay.

- Organize your ideas effectively.

- Include specific details that develop your writing.

- Edit your writing for standard grammar and language usage.

# ITBS PRACTICE TEST

## Vocabulary

**DIRECTIONS**

This is a test about words and their meanings.

■ For each question, you are to decide which one of the four answers has most nearly the same meaning as the underlined word above it.

■ Then, on your answer folder, find the row of answer spaces numbered the same as the question. Fill in the answer space that has the same letter as the answer you picked.

The sample on this page shows you what the questions are like and how to mark your answers.

**SAMPLE**

**S1** To <u>embrace</u> a friend

   **A** find
   **B** hug
   **C** listen to
   **D** smile at

**ANSWER**

**S1** A B C D

# Vocabulary

**1** A <u>clogged</u> drain

  **A** blocked
  **B** broken
  **C** loose
  **D** rusty

**2** A freshly painted <u>exterior</u>

  **J** building
  **K** floor
  **L** outside
  **M** trimming

**3** To <u>generate</u> responses

  **A** display
  **B** interpret
  **C** grade
  **D** produce

**4** A <u>fictional</u> character

  **J** cruel
  **K** fascinating
  **L** make-believe
  **M** well-known

**5** To <u>highlight</u> questions

  **A** answer
  **B** ask
  **C** cancel
  **D** stress

**6** A <u>grouchy</u> dog

  **J** crabby
  **K** curious
  **L** helpless
  **M** watchful

**7** Feeling <u>lightheaded</u>

  **A** cranky
  **B** dizzy
  **C** happy
  **D** sleepy

**8** To <u>loathe</u> an enemy

  **J** despise
  **K** put up with
  **L** scare
  **M** talk to

**9** A speedy <u>recovery</u>

  **A** change
  **B** completion
  **C** healing
  **D** trip

**10** A different <u>aspect</u>

  **J** feature
  **K** file
  **L** answer
  **M** scene

**11** A loud <u>clamor</u>

  **A** ballad
  **B** color
  **C** machine
  **D** racket

**12** A <u>bewildering</u> action

  **J** amusing
  **K** annoying
  **L** horrifying
  **M** puzzling

**13** A humble <u>abode</u>

  **A** attitude
  **B** home
  **C** letter
  **D** style

**14** To <u>devise</u> a plan

  **J** come up with
  **K** put into action
  **L** repeat
  **M** take over

# Reading Comprehension

## DIRECTIONS

This is a test of how well you understand what you read.

- This test consists of reading passages followed by questions.

- Read each passage and then answer the questions.

- Four answers are given for each question. You are to choose the answer that you think is better than the others.

- Then, on your answer folder, find the row of answer spaces numbered the same as the question. Fill in the answer space for the best answer.

The sample on this page shows you what the questions are like and how to mark your answers.

**SAMPLE**

As Lisa walked home from school, she thought about Mason and how sad he looked when Ms. Felter told him his science grade. "I should have helped him study," she said out loud. "He would have done that much for me." Lisa remembered all the times Mason had been there for her. When she had fallen off her bike, he had helped her up and brushed her off. When she had forgotten her lunch, he had given her half of his. He was the best friend anyone could ever have.

**S1** **How does Lisa feel about Mason's science grade?**

**A** angry
**B** guilty
**C** surprised
**D** unconcerned

**ANSWER**
**S1** A B C D

*from* "The Life of a Spartan in Ancient Greece"
# The Life of a Spartan in Ancient Greece

In ancient Greece, the city-state of Sparta was known for its military strength. All of its male citizens were trained to serve as soldiers. The women of Sparta were also trained to fight. In order to keep its position as the most powerful Greek city-state, Sparta was often in conflict with its neighbors. How did Sparta deal with conflict?

## A Military City-State

Protected by mountain ranges, Sparta was located in a river valley. Although the mountains helped to keep Sparta's enemies out, the Spartans were happy to set off across those mountains in search of conquests.

One of the most famous stories that involves ancient Sparta is the legend of the Trojan War. This was a conflict between Sparta and Troy, a city whose ruins are in modern-day Turkey.

Scholars argue about the facts of the Trojan War. However, tales indicate that the Trojan War happened about 1200 B.C. It began when Helen, the Queen of Sparta, ran away with Paris, a prince of Troy. Helen and Paris's actions would affect the lives of many people. After ten years of war, the Greeks used trickery to bring the war to an end. They pretended to withdraw their forces at the gates of Troy, but left behind a huge wooden horse filled with warriors. The Trojans, celebrating their victory, moved the horse inside the gates. The Greek soldiers then escaped from the horse and opened the gates to admit their comrades. In this way, Greece was able to accomplish its defeat of Troy.

## The Rise of Sparta

Over the years, Sparta's power grew. In 640 B.C., the Messenians, people whom the Spartans had conquered, decided to revolt. They almost defeated the Spartans. After that, a Spartan man named Lycurgus helped to strengthen Sparta's government. It became a military government, one that excelled at crushing its enemies.

**Sparta's Government** Ancient Greece was made up of many independent city-states. A city-state included the city and the land it controlled. Sparta became the most powerful city-state in all of Greece.

Sparta had an unusual government. It included a council made up of two kings and 28 nobles, five overseers, and an Assembly of male citizens. Sparta's two kings were descended from two great houses of early Sparta. The kings acted as generals in the military. They also had some religious duties. The nobles were elected for life. The council members worked together to establish the laws Sparta needed.

The members of the Assembly, or Spartiate, could approve or veto the council's decisions. The overseers, called the Ephorate, could veto anything approved by the council *or* the Spartiate. Thus, these five men had the most powerful roles in the government.

**The Values of Sparta** Spartans were taught to dedicate themselves to the state. They learned to appreciate courage, strength, and a simple life. Spartans followed rules and believed in an orderly life. They were able to get by with very little, owning few possessions. Citizens were not allowed to own silver or gold. They also ate plain foods. In addition, Spartans believed in using as few words as possible when speaking.

Like people in the rest of Greece, Spartans worshipped many gods. The patron goddess of Sparta was Artemis. She was the goddess of hunting and wild animals. Aries, the god of war, was Sparta's patron god.

1. **How did the Greeks finally win the Trojan War?**
   A. They used military strength.
   B. They used trickery.
   C. They did not win; they withdrew their forces.
   D. They stormed Troy's gates.

2. **Which of the following *best* describes the Spartans?**
   J. They were content to stay in Sparta, protected by the mountains.
   K. They collected wealth and riches.
   L. They had a strong military and wanted to conquer new lands.
   M. They enjoyed fancy banquets.

3. **Who had the most powerful position in Sparta's government?**
   A. the Ephorate, or the overseers
   B. Sparta's two kings who were also military generals
   C. the Assembly
   D. the nobles who were elected for life

4. **Reread the "Values of Sparta" section. Based on the context, what is the meaning of the word *dedicate*?**
   J. to be dishonored
   K. to be devoted
   L. to be disrespectful
   M. to sign a paper

5. **Which of the following statements does *not* accurately describe the city of Troy and the Trojans?**
   A. The Trojans celebrated their victory in the Trojan War too soon.
   B. The ruins of the city of Troy are located in modern-day Turkey.
   C. Before the start of the war, Helen was Queen of Troy.
   D. Paris was a prince of Troy.

6. **Which of the following statements best describes the people of Sparta?**
   J. Men were great speakers.
   K. Women were members of the Assembly.
   L. Citizens could own gold.
   M. Women were trained to fight.

### from "Delta Blues"

**In this excerpt from "The Delta Blues, the author discusses the importance of music to the African-Americans during slavery.**

1. Since the earliest days of slavery, African Americans have expressed through music how they feel about themselves and the events that affect their lives. Early black music, with its distinctive rhythms and soulful sounds, linked the slaves to their native lands, to their faith, and to each other. From this music emerged a new rhythm and a new sound. This music, too, reflected the everyday lives of the black community. It *belonged* to the black community. It was called The Blues.

2. Slaves, brought to America from Africa and the West Indies, were not all alike. They came from different tribes and groups. Although they shared cultural similarities, they were dissimilar in many ways. It was the hard experience of slavery that united these various people into a community. This communal experience created a whole new culture. It did, however, preserve some native customs, especially music. "During my childhood," recalled one Southern woman of the time, ". . . I came to the conclusion . . . that the greater part of the [slaves'] music, their methods, their scale, their type of thought, their dancing, their patting of feet, their clapping of hands, their grimaces and pantomime . . . came straight from Africa."

3. Slave songs were communal and anonymous. They were folk tunes created by a shared condition rather than an individual talent. That's how it would be throughout the years of slavery. Not until after the Emancipation would the black community begin to produce musicians who stood alone with their music. Yet, as might be expected, the rhythms and patterns of slave songs echoed within their work.

4. During the last half of the 19th century a new kind of music emerged from the black community. Its origins are obscure, but most believe it was born where it was discovered, in the Mississippi Delta. The music still contained elements from the old slave songs and spirituals. It was soulfully sad and sweet, filled with African tonalities and rhythms. But the music was not African. It was born out of two cultures: black and white. Its scale, its folk traditions, and its instruments were all part of the white musical culture. Black and white music, just like the black and white communities of the time, were merging and growing separately and together.

---

**7. Based on the context of paragraph 2, what is meant by the phrase *communal* experience?**
A. shared living conditions
B. religious event
C. something that the entire community participates in and shares
D. a happy and comforting event

**8. The early black music did *not* do which of the following?**
J. allow individual musicians to create music
K. link the slaves to their native lands
L. express how the slaves felt about themselves
M. express how the slaves felt about their lives

**9. In paragraph 4, what is the meaning of the word *obscure*?**
A. not well known
B. out of date
C. from long ago
D. familiar

**10. Why *most likely* did a new type of music develop in the last half of the 19th century?**
J. The black community was given their freedom.
K. The music from Africa was being forgotten.
L. The new music was the merging of the black and white musical cultures.
M. People were tired of their native music.

In **"The Dumb Soldier,"** by Robert Louis Stevenson, the speaker tells of his toy soldier which he has hidden in the lawn.

(1)     When the grass was Closely mown,
      Walking on the lawn alone,
      In the turf a hole I found,
      And hid a soldier underground.

(2)     Spring and daisies came apace;
      Grasses hide my hiding place;
      Grasses run like a green sea
      O'er the lawn up to my knee.

(3)     Under grass alone he lies,
      Looking up with leaden eyes,
      Scarlet coat and pointed gun,
      To the stars and to the sun.

(4)     When the grass is ripe like grain,
      When the scythe is stoned again,
      When the lawn is shaven clear,
      Then my hole shall reappear.

(5)     I shall find him, never fear,
      I shall find my grenadier;
      But for all that's gone and come,
      I shall find my soldier dumb.

(6)     He has lived, a little thing,
      In the grassy woods of spring;
      Done, if he could tell me true,
      Just as I should like to do.

(7)     He has seen the starry hours
      And the springing of the flowers;
      And the fairy things that pass
      In the forests of the grass.

(8)     In the silence he has heard
      Talking bee and ladybird,
      And the butterfly has flown
      O'er him as he lay alone.
      Not a word will he disclose,
      Not a word of all he knows.
      I must lay him on the shelf,
      And make up the tale myself.

11. **In stanza 6, what is the meaning of the line, "Just as I should like to do."**
    A. The speaker would like to spend spring in the woods.
    B. The speaker would like to be a soldier.
    C. The speaker wants to hide more soldiers.
    D. The speaker wants to tell the truth about the soldier.

12. **Who *most probably* is the speaker in the poem?**
    J. a toy soldier
    K. a young boy
    L. a toy soldier who has come to life
    M. a talking bee and ladybird

13. **What does the speaker mean in the last line of the poem?**
    A. The speaker does not want to tell his parents that he lost the soldier.
    B. The soldier was never missing.
    C. The speaker tells many lies rather than tell the truth.
    D. The speaker will use his imagination to create a story about what the soldier did while he was lost.

14. **In stanza 5, when the speaker says the soldier is "dumb," the speaker means the soldier is**
    J. not intelligent
    K. unable to speak
    L. unable to hear
    M. unable to see

# Spelling

## DIRECTIONS

This test will show how well you can spell.

■ Many of the questions in this test contain mistakes in spelling. Some do not have any mistakes at all.

■ You should look for mistakes in spelling.

■ When you find a mistake, fill in the answer space on your answer folder that has the same letter as the **line** containing the mistake.

■ If there is no mistake, fill in the last answer space.

The samples on this page show you what the questions are like and how to mark your answers.

## SAMPLES

**S1**
- A explane
- B hornet
- C brilliance
- D devote
- E *(No mistakes)*

**S2**
- J hopeless
- K parcel
- L radar
- M repair
- N *(No mistakes)*

## ANSWERS

**S1** **A** B C D E

**S2** J K L M **N**

## Spelling

**1**
A  harmful
B  greatful
C  healthful
D  playful
E  *(No mistakes)*

**2**
J  clamor
K  docter
L  flounder
M  sailor
N  *(No mistakes)*

**3**
A  hoarse
B  cinch
C  ought
D  drought
E  *(No mistakes)*

**4**
J  plague
K  leegue
L  earn
M  turn
N  *(No mistakes)*

**5**
A  impresion
B  infection
C  reflection
D  inscription
E  *(No mistakes)*

**6**
J  protector
K  encountor
L  deliver
M  producer
N  *(No mistakes)*

**7**
A  amazement
B  element
C  improvment
D  refreshment
E  *(No mistakes)*

**8**
J  diagram
K  absolute
L  buttermilk
M  canary
N  *(No mistakes)*

**9**
A  deliteful
B  forgetful
C  regretful
D  plentiful
E  *(No mistakes)*

**10**
J  gourmet
K  bouquet
L  context
M  afflict
N  *(No mistakes)*

**11**
A  detergent
B  principal
C  accompliss
D  computer
E  *(No mistakes)*

**12**
J  dwarf
K  moose
L  ounce
M  raise
N  *(No mistakes)*

**13**
A  reaction
B  election
C  collection
D  atraction
E  *(No mistakes)*

**14**
J  feilder
K  welder
L  flutter
M  glitter
N  *(No mistakes)*

# Capitalization

## DIRECTIONS

This is a test on capitalization. It will show how well you can use capital letters in sentences.

■ You should look for mistakes in capitalization in the sentences on this test.

■ When you find a mistake, fill in the answer space on your answer folder that has the same letter as the **line** containing the mistake.

■ Some sentences do not have any mistakes at all. If there is no mistake, fill in the last answer space.

The samples on this page show you what the questions are like and how to mark your answers.

## SAMPLES

**S1**  **A**  Anne Tyler, the author
       **B**  of *Breathing lessons,* is one
       **C**  of my all-time favorite writers.
       **D**  *(No mistakes)*

**S2**  **J**  Kristina's father bought
       **K**  her a new blue Convertible
       **L**  for her sixteenth birthday.
       **M**  *(No mistakes)*

**S3**  **A**  If you ever visit Norway, be
       **B**  sure to see the ancient ships
       **C**  kept in the museums.
       **D**  *(No mistakes)*

## ANSWERS

**S1**  A B C D
**S2**  J K L M
**S3**  A B C D

# Capitalization

**1**
A My teacher rolled his eyes
B and said, "please don't tell me
C the dog ate your homework."
D *(No mistakes)*

**2**
J A Tanager is a beautiful, colorful
K bird that is very common in the
L Southwest and in southern
California.
M *(No mistakes)*

**3**
A "Would you be kind enough to
carry
B this great big suitcase for me?"
the sweet
C old woman asked the worried
little boy.
D *(No mistakes)*

**4**
J Last winter we visited aunt Carrie
K in Mesa, Arizona, where
L she owns a small summer home.
M *(No mistakes)*

**5**
A *The Horse whisperer,* a novel by
B Nicholas Evans, about a man who
talks
C to horses, is set in Montana.
D *(No mistakes)*

**6**
J Jamie lives West of our
K house, on Hamilton Street, in
L a town called Wyoming.
M *(No mistakes)*

**7**
A In the late 1800s, the Brontë
B Sisters published novels under
the
C names Currier, Ellis, and Acton
Bell.
D *(No mistakes)*

**8**
J 155 Hightop Drive, Apt. 4
K Binghamton, NY
L September 27, 2001
M *(No mistakes)*

**9**
A Dr. Carol Harris
B Riverview college
C Dear Dr. Harris:
D *(No mistakes)*

**10**
J I am writing this letter to
tell you how
K much I enjoyed your book,
*Planetary Wonders.*
L I particularly enjoyed the
chapter about mars.
M *(No mistakes)*

**11**
A I would also like to ask
you if I may
B photocopy chapter 9 for an
oral presentation
C I am giving on the solar
system.
D *(No mistakes)*

**12**
J I'm in the sixth grade at
Montgomery Elementary.
K Sincerely yours,
L Charles Moyerowski
M *(No mistakes)*

**13**
A My sister Cara is a successful
B photographer who worked her way
C through College and supported me
as well.
D *(No mistakes)*

Name _____ Date _____

## Punctuation

### DIRECTIONS

This is a test on punctuation. It will show how well you can use periods, question marks, commas, and other kinds of punctuation marks.

■ You should look for mistakes in punctuation in the sentences on this test.

■ When you find a mistake, fill in the answer space on your answer folder that has the same letter as the **line** containing the mistake.

■ Some sentences do not have any mistakes at all. If there is no mistake, fill in the last answer space.

The samples on this page show you what the questions are like and how to mark your answers.

### SAMPLES

**S1**
A   The three girls earned the
B   money for the trip by baby-sitting
C   and saving their allowances.
D   *(No mistakes)*

**S2**
J   Because of the upcoming
K   snowstorm school was
L   dismissed at noon today.
M   *(No mistakes)*

**S3**
A   The dog liked three things
B   best, running in the field,
C   chasing the ball, and eating.
D   *(No mistakes)*

### ANSWERS

**S1**   A B C **D**

**S2**   J **K** L M

**S3**   A **B** C D

Name _____ Date _____

## Punctuation

**1**  A  The Norway Spruce an evergreen
   B  tree, was brought to the United
   C  States from Europe.
   D  *(No mistakes)*

**2**  J  On December 10 1949 the
   K  AAFC and NFL merged and made
   L  the Cleveland Browns part of the
      NFL.
   M  *(No mistakes)*

**3**  A  Sara knew her little sister wasn't
      telling
   B  the truth because she rolled her
      eyes and
   C  said "Give me a break already,
      will you?"
   D  *(No mistakes)*

**4**  J  Even though Arthur Harris earned
      straight
   K  A's since the first grade, each time
      he took a
   L  test he asked the teacher, "How
      did I do."
   M  *(No mistakes)*

**5**  A  My 71-year-old mother writes
      novels,
   B  paints pictures, sings in the
   C  choir, and is a devout baseball
      fan.
   D  *(No mistakes)*

**6**  J  The clavicle is a long thin bone
   K  located at the root of the neck.
      Just below
   L  the skin in front of the first rib.
   M  *(No mistakes)*

**7**  A  Michelangelo who spent his life
   B  in Florence and Rome, was a
      talented
   C  painter, sculptor, poet, and
      architect.
   D  *(No mistakes)*

**8**  J  Brackton Middle School
   K  Brackton, PA 18641
   L  January 10 2000
   M  *(No mistakes)*

**9**  A  Dear Friend:
   B  The students at Brackton
      Area Middle School are
   C  holding the annual
      Valentine's Day dance on
      February 14.
   D  *(No mistakes)*

**10**  J  Would you consider
      donating party supplies
   K  for the dance. The proceeds
      from ticket sales
   L  to the dance will benefit local
      charities.
   M  *(No mistakes)*

**11**  A  Thank you for your
      consideration.
   B  Sincerely,
   C  The Students at
      Brackton Middle
      School
   D  *(No mistakes)*

**12**  J  Because of rising airline costs
   K  many people are choosing to drive
   L  to vacation spots instead of flying.
   M  *(No mistakes)*

Name _____ Date _____

# Usage and Expression

### DIRECTIONS

This is a test on the use of words. It will show how well you can use words according to the standards of correctly written English.

■ You should look for mistakes in the sentences on this test.

■ When you find a mistake, fill in the answer space on your answer folder that has the same letter as the **line** containing the mistake.

■ Some sentences do not have any mistakes at all. If there is no mistake, fill in the last answer space.

The samples on this page show you what the questions are like and how to mark your answers.

### SAMPLES

**S1**   **A**   When it comes to science, both of
      **B**   my favorite teachers, Mrs. Keton and
      **C**   Ms. Connelly, knows her stuff.
      **D**   *(No mistakes)*

**S2**   **J**   Ernest Hemingway was a
      **K**   famous writer who living in a mansion
      **L**   in Key West with over 60 cats.
      **M**   *(No mistakes)*

### ANSWERS
**S1**   A B **C** D
**S2**   J **K** L M

# Usage

**1**
  **A**   Each of the girls knows the
  **B**   combination to their locker as well
  **C**   as her identification number.
  **D**   *(No mistakes)*

**2**
  **J**   Stephen King, a famous horror
  **K**   writer, usually writing his
        novels in
  **L**   the basement of his home.
  **M**   *(No mistakes)*

**3**
  **A**   Shelby said she don't have no idea
  **B**   why her brother didn't show
        up for
  **C**   band practice last Tuesday.
  **D**   *(No mistakes)*

**4**
  **J**   A cat named Shade McCorkle
  **K**   once saved his owner's life
  **L**   by fending off an intruder.
  **M**   *(No mistakes)*

**5**
  **A**   Most physicians agree that, in
  **B**   addition to improving your muscle
  **C**   tone, exercise can lifting your
        spirits.
  **D**   *(No mistakes)*

**6**
  **J**   Some people believe that e-mail will
  **K**   eventually replace mail as the primary
  **L**   means of written correspondence.
  **M**   *(No mistakes)*

**7**
  **A**   After scuba diving for three
  **B**   days, we found the rare puffer fish,
  **C**   just what we was looking for.
  **D**   *(No mistakes)*

**8**
  **J**   A recent survey showed that many
  **K**   Americans don't realize that 220
  **L**   is a high cholesterol level.
  **M**   *(No mistakes)*

**9**
  **A**   My mother's store of
  **B**   patience is great, but my father's
  **C**   is even more greater.
  **D**   *(No mistakes)*

**10**
  **J**   For all their power, the human
  **K**   heart is amazingly small—about
  **L**   the size of two fists.
  **M**   *(No mistakes)*

Name _____ Date _____

# Expression

## DIRECTIONS

This is Part 2 of the test about the use of words. It will show how well you can express ideas correctly and effectively. There are several sections to this part of the test. Read the directions to each section carefully. Then mark your answers on your answer folder.

**Directions:** Use this paragraph to answer questions 11–14.

[1]The *Tyrannosaurus Rex*, or T-Rex as it is commonly called, was a gigantic dinosaur that roamed North America more than 70 million years ago. [2]Its head was more than 4 feet long, and some of its teeth were larger than a human hand. [3]T-Rex stood about 19 feet high and was <u>pretty close to</u> 47 feet long. [4]Its massive tail was probably used to balance its heavy head. [5]Dimetrodon was the most common meat-eating dinosaur and lived in Permian times, almost 260 million years ago.

**11** Which is the best place for sentence 2?

A  Where it is now
B  Before Sentence 1
C  Between Sentences 3 and 4
D  After Sentence 5

**12** Which sentence should be left out of this paragraph?

J  Sentence 1
K  Sentence 2
L  Sentence 4
M  Sentence 5

**13** Which is the best way to rewrite the underlined part of sentence 3?

A  about
B  probably almost
C  somewhere around
D  *(No change)*

**14** Which is the best concluding sentence for this paragraph?

J  Scientists are still unsure what happened to T-Rex that made it become extinct.
K  Although the T-Rex was massive, it was not as feared as the Velociraptor, a smaller dinosaur that hunted in packs.
L  The T-Rex has been featured in many movies, some of them enormously popular.
M  Scientists believe T-Rex mothers were extremely protective of their young.

Name _____ Date _____

**Directions:** In questions 15–16, choose the best way to express the idea.

**15** A Many experts believe that a fear of public speaking can be conquered with practice.
B With practice, a fear of public speaking can be conquered, many experts believe.
C A belief held by many experts is that a fear of public speaking can be conquered with practice.
D That a fear of public speaking can be conquered with a practice, is a belief held by many experts.

**16** J The gray squirrel is common in the North, but frequently raids bird feeders and garbage cans.
K The gray squirrel, which is common in the North, frequently raids bird feeders and garbage cans.
L While the gray squirrel is common in the North, it frequently raids bird feeders and garbage cans.
M A frequent raider of bird feeders and garbage cans is the gray squirrel that's common in the North.

**Directions:** In questions 17–19, choose the best way to write the underlined part of the sentence.

**17** My little sister Kelsy likes to sing, <u>dancing</u>, and play the piano.
A will dance    B dance    C to dance    D *(No change)*

**18** I should <u>have went</u> to the game, instead of just watching television all evening.
J have gone    K had went    L going    M *(No change)*

**19** **Which of these would be most persuasive in a letter to the school board?**

A We students feel the new mandatory community service requirement for all graduating seniors is unfair. Many of us have after-school jobs and can't spare 10 hours a month. In addition, some of our parents can't provide us with the necessary transportation to and from the service facility we are assigned.

B Some of us seniors don't like the new mandatory community service requirement. Making us serve the community in order to graduate isn't fair. We want to spend our time in other ways. How can we find time to study and serve the community? Please reconsider this requirement.

C We're attending this meeting to try to persuade you to change the new mandatory community service requirement. You're forcing us to do something we may not want to do.

D The new community service requirement is completely unfair. Seniors don't want to do this. We need to spend time with our friends. We have a petition with us. Basically, we refuse to do this.

# TERRANOVA PRACTICE TEST

## Reading and Language Arts

### Sample Passage

### Respect

People from various cultures have different ways of showing respect toward one another. In some cultures people shake hands upon meeting. In others, people hug each other as a way of greeting. In the United States, eye contact is encouraged, but in some cultures, eye contact is a sign of rudeness.

### Sample A

**This passage is mostly about**

Ⓐ  how people show respect

Ⓑ  how people shake hands

Ⓒ  why eye contact is rude

Ⓓ  why greetings are important

Name _____ Date _____

## Directions

**A student wrote a paragraph about his older brother. There are some mistakes that need correcting.**

> [1]For as long as I can remember, my older brother Mark has been there. [2]Mark has always been there for me. [3]He taught me how to have faith in myself and to stand up for what I believe in. [4]I always knew that whenever I had a problem, Mark would be there for me, trying to make things better.

## Sample B

**Which of these best combines Sentences 1 and 2?**

(F) For as long as I can remember, my older brother Mark has been there for me.

(G) My older brother Mark, for as long as I can remember, has been there for me.

(H) Because my older brother Mark has been there, for as long as I can remember.

(J) My older brother Mark has always been there for me, at least as long as I can remember.

## Sample C

**Where would this sentence best fit into the paragraph?**

*I know he'll also be there for me in the future.*

(A) after Sentence 1

(B) after Sentence 2

(C) after Sentence 3

(D) after Sentence 4

Name _____ Date _____

*from* "Searching for Pompeii" in Discoveries: Digging for Answers
# Searching for Pompeii

Vesuvius is the name of an immense mountain in southern Italy. Vesuvius is not an ordinary mountain. It is a volcano. This is an opening in the Earth's crust through which melted rock, called lava, and gases sometimes erupt. Long periods of time can pass between eruptions. This was true of Vesuvius.

In the year 79, no one living near Vesuvius knew that it was a volcano. Nearly 20,000 people lived in a grand city in its shadow. That city was Pompeii. Today, we know that Pompeii was built on lava from Vesuvius eruptions in prehistoric times. We know many other important and interesting things about the ancient city of Pompeii. We have the careful work of archaeologists to thank.

On the afternoon of August 24, in the year 79, Vesuvius awoke from its long sleep. The first explosion from the volcano created panic in Pompeii. Many more explosions followed. By the next morning Pompeii was buried under 12 feet of hot ash, rocks, and debris. Few people survived. Anyone who did manage to escape and who returned to Pompeii would have been lost in a strange landscape. They might question that Pompeii had ever really been there. Earthquakes caused by the eruption of Vesuvius had created new hills and valleys. The city had vanished. Pompeii's secrets would remain hidden for centuries.

## The Rediscovery of a Buried City

For nearly 1600 years, Pompeii lay buried and forgotten. New towns, such as Naples and Torre Annunziata, grew up around the ancient site. In 1592, the citizens of Torre Annunziata came up with a plan. The townspeople wanted to utilize water from the nearby Sarno River. They hired Italian architect Domenico Fontana to undertake the construction of a tunnel. It would be dug across the plateau where Pompeii had once stood. As Fontana's workmen started cutting through the rock, they began to uncover many statues and wall paintings. Their discoveries, however, did not interest Fontana. He decided not to stop work. He did not want to fully investigate what they had found.

In 1734, Spain conquered both Sicily and Naples. Several years later, the Spanish King Charles III ordered the first official excavation of Pompeii. His intent was to find treasures to enrich the royal court. Charles hired a military engineer named Alcubierre to supervise the work. Alcubierre knew of the underground tunnel that had been dug over a century earlier by Domenico Fontana. He hoped he would be able to follow it to the ruins of ancient Pompeii. Unlike Fontana, Alcubierre wanted to examine what was there. He hoped to find objects of value.

## An Amazing Find!

Twenty days after Alcubierre's crew of 24 men began digging, they made a significant find. They uncovered the skeleton of a man who had died during the eruption of Vesuvius in 79. Near the skeleton Alcubierre found 18 coins. Could the man have been running away from the eruption, carrying what few valuables he had? Was he killed by the ash and debris? These were interesting questions. Yet, Alcubierre did not want to pursue them and find possible answers. He had not come to Pompeii to find answers. He had come to find treasures. Days later, Alcubierre's men found ruined structures. These may have been the remains of a private home or public building in Pompeii. In his report on the day of this discovery, Alcubierre wrote, "Nothing was found."

Alcubierre soon lost interest in Pompeii. Teams of workmen persisted in digging at the site. In 1771, they made an amazing discovery. A large house was uncovered. Two skeletons were found in the house. One of them was wearing a gold ring and holding a key. Many gold and silver coins were found near this skeleton. The coins were found wrapped in cloth. Perhaps the coins had been locked up. As Vesuvius erupted, the man may have taken the key to get the coins from their hiding place. Then he ran through the house. But he could not escape the ash and debris. He died with the key still in his hand.

The following year even more skeletons were uncovered at the house. Eighteen adults and two children were found together. They were in an underground room. One of the women had a large amount of jewelry. She was wearing necklaces, bracelets, and rings. She was found with the skeleton of a young boy in her arms. Her remains were very well preserved. The excavators were able to determine that she was wearing very beautiful and expensive clothing when she died.

Other skeletons found nearby were not dressed the same way. They wore very simple clothes. Many of them were not wearing shoes. Based on this evidence, the diggers who had discovered the skeletons were able to identify the woman as the wife of a wealthy man. The other skeletons were probably the remains of her servants. It is also possible that these people were slaves. The young boy the woman was carrying in her arms might have been her son.

By the end of the eighteenth century, those in charge of uncovering Pompeii began to use a new strategy. They started to leave the buildings they found in plain view. Many objects that were not considered valuable were left inside. Pompeii was slowly becoming what it is today: a museum-city open to visitors. People came from all over the world to see the ruins. They also wanted to see the skeletons that had been uncovered. Unfortunately, a number of these tourists stole bones from the skeletons. They took them home as souvenirs. The ancient site of Pompeii was not well guarded. Soon artwork and other artifacts also began to disappear. In addition, in spite of all that had been uncovered, very few questions about Pompeii had been answered. Who were the people who lived here? When and how was the city destroyed? Before these questions could be answered, new methods would have to be put in place to uncover and excavate the rest of the ancient city.

**1.** **Choose the sentence that best describes what the passage is about.**
- Ⓐ the destruction caused by the eruption of the volcano in Pompeii
- Ⓑ several of the searches and discoveries made at Pompeii
- Ⓒ Alcubierre's search for treasures at Pompeii
- Ⓓ new advances in archaeology

**2.** **According to the passage, the author says that "twenty days after Alcucbierre's crew of 24 men began digging, they made a significant find." The word *significant* means**
- Ⓕ strange
- Ⓖ large
- Ⓗ valuable
- Ⓙ scientific

**3.** **Which of these best describes Alcubierre?**
- Ⓐ He was curious about the people of Pompeii.
- Ⓑ He was determined to bring water from the Sarno River.
- Ⓒ He was excited about the discovery of a skeleton at Pompeii.
- Ⓓ He was interested in Pompeii's treasures.

Name _____ Date _____

**4.** The answer you chose for Number 3 is best because you learned from the passage that
 (F) Alcubierre's men discovered ruined structures at Pompeii.
 (G) Alcubierre lost interest when skeletons and structures were discovered rather than treasures.
 (H) Alcubierre's men continued working and found more skeletons.
 (J) Alcubierre set up Pompeii as a museum for visitors.

**5.** Why might anyone question that Pompeii had ever existed?
 (A) All evidence of the city was washed away by strong storms.
 (B) The eruption of Mount Vesuvius was one of the worst disasters in history.
 (C) Earthquakes caused by the eruption changed the landscape by creating new hills and valleys.
 (D) There were no survivors from the eruption of Mount Vesuvius.

**6.** In the passage, the author says that people "wanted to utilize water from the nearby Sarno River." The word *utilize* means
 (F) to buy or purchase
 (G) to move or change the direction
 (H) to use  for a particular purpose.
 (J) to re-use

Name _____ Date _____

## Directions

Ms. Chan's class is writing about places they have visited or places they would like to visit. Carol wrote about a visit to see her aunt and uncle in Ocean City, Maryland. Here is her essay. There are several mistakes that need correcting.

[1]Last summer, my Aunt Deeny and Uncle Phil invited my brother Marc and me to spend two weeks with them at their home in Ocean City, Maryland. [2]Marc and I live in Ohio, we had never been to the ocean, so we were very excited. [3]Aunt Deeny and Uncle Phil live in a house that's next to a beautiful bay. [4]They have a dock in the back of the house, so they can driving their boat right up to their back door. [5]Marc and I spent most of our days at the beach, which is beautiful. [6]The beach is very crowded in the summer. [7]Uncle Phil taught Marc and I to learn how to bodyboard. [8]You put the bodyboard underneath your stomach and glide on the waves. [9]We weren't very good at it when we first tried it. [10]I scraped my arms and swallowed some sea water. [11]However, by the end of the trip, we was very good. [12]Even though the beach was a blast, the best part of the trip was spending time with Aunt Deeny and Uncle Phil. [13]I hope we can visit them again next summer.

**7** Which sentence contains two complete thoughts and should be written as two sentences?

Ⓐ  Sentence 1

Ⓑ  Sentence 2

Ⓒ  Sentence 11

Ⓓ  Sentence 12

**8** The best way to write Sentence 4 is

Ⓕ  In the back of their house, they have a dock so they drive their boat right up to the back.

Ⓖ  They have a dock in the back of the house, so they can drive their boat right up to their back door.

Ⓗ  They will drive their boat right up to the back door, because they have a dock in the back of the house.

Ⓙ  Best as it is

**9** **Which of these best combines Sentences 5 and 6?**

   Ⓐ  Marc and I spent most of our days at the beach, which is beautiful and very crowded in the summer.

   Ⓑ  Marc and I spent most of our days at the beautiful beach, which is also very crowded in the summer.

   Ⓒ  The beach is beautiful in the summer and very crowded, but Marc and I spent most of our days there.

   Ⓓ  The beach is very crowded in the summer and Marc and I spent most of our days at the beach, which is beautiful.

**10** **Which is the best way to write Sentence 7?**

   Ⓕ  Uncle Phil taught Marc and me how to bodyboard.

   Ⓖ  Marc and I were taught by Uncle Phil how to bodyboard.

   Ⓗ  Marc and I learned how to bodyboard from Uncle Phil, who taught us.

   Ⓙ  Best as it is

**11** **Choose the best way to write Sentence 11.**

   Ⓐ  We was very good by the end of the trip, however.

   Ⓑ  When the trip ended, we were very good, however.

   Ⓒ  However, by the end of the trip, we were very good.

   Ⓓ  Best as it is

**12** **Where would this sentence best fit in the paragraph?**

*A bodyboard looks like a small surfboard.*

   Ⓕ  after Sentence 7

   Ⓖ  after Sentence 8

   Ⓗ  after Sentence 9

   Ⓙ  after Sentence 10

# Excerpts from an interview with Barbara Morgan, Mission Specialist on Space Shuttle Endeavor's STS-118

## Directions

**In this interview, Barbara Morgan, a teacher and a full-trained astronaut, answers some questions. On Aug. 8, 2007, Barbara Morgan, who was 55 years old, traveled on the space shuttle Endeavor to the International Space Station. She returned to earth on Aug. 21, 2007. Before traveling in space, Barbara spent more than 20 years teaching second, third and fourth grades in McCall, Idaho. Read the interview. Then, do numbers 13 to 18.**

**How would you describe the mission to kids and what your role and duties are on the flight?**

Well, my first word would be "exciting." Actually, it's more than a word. Exciting, interesting, amazing, and fun. We are going to the International Space Station; we call it an assembly mission. We are going to the International Space Station to help finish building it. In our cargo bay, or in the back end of the shuttle, we're taking up a couple of big pieces that are part of the station. We're also going to take up, it's kind of like a small room that's cram-packed full of stuff, full of equipment and supplies for our crew members who are living and working aboard the International Space Station. We'll be transferring all the things over that they need and bringing the things that they don't need back home with us. I'll be one of the robotic arm operators, so I'll be using the space shuttle arm and the space station arm to help us move some of these pieces of equipment as we attach them onto the station.

**Kids always love spaceflight. What should they pay particular attention to on your flight? And ultimately, what do you think they're going to learn from this mission?**

You're going to laugh at this, but what I really want them to do is to pay attention to themselves and to look very deep within themselves and dig up all the questions that they can that they have about our world, our universe, and about space exploration. Because this is all about learning, and we're here to help and we want to know from them—what is it that they really want to know and learn? Because this is their future and it's open-ended for them. I also hope that they'll see an ordinary person doing the things that they can be doing. It's all about learning and exploring, and we want them to come with us.

**As the mission nears, what is it about the mission that you're most excited about now?**

I'm actually excited about going up and doing the work. We've been training really hard. There's been so much to learn to be able to do our jobs

well. And so, I'm really excited about going up and doing our jobs, and doing them well. And I'm excited about experiencing the whole spaceflight, seeing Earth from space for the very first time and experiencing weightlessness and what that's all about—seeing what it's like living and working on board the International Space Station.

**Is it hard to eat in microgravity?**

It's not hard to eat in microgravity, it's pretty easy. In fact, it's pretty fun because you can even play with your food. For example you can ... my crewmate right here has his food floating in mid-air, and he's reaching for it with his tongue. Also he's playing with a can and spinning it around. At first it was hard to get the food to actually go down when you swallowed it. It felt like it stayed up near your throat. That lasted for two or three days, but then that went away.

**How do you exercise on the space station?**

On the space station, we have three different tools for exercising. There's an exercise bicycle, there's a treadmill so that you can run. You strap yourself into it or you strap yourself into the bike. And we also have what we call resistant exercise. It's a lot like lifting weights, only you're pulling on cables that are attached to these canisters that you pull against.

**If you had to choose one, would you be an astronaut or a teacher?**

Do I have to choose one or can I do both, please? Actually, both are excellent jobs and they're both very, very similar. In both you're exploring, you're learning, you're discovering and you're sharing. And the only difference really to me is that as an astronaut you do that in space and as a teacher you get to do that with students. And they're both wonderful jobs. I highly recommend both.

Name _____ Date _____

**13.** The interview you have just read is mostly about
    Ⓐ an astronaut's thoughts on space travel
    Ⓑ an astronaut's eating habits
    Ⓒ the differences between being an astronaut and a teacher
    Ⓓ the work done by astronauts

**14.** Barbara Morgan had difficulty eating at first because
    Ⓕ the food did not taste good.
    Ⓖ she became dizzy.
    Ⓗ she found it difficult to swallow.
    Ⓙ the food floated away.

**15.** According to the interview, why does Barbara Morgan want students to pay attention to this space flight?
    Ⓐ to ask questions and learn
    Ⓑ to prove a teacher can be an astronaut
    Ⓒ to learn how to eat and sleep in space
    Ⓓ to become astronauts

**16.** What was Barbara Morgan most excited about as she left on her trip into space?
    Ⓕ exercising on a treadmill in space
    Ⓖ eating food that flies away
    Ⓗ being an astronaut rather than a teacher
    Ⓙ going and doing her job well

**17.** The author's purpose in writing this article was probably to report on Barbara Morgan's
    Ⓐ experiences in space
    Ⓑ feeling that being an astronaut was even better than being a teacher
    Ⓒ operation of the robotic arm
    Ⓓ problems eating

**18.** **Here are two sentences related to the passage.**
Barbara Morgan traveled in space aboard the Space Shuttle *Endeavor*. She was 55 years old.
**Which of these best combines the two sentences into one?**

(F) She was a 55 years old, but Barbara Morgan traveled in space aboard the Space Shuttle *Endeavor*.

(G) When she was 55 years old, Barbara Morgan traveled in space aboard the Space Shuttle *Endeavor*.

(H) While Barbara Morgan traveled in space aboard the Space Shuttle *Endeavor*, she was 55 years old.

(J) Barbara Morgan traveled in space aboard the Space Shuttle *Endeavor*, and she was 55 years old.

Name _____ Date _____

# Let's Write

## Sample D

**There are <u>four</u> mistakes in this paragraph. Let's correct them together.**

---

Last winter, my friend Clara asking me to go on a three-day skiing trip with her. It sounded like fun, but skiing is more harder than you would think. I couldn't even stand the first day. I fell off the ski lift. I felled all the way down the bunny slope. I lost one of my poles in the Woods. I crashed into a fence. Eventually, however, I got the hang of it. I'm still not a great skier, but I have mastered the bunny slope.

---

**19** **A student wrote this paragraph about imaginary trips he takes while camping outdoors with his brother. There are <u>five</u> mistakes in the paragraph. Draw a line through each part that has a mistake, and write the correction above it.**

---

In the summer my older brother Matt and me sleep in a tent in our backyard. Sometimes we pretending the tent is a space ship that takes us to all kinds of places. Every now and then, we go to the moon in our space ship, although once I fell in a crater and hurted my knee. Other times, we travel from star to star in the ship, and sometimes we stop at a planet to get a bite to eat. Matt can even make our space ship travel back in time, once we pretended we were Cowboys riding our horses across the Great Plains. We never know quite where we'll end up.

---

Name _____ Date _____

## Directions

**Study this poster encouraging students to attend a ski trip.**

---

**The Middle View Area Ski Club will hold a**

**Ski Trip to Camelback Ski Resort**

**on January 10**

Students, friends, and family of all ages welcome!

Bus leaves the school at 8:30 A.M. and returns at 10:30 P.M.

Cost is $45 a person, including ski rental, lunch, and dinner.

Tickets available at the school office.

---

The Ski Club needs your help! Students and parents need to organize and supervise the trip.

Call Tony Parks at 555-234-8897 for more information.

---

**20** **Now use the information from the poster to do the following:**

Write the information that is most important if you plan to attend the ski trip.

_____

Write the information that is most important if you want to help with the trip.

_____

Write one phrase from the poster that is meant to persuade you to help.

_____

Name _____ Date _____

**21** Look back at the excerpt from an interview with Barbara Morgan. Now think about Barbara Morgan's experience in outer space. If you could travel to any place in the universe, where would you go and why? What would you do on your trip? Write a paragraph discussing your answer.

For this answer, be sure to use complete sentences and check your work for correct spelling, capitalization, and punctuation.

_____

_____

_____

_____

_____

_____

_____

_____

# SAT 10 PRACTICE TEST

## Vocabulary

**Directions:**

Look at each underlined word. Choose the word that means about the same thing.

**1 To <u>supervise</u> is to—**

A lose

B win

C argue

D oversee

**2 Something that is <u>vacant</u> is—**

F noisy

G empty

H round

J nearby

**3 <u>Mobility</u> refers to—**

A motion

B speed

C distance

D height

**4 <u>Accurately</u> means—**

F purposely

G correctly

H quickly

J recently

**Directions:**

Read each boxed sentence. Then, read the sentences that follow. Choose the sentence that uses the underlined word in the same way as in the box.

**5**

> <u>Kick</u> the ball into the goal.

In which sentence does the word <u>kick</u> mean the same thing as in the sentence above?

A Janet got a <u>kick</u> out of the comedy show.

B Please don't <u>kick</u> me out of the club.

C Barney should <u>kick</u> the habit of oversleeping.

D It is mean to <u>kick</u> other people.

**6**

> The tree branches <u>shake</u>.

In which sentence does the word <u>shake</u> mean the same thing as in the sentence above?

F Boris drank a chocolate milk <u>shake</u>.

G His hand<u>shake</u> was very strong.

H I can't <u>shake</u> the cold I've had all week.

J The baby likes to <u>shake</u> the rattle.

Name _____ Date _____

## Reading Comprehension

# *from* Appreciating Our Heritage

### Directions:

**Read this excerpt from "Appreciating Our Heritage." Then complete numbers 1 through 4 by choosing the best answer.**

1. Honoring native traditions is making a comeback. It's happening all over North America. In the early 1900s, Native American children were not allowed to wear their own dress or use their language. Many have waited wistfully for a time when they could once again express their people's way of life. Today, from Alaska to Mexico, we are all rediscovering the importance of heritage. Let's take a look at how several groups in North America say "This is who I am."

**Finding Common Ground**

2. In 2004, Alaska's Perseverance Theatre did something extraordinary. It produced William Shakespeare's Scottish play, *Macbeth*, in the traditional dress of the Tlingit (pronounced *KLINK-it*) people. Some of the dialogue was in Tlingit too. At the time of the production, fewer than 300 people still spoke the Tlingit language.

3. In this *Macbeth*, young people became *Kushdaakaa*, land otter people, to portray Shakespeare's three witches. The ghost of Banquo wore a traditional raven mask. At one point, it split in half to reveal Banquo's face. The malicious Macbeth appeared in Tlingit war armor and a raven's tail robe. The effect was astounding. The Smithsonian Institution brought the play to Washington, D.C. The National Museum of the American Indian produced it in March of 2007.

4. The play's director was Anita Maynard-Losh. Maynard-Losh was living in a Tlingit village when she had the idea. (The Tlingit live in southeast Alaska and Canada.) As she got to know the Tlingit culture, she started to compare it with Shakespeare's Scotland. She found many connections! That's what motivated her to produce *Macbeth* and set it within the Tlingit culture. She put some of the words in Tlingit, too.

5. The play drove home an important point. We are all connected. As we each honor our own cultures, we gain understanding for the cultures of others. We see the qualities that connect us to one another.

**1** **Why did Maynard-Losh to produce *Macbeth* using the traditional dress of the Tlingit people?**
   A  She found many connections between the two cultures.
   B  She knew many Tlingit people who were also actors.
   C  She was living in a Tlingit village.
   D  She was asked to do this by the National Museum.

**2** **In paragraph 3, what does the word *malicious* mean?**
   F  military
   G  fully satisfied
   H  showing strength
   J  having evil intentions

**3** **What is the main idea of this passage?**
   A  Once we understand other cultures, we see connections between them.
   B  The Tlingit version of *Macbeth* was very successful.
   C  There are very few people who still speak the Tlingit language.
   D  Alaskan theater is the most creative in the country.

**4** **What is the literary point of view in this passage?**
   F  A first-person narrator describes her own thoughts and actions.
   G  A third-person narrator describes the actions but not the thoughts of others.
   H  A first-person narrator describes all the thoughts and actions of others.
   J  A third-person narrator describes the thoughts of several other people.

## Reading Comprehension

# from "Hard as Nails" by Russell Baker

### Directions:

**Here is an excerpt from *Hard as Nails* by Russell Baker. This essay describes Baker's first job—delivering newspapers in Baltimore. Read this excerpt. Then, complete numbers 5 and 6 by choosing the best answer.**

As we walked back to the house she [Baker's mother] said I couldn't have a paper route until I was twelve. And all because of some foolish rule they had down here in Baltimore. You'd think if a boy wanted to work they would encourage him instead of making him stay idle so long that laziness got embedded in his bones.

That was April. We had barely finished the birthday cake in August before Deems came by the apartment and gave me the tools of the newspaper trade: an account book for keeping track of the customers' bills and a long, brown web belt. Slung around one shoulder and across the chest, the belt made it easy to balance fifteen or twenty pounds of papers against the hip. I had to buy my own wire cutters for opening the newspaper bundles the trucks dropped at Wisengoff's store on the corner of Stricker and West Lombard streets.

In February my mother had moved us down from New Jersey, where we had been living with her brother Allen ever since my father died in 1930. This move of hers to Baltimore was a step toward fulfilling a dream. More than almost anything else in the world, she wanted "a home of our own." I'd heard her talk of that "home of our own" all through those endless Depression years when we lived as poor relatives dependent on Uncle Allen's goodness. "A home of our own. One of these days, Buddy, we'll have a home of our own."

That winter she had finally saved just enough to make her move, and she came to Baltimore. There were several reasons for Baltimore. For one, there were people she knew in Baltimore, people she could go to if things got desperate. And desperation was possible, because the moving would exhaust her savings, and the apartment rent was twenty-four dollars a month. She would have to find a job quickly. My sister Doris was only nine, but I was old enough for an after-school job that could bring home a few dollars a week. So as soon as it was legal I went into newspaper work.

**5** **The author and his family moved to Baltimore because—**

   **A** his mother thought the rent was lower in Baltimore.

   **B** his mother wanted them to be near Doris.

   **C** his mother wanted them to have their own home.

   **D** his mother found a job in Baltimore.

**6** **The author probably wrote this passage to—**

   **F** persuade children to get after-school jobs

   **G** show readers the unfairness of child labor

   **H** explain what it is like to live in Baltimore

   **J** entertain readers with a memory from his youth

# *from* Statistics Don't Lie (But People Do)

**Directions:**

**Read this excerpt from "Statistics Don't Lie (But People Do)." The complete numbers 7 and 8 by choosing the best answer.**

Facts tell us what is real. If you want to persuade someone, facts help you prove your point. Facts with numbers seem especially true, don't they? Well, even if they seem true, number facts don't always give you a good picture of what's real. People can use numbers to prove almost anything. It's up to you to be an active reader. You have to challenge what you read, or you could be fooled.

People say that statistics don't lie. That might be true, but unfortunately, people do. And they don't need words to do it. Anyone can "bend the truth" with statistics.

Statistics are number facts. People love to use statistics to back up their opinions. Numbers seem neutral. Compare these two statements:

• It's shocking how terribly dangerous our playground has become.
• Last year, accidents at our playground increased by 57%.

The first statement sounds very emotional. It makes a claim, but doesn't back it up. The second statement includes a statistic. It sounds impressive.

Writers know that readers are more likely to respond favorably to statistics. That's why you read number facts every day. You find them in newspapers and magazines. You hear them on the television and radio news. Advertisements cite them to sell products. Can you trust every statistic you read? Of course not. You need to learn some of the tricks people can use to lie with statistics.

**7** **What is the major purpose of this selection?**
  A. to persuade people to read carefully because number facts are not always true
  B. to prove that you should believe any fact that uses numbers
  C. to persuade people to use statistics to prove their points
  D. to tell people how dangerous playgrounds are today

**8** **What does the writer mean by the sentence: "You need to learn some of the tricks people can use to lie with statistics"?**
  F. Everyone should learn how to lie by using numbers.
  G. Using numbers to prove a point is always the right thing to do.
  H. You need to understand how people lie using numbers.
  J. Statistics usually trick people, so they should not be used to back up opinions.

## Reading Comprehension

# from "Becky and the Wheels-and-Brake Boys"
# by James Berry

### Directions:

**Read this excerpt from "Becky and the Wheels-and-Brake Boys" by James Berry. Then, complete numbers 9 and 10 by choosing the best answer.**

Over and over I told my mum I wanted a bike. Over and over she looked at me as if I was crazy. "Becky, d'you think you're a boy? Eh? D'you think you're a boy? In any case, where's the money to come from? Eh?"

Of course I know I'm not a boy. Of course I know I'm not crazy. Of course I know all that's no reason why I can't have a bike. No reason! As soon as I get indoors I'll just have to ask again—ask Mum once more.

**9 Which sentence best describes the literary point of view used in this passage?**

**A** A third-person narrator describes the thoughts and actions of several other people.

**B** A first-person narrator describes only her own thoughts and actions.

**C** A first-person narrator describes her own thoughts and the actions of herself and others.

**D** A third-person narrator describes the action through the eyes of one person.

**10 Becky's mother does not want her to have a bicycle because—**

**F** she thinks only boys should ride bicycles.

**G** Becky does not do her chores.

**H** she wants Becky to watch her sister.

**J** Becky is too young.

Name _____ Date _____

## Reading Comprehension

*Directions:*

**Read this excerpt from a textbook. Then, complete number 11 by choosing the best answer.**

---

   The National Aeronautics and Space Administration (NASA) is responsible for running the United States space program. NASA's Project Mercury put the first Americans in space. This project also established NASA's ability to launch Earth-orbiting spacecraft. Project Apollo was designed to land Americans on the moon, a goal that was accomplished in July 1969 with the *Apollo 11* mission. Five additional lunar landings followed this success, ending with *Apollo 17* in 1972. As the space shuttle program continues, astronauts use their unique zero-gravity environment to conduct experiments and gather information for the benefit of earthbound humankind and future space travelers.

---

**11 What is this passage mostly about?**

   **A** future space travelers

   **B** the importance of the space shuttle

   **C** astronauts' specialized training

   **D** NASA's accomplishments

# Reading Comprehension

*Directions:*

**Read the following poster. Then, complete number 12 by choosing the best answer.**

---

**The Middle View Area Ski Club will hold**

**a Ski Trip to Silver Bells Ski Resort**

**on January 10**

Students, friends, and family of all ages welcome!

Bus leaves the school at 8:30 A.M. and returns at 10:30 P.M.

Cost is $45 per person, including ski rental, lunch, and dinner.

Tickets are available at the school office.

---

The Ski Club needs your help! Students and parents need

to organize and supervise the trip.

Call Tony Parks at 555-2378 for more information.

---

**12 Which of the following sentences from the poster is meant to persuade you to volunteer to organize the trip?**

**F** Tickets are available at the school office.

**G** Call Tony Parks at 555-2378 for more information.

**H** The Ski Club needs your help!

**J** Bus leaves the school at 8:30 A.M. and returns at 10:30 P.M.

# Spelling

## Directions:

**Read each group of sentences. For each item on the answer sheet, fill in the bubble for the answer that has a mistake in spelling. If there is no mistake, fill in the last answer choice.**

1  **A** <u>Science</u> is Lee's favorite subject.

   **B** Are the <u>tomatoes</u> ripe yet?

   **C** Valentine's Day is in <u>Febuary</u>.

   **D** No mistake

2  **F** The <u>secetary</u> typed the letter.

   **G** Most kittens are <u>curious</u>.

   **H** <u>Whales</u> are mammals, not fish.

   **J** No mistake

3  **A** Lucy ate <u>ninety</u> peanuts.

   **B** The shirt was a <u>bargin</u> at $3.00.

   **C** <u>Parallel</u> lines never meet.

   **D** No mistake

4  **F** <u>Answer</u> all of the questions.

   **G** We will buy a new <u>calendar</u> in December.

   **H** Gary saw a movie at the <u>theater</u>.

   **J** No mistake

5  **A** They ate lunch in the <u>cafeteria</u>.

   **B** The next street is Sixth <u>Avenue</u>.

   **C** Did you take <u>medicin</u> for your cold?

   **D** No mistake

6  **F** Mom cooked <u>spagetti</u> and meatballs.

   **G** Darla's birthday is on <u>Wednesday</u>.

   **H** Would you like more mashed <u>potatoes</u>?

   **J** No mistake

7  **A** Luke <u>weighs</u> 85 pounds.

   **B** Is that word <u>misspelled</u>?

   **C** It takes <u>coperation</u> to succeed.

   **D** No mistake

8  **F** There was a <u>mysterious</u> noise in the woods.

   **G** The boys paddled the <u>canoe</u>.

   **H** In the fall the <u>leaves</u> change color.

   **J** No mistake

9  **A** It is <u>neccesary</u> to finish high school.

   **B** Sign the letter "Yours <u>truly</u>."

   **C** Winter is Bart's favorite <u>season</u>.

   **D** No mistake

10  **F** The fans shouted <u>encouragement</u> at the runners.

   **G** The puppy <u>excaped</u> from the yard.

   **H** Measure the <u>width</u> of the table.

   **J** No mistake

11  **A** <u>Abbreviate</u> Alabama as AL.

   **B** A drum is a <u>rythm</u> instrument.

   **C** That <u>restaurant</u> serves tacos.

   **D** No mistake

## Spelling

**12 F** Do tests give you <u>anxiety</u>?

   **G** Pay the <u>cashier</u> for your lunch.

   **H** What is your <u>opinon</u> of rap music?

   **J** No mistake

**13 A** An eclipse will <u>ocurr</u> tomorrow.

   **B** Those <u>scissors</u> are very sharp.

   **C** A <u>nickel</u> equals five cents.

   **D** No mistake

**14 F** A <u>censis</u> counts all the people.

   **G** He ate ice cream for <u>dessert</u>.

   **H** The bride walked down the <u>aisle</u>.

   **J** No mistake

**15 A** Look up the word in a <u>dictionary</u>.

   **B** The Civil War was in the <u>ninteenth</u> century.

   **C** How old will you be in <u>ninety</u> years?

   **D** No mistake

**16 F** The ending of the book <u>satisfied</u> Selma.

   **G** The ending <u>surprised</u> Rita.

   **H** Brandon liked the <u>eighth</u> chapter best.

   **J** No mistake

**17 A** The flower garden is <u>beautiful</u>.

   **B** Let's take a <u>photograph</u> of the parade.

   **C** It is impolite to <u>interrupt</u>.

   **D** No mistake

**18 F** 100 percent is the <u>maximum</u> score.

   **G** Read the <u>paragraf</u> about Mars.

   **H** Encyclopedia Brown is an <u>amateur</u> detective.

   **J** No mistake

**19 A** A chameleon's color is <u>changeable</u>.

   **B** Daily <u>exercise</u> helps make people healthy.

   **C** Give the dog a <u>biskit</u> as a treat.

   **D** No mistake

**20 F** Will you <u>persue</u> computers as a career?

   **G** The actors <u>rehearsed</u> the play.

   **H** Malik fell and <u>bruised</u> his knee.

   **J** No mistake

**21 A** The <u>physician</u> looked at Sue's tonsils.

   **B** Many scientists work in a <u>labertory</u>.

   **C** Return the books to the <u>library</u>.

   **D** No mistake

**22 F** The surprise party was a <u>sucess</u>.

   **G** The pyramids are <u>ancient</u> tombs.

   **H** A weather <u>satellite</u> orbits Earth.

   **J** No mistake

## Language

*Directions:*

**Read each passage. Then decide which type of error, if any, appears in each underlined section. For each item on the answer sheet, fill in the bubble for the answer. If there is no error, fill in the last answer choice.**

---

<u>The worlds largest library is the Library of Congress,</u> which is in Washington, D.C.
1

The original <u>library was burned by british troops during</u> the War of 1812. The federal
2

<u>government had very little money to build a new one, but</u> a former president stepped in
3

to help. <u>Thomas Jefferson, donated more than six thousand of his own books</u> to get the
4

new library going. From this <u>humble begining, the Library of Congress has grown to</u>
5

<u>include</u> more than 20 million books, 10 million prints and photographs, and 4 million

atlases and maps. <u>To hold these books, their are more than 530 miles of shelves.</u>
6

---

**1 A** Spelling error

  **B** Capitalization error

  **C** Punctuation error

  **D** No error

**2 F** Spelling error

  **G** Capitalization error

  **H** Punctuation error

  **J** No error

**3 A** Spelling error

  **B** Capitalization error

  **C** Punctuation error

  **D** No error

**4 F** Spelling error

  **G** Capitalization error

  **H** Punctuation error

  **J** No error

**5 A** Spelling error

  **B** Capitalization error

  **C** Punctuation error

  **D** No error

**6 F** Spelling error

  **G** Capitalization error

  **H** Punctuation error

  **J** No error

## Language

Many people believe, that animals cannot see colors, but this is not true. Dogs,
        7

horses, and sheep are able to see some colors, although not as well as Humans can.
                                                                    8

Monkeys are able to see colors, to. In fact, their color vision is almost equal to our own.
                    9

It is also obvious that birds' can see colors. There are different ways they attract other
10                                                                                      11

birds, one of these ways is through their natural color.

But there are many animals that apparently cannot see colors. Bulls, for example, are
                                                                    12

probly not excited by the color red in a bullfighter's cape. Instead, they are excited only
                                                                                    13

by the movement of the cape in the bullfighter's hands.

**7 A** Spelling error

**B** Capitalization error

**C** Punctuation error

**D** No error

**8 F** Spelling error

**G** Capitalization error

**H** Punctuation error

**J** No error

**9 A** Spelling error

**B** Capitalization error

**C** Punctuation error

**D** No error

**10 F** Spelling error

**G** Capitalization error

**H** Punctuation error

**J** No error

**11 A** Spelling error

**B** Capitalization error

**C** Punctuation error

**D** No error

**12 F** Spelling error

**G** Capitalization error

**H** Punctuation error

**J** No error

**13 A** Spelling error

**B** Capitalization error

**C** Punctuation error

**D** No error

# Language

## Directions:

**Read the passage. Then, choose the word or group of words that belongs in each space. For each item on the answer sheet, fill in the bubble for the answer that you think is correct.**

> The writer Bailey White has an —(1)— story to tell of how, as a child, she hatched sixteen wild turkeys! White's mother had long been a friend of local ornithologists, or bird experts. The ornithologists were worried that the wild turkey was headed for extinction [dying out]. When they found a nest of eggs, they could hardly control their excitement. They camped out in the woods to protect the —(2)— nest from people or animals that might harm it. Unfortunately, however, they scared off the mother turkey, and she —(3)— her nest on the night the eggs were supposed to hatch.
>
> Six-year-old Bailey White was suffering from a case of the measles and a temperature that —(4)— to 102 degrees. She barely remembers the ornithologists creeping into —(5)— room with a cardboard box, but she remembers very clearly what happened the next morning. When she woke up, the little girl was surprised to find sixteen baby turkeys —(6)— her bed! White helped take care of the turkeys until one day in late summer. Then, with the ornithologists and White —(7)— watching, the wild turkeys were set free.

1  **A** interested
   **B** interesting
   **C** interest
   **D** interests

2  **F** rarest
   **G** rarer
   **H** rare
   **J** rarely

3  **A** abandoned
   **B** would have abandoned
   **C** abandoning
   **D** was abandoned

4  **F** had risen
   **G** will rise
   **H** rises
   **J** is rising

5  **A** their
   **B** her
   **C** she
   **D** our

6  **F** sharing
   **G** are sharing
   **H** share
   **J** shares

7  **A** most careful
   **B** careful
   **C** carefully
   **D** more careful

## Language

### Directions:

**Read each passage. Some sections are underlined. The underlined sections may be one of the following:**

- **Incomplete sentences**
- **Run-on sentences**
- **Correctly written sentences that should be combined**
- **Correctly written sentences that do not need to be rewritten**

**Choose the best way to write each underlined section and mark the letter for your answer. If the underlined section needs no change, mark the choice "Correct as is."**

---

Without the hard work of Noah Webster. We might never have had spelling bees!
8

In the early days of the United States no uniform spelling of words existed. Webster
9                                                                                          10

changed all that with his *American Dictionary of the English Language.* It was published
11

in 1828. It included 70,000 words.

---

**8 F** Without the hard work of Noah Webster, we might never have had spelling bees!

**G** Without the hard work. Of Noah Webster we might never have had spelling bees!

**H** Without the hard work of Noah Webster, which we might never have had spelling bees!

**J** Correct as is

**9 A** In the early days of the United States. No uniform spelling of words existed.

**B** In the early days of the United States, no uniform spelling of words existed.

**C** No uniform spelling of words existed until the early days of the United States.

**D** Correct as is

**10 F** Webster changed all that. With his *American Dictionary of the English Language.*

**G** Webster, changed all that, with his *American Dictionary of the English Language.*

**H** Changing all that, Webster did with his *American Dictionary of the English Language.*

**J** Correct as is

**11 A** It was published in 1828 and the dictionary also included 70,000 words.

**B** Published in 1828, it included 70,000 words.

**C** It was published in 1828, it included 70,000 words.

**D** Correct as is

# Language

---

It was spring of the year 1836. <u>The Texas Revolution had been going on for several</u>
                                                    12

<u>months. It had started in October 1835.</u> Many lives had already been lost. <u>The Texans</u>
                                                                                    13

<u>had suffered a serious defeat at the Alamo mission. The Alamo was a mission in San</u>

<u>Antonio.</u> <u>The 189 men there had fought against more than 3,000 Mexican troops, and</u>
                14

<u>every one of them had died in the battle.</u>

On April 21, 1836, the Texans' luck turned when Sam Houston's army crept up on

the Mexican troops near the San Jacinto River. <u>There they sprang a surprise attack.</u>
                                                                15

<u>Which turned out to be more successful than they had imagined.</u> The Battle of San

Jacinto lasted less than 20 minutes and ended when the Texans captured the Mexican

leader, Santa Anna. <u>In return for setting him free, the Texans demanded their immediate</u>
                        16

<u>independence.</u> The Mexican leader had little choice but to agree. A treaty was quickly

signed. <u>Texas was no longer part of Mexico it was an independent country.</u>
        17

---

**12 F** The Texas Revolution had been going on for several months, it had started in October 1835.

**G** The Texas Revolution had started in October 1835 and the Texas Revolution had been going on for several months.

**H** The Texas Revolution, which had started in October 1835, had been going on for several months.

**J** Correct as is

**13 A** The Alamo was a mission in San Antonio, which Texans had suffered a serious defeat there.

**B** The Texans had suffered a serious defeat at the Alamo mission in San Antonio.

**C** Suffering a serious defeat, the Alamo was a mission in San Antonio.

**D** Correct as is

# Language

**14 F** The 189 men there had fought against more than 3,000 Mexican troops, every one of them had died in the battle.

**G** The 189 men there had fought. Against more than 3,000 Mexican troops, who had all died in the battle.

**H** Against more than 3,000 troops were what the 189 men had fought against and died there.

**J** Correct as is

**15 A** There they sprang a surprise attack and the surprise attack turned out to be more successful than they had imagined.

**B** There they sprang a surprise attack, which turned out to be more successful than they had imagined.

**C** They were more successful than they had imagined. When they sprang a surprise attack there.

**D** Correct as is

**16 F** In return for setting him free. The Texans demanded their immediate independence.

**G** In return, the Texans demanded their immediate independence, for setting him free.

**H** The Texans demanded their immediate independence, in return they set him free.

**J** Correct as is

**17 A** Texas was no longer part of Mexico; it was an independent country.

**B** Texas was no longer part of Mexico and Texas was an independent country.

**C** Texas, no longer part of Mexico, an independent country.

**D** Correct as is

# Language

## Directions:

Read the following questions. Then, complete number 18 by choosing the best answer.

18 Suppose that you are writing an essay comparing your favorite class and your least favorite class. Which of the following organizers would be most useful?

F time line

G cause-effect frame

H Venn diagram

J character-change map

## Directions:

Kenny is working on an essay about his pet hamster. Several mistakes need to be corrected. Read the following paragraph. Then, complete numbers 19 through 21 by choosing the best answer.

[1]When my brother and I asked our parents for a pet, we were hoping for a dog, so we were disappointed when our father bought us a hamster, but we weren't sad for long. [2]Sammy is our hamster. [3]Sammy is really cute. [4]He also spends a lot of time digging. [5]My father told my brother and me that Sammy does this because hamsters dig burrows in the wild. [6]Sammy is the most lovable hamster I have ever seen. [7]He loves to come out of his cage and be held. [8]Sometimes he crawls up my arm, onto my shoulder, and nibbles my ear. [9]Show me a dog do that!

19 Which of these best combines Sentences 2 and 3 into one?

A Sammy is our hamster, but he is really cute.

B Sammy is our hamster and really cute.

C Sammy is our hamster; Sammy is really cute.

D Sammy, our hamster, is really cute.

20 Which sentence should be rewritten as two complete sentences?

F Sentence 1

G Sentence 5

H Sentence 6

J Sentence 7

21 If Kenny wanted to add a paragraph to his essay, a good topic would be

A what hamsters eat

B what kind of dog Kenny wants

C why hamsters are cute

D who takes care of Sammy

# Listening

***Directions:***

**Suppose that the following paragraph is being read aloud. Read the paragraph. Then, complete numbers 1 and 2 by choosing the best answer.**

> My first apartment in New York was in a <u>gritty</u> warehouse district, the kind of place that makes your parents wince. A lot of old Italians lived around me, which suited me just fine because I was the granddaughter of old Italians. Their own children and grandchildren had moved to Long Island and New Jersey. All they had was me. All I had was them.
>
> —from "Melting Pot" by Anna Quindlen

**1 You can tell from the passage that the word <u>gritty</u> means—**

**A** tough

**B** lovely

**C** urban

**D** old

**2 This passage gives you enough information to believe that the speaker and her neighbors—**

**F** were related by blood

**G** got on each other's nerves

**H** grew up in New Jersey and then moved to New York City

**J** became important to each other

Name _____ Date _____

# Listening

## Directions:

The Brentwood School Board decided to require student athletes to attend physical education (P.E.) classes. Sandra delivered the following speech during a class debate. Read the paragraph. Then, complete numbers 3 through 5 by choosing the best answer.

---

Playing a team sport at school requires the same type of physical activity as a P.E. course. Athletes may exhaust or injure themselves if they take part in both activities. In addition, the time spent in P.E. courses can be put to use by coaches as training time. That way, athletes would not have to spend so much time training after school and would have more time to study. Finally, as I understand it, P.E. courses are supposed to develop an interest in athletics. Students who take part in team sports already have this interest. For athletes, P.E. is unnecessary, and it might even be harmful—both physically and academically.

---

**3 What does Sandra mean when she says that P.E. classes could be academically harmful for athletes?**

**A** P.E. classes would be difficult for athletes, and they might fail.

**B** P.E. classes take up time that athletes could use to study for their other classes.

**C** Athletes who take P.E. classes would have to drop out of one of their other courses.

**D** P.E. classes would create too much homework for athletes.

**4 This speech was given in order to—**

**F** complain about athletic teams

**G** explain why the school board should change its decision

**H** explain why the school board should not change its decision

**J** express the school board's opinions about its decision

**5 Suppose that while listening to Sandra's speech, you had to write her words. Which of the following would be the best listening technique?**

**A** listening to the first sentence of the speech

**B** listening for information in the speech that you find interesting

**C** listening for the most important points of the speech

**D** listening to the last sentence of the speech

Name _____    Date _____

# Answer Sheet: Screening Test

| | | |
|---|---|---|
| 1. (A)(B)(C)(D) | 15. (A)(B)(C)(D) |
| 2. (F)(G)(H)(J) | 16. (F)(G)(H)(J) |
| 3. (A)(B)(C)(D) | 17. (A)(B)(C)(D) |
| 4. (F)(G)(H)(J) | 18. (F)(G)(H)(J) |
| 5. (A)(B)(C)(D) | 19. (A)(B)(C)(D) |
| 6. (F)(G)(H)(J) | 20. (F)(G)(H)(J) |
| 7. (A)(B)(C)(D) | 21. (A)(B)(C)(D) |
| 8. (F)(G)(H)(J) | 22. (F)(G)(H)(J) |
| 9. (A)(B)(C)(D) | 23. (A)(B)(C)(D) |
| 10. (F)(G)(H)(J) | 24. (F)(G)(H)(J) |
| 11. (A)(B)(C)(D) | 25. (A)(B)(C)(D) |
| 12. (F)(G)(H)(J) | 26. (F)(G)(H)(J) |
| 13. (A)(B)(C)(D) | 27. (A)(B)(C)(D) |
| 14. (F)(G)(H)(J) | 28. (F)(G)(H)(J) |

Name _____ Date _____

# Answer Sheet: Practice Test 1

1. (A) (B) (C) (D)    14. (A) (B) (C) (D)
2. (A) (B) (C) (D)    15. (A) (B) (C) (D)
3. (A) (B) (C) (D)    16. (A) (B) (C) (D)
4. (A) (B) (C) (D)    17. (A) (B) (C) (D)
5. (A) (B) (C) (D)    18. (A) (B) (C) (D)
6. (A) (B) (C) (D)    19. (A) (B) (C) (D)
7. (A) (B) (C) (D)    20. (A) (B) (C) (D)
8. (A) (B) (C) (D)    21. (A) (B) (C) (D)
9. (A) (B) (C) (D)    22. (A) (B) (C) (D)
10. (A) (B) (C) (D)   23. (A) (B) (C) (D)
11. (A) (B) (C) (D)   24. (A) (B) (C) (D)
12. (A) (B) (C) (D)   25. (A) (B) (C) (D)
13. (A) (B) (C) (D)

Name _____ Date _____

# Answer Sheet: Practice Test 2

| | |
|---|---|
| 1. Ⓐ Ⓑ Ⓒ Ⓓ | 14. Ⓐ Ⓑ Ⓒ Ⓓ |
| 2. Ⓐ Ⓑ Ⓒ Ⓓ | 15. Ⓐ Ⓑ Ⓒ Ⓓ |
| 3. Ⓐ Ⓑ Ⓒ Ⓓ | 16. Ⓐ Ⓑ Ⓒ Ⓓ |
| 4. Ⓐ Ⓑ Ⓒ Ⓓ | 17. Ⓐ Ⓑ Ⓒ Ⓓ |
| 5. Ⓐ Ⓑ Ⓒ Ⓓ | 18. Ⓐ Ⓑ Ⓒ Ⓓ |
| 6. Ⓐ Ⓑ Ⓒ Ⓓ | 19. Ⓐ Ⓑ Ⓒ Ⓓ |
| 7. Ⓐ Ⓑ Ⓒ Ⓓ | 20. Ⓐ Ⓑ Ⓒ Ⓓ |
| 8. Ⓐ Ⓑ Ⓒ Ⓓ | 21. Ⓐ Ⓑ Ⓒ Ⓓ |
| 9. Ⓐ Ⓑ Ⓒ Ⓓ | 22. Ⓐ Ⓑ Ⓒ Ⓓ |
| 10. Ⓐ Ⓑ Ⓒ Ⓓ | 23. Ⓐ Ⓑ Ⓒ Ⓓ |
| 11. Ⓐ Ⓑ Ⓒ Ⓓ | 24. Ⓐ Ⓑ Ⓒ Ⓓ |
| 12. Ⓐ Ⓑ Ⓒ Ⓓ | 25. Ⓐ Ⓑ Ⓒ Ⓓ |
| 13. Ⓐ Ⓑ Ⓒ Ⓓ | |

Name _____ Date _____

# Answer Sheet: Practice Test 3

| | | |
|---|---|---|
| 1. (A) (B) (C) (D) | 20. (A) (B) (C) (D) | 39. (A) (B) (C) (D) |
| 2. (A) (B) (C) (D) | 21. (A) (B) (C) (D) | 40. (A) (B) (C) (D) |
| 3. (A) (B) (C) (D) | 22. (A) (B) (C) (D) | 41. (A) (B) (C) (D) |
| 4. (A) (B) (C) (D) | 23. (A) (B) (C) (D) | 42. (A) (B) (C) (D) |
| 5. (A) (B) (C) (D) | 24. (A) (B) (C) (D) | 43. (A) (B) (C) (D) |
| 6. (A) (B) (C) (D) | 25. (A) (B) (C) (D) | 44. (A) (B) (C) (D) |
| 7. (A) (B) (C) (D) | 26. (A) (B) (C) (D) | 45. (A) (B) (C) (D) |
| 8. (A) (B) (C) (D) | 27. (A) (B) (C) (D) | 46. (A) (B) (C) (D) |
| 9. (A) (B) (C) (D) | 28. (A) (B) (C) (D) | 47. (A) (B) (C) (D) |
| 10. (A) (B) (C) (D) | 29. (A) (B) (C) (D) | 48. (A) (B) (C) (D) |
| 11. (A) (B) (C) (D) | 30. (A) (B) (C) (D) | 49. (A) (B) (C) (D) |
| 12. (A) (B) (C) (D) | 31. (A) (B) (C) (D) | 50. (A) (B) (C) (D) |
| 13. (A) (B) (C) (D) | 32. (A) (B) (C) (D) | 51. (A) (B) (C) (D) |
| 14. (A) (B) (C) (D) | 33. (A) (B) (C) (D) | 52. (A) (B) (C) (D) |
| 15. (A) (B) (C) (D) | 34. (A) (B) (C) (D) | 53. (A) (B) (C) (D) |
| 16. (A) (B) (C) (D) | 35. (A) (B) (C) (D) | 54. (A) (B) (C) (D) |
| 17. (A) (B) (C) (D) | 36. (A) (B) (C) (D) | 55. (A) (B) (C) (D) |
| 18. (A) (B) (C) (D) | 37. (A) (B) (C) (D) | |
| 19. (A) (B) (C) (D) | 38. (A) (B) (C) (D) | |

Name _____ Date _____

**Writing Prompt 1:**

_____
_____
_____
_____
_____
_____
_____
_____
_____
_____
_____
_____
_____
_____
_____
_____
_____
_____
_____
_____
_____
_____
_____
_____
_____
_____
_____
_____
_____

Name _____ Date _____

**Writing Prompt 2:**

_____
_____
_____
_____
_____
_____
_____
_____
_____
_____
_____
_____
_____
_____
_____
_____
_____
_____
_____
_____
_____
_____
_____
_____
_____
_____
_____

Name _____ Date _____

# Answer Sheet for ITBS

## Vocabulary

| | | | | |
|---|---|---|---|---|
| 1. (A) (B) (C) (D) | 4. (J) (K) (L) (M) | 7. (A) (B) (C) (D) | 10. (J) (K) (L) (M) | 13. (A) (B) (C) (D) |
| 2. (J) (K) (L) (M) | 5. (A) (B) (C) (D) | 8. (J) (K) (L) (M) | 11. (A) (B) (C) (D) | 14. (J) (K) (L) (M) |
| 3. (A) (B) (C) (D) | 6. (J) (K) (L) (M) | 9. (A) (B) (C) (D) | 12. (J) (K) (L) (M) | |

## Reading Comprehension

| | | | | |
|---|---|---|---|---|
| 1. (A) (B) (C) (D) | 4. (J) (K) (L) (M) | 7. (A) (B) (C) (D) | 10. (J) (K) (L) (M) | 13. (A) (B) (C) (D) |
| 2. (J) (K) (L) (M) | 5. (A) (B) (C) (D) | 8. (J) (K) (L) (M) | 11. (A) (B) (C) (D) | 14. (J) (K) (L) (M) |
| 3. (A) (B) (C) (D) | 6. (J) (K) (L) (M) | 9. (A) (B) (C) (D) | 12. (J) (K) (L) (M) | |

## Spelling

| | | | | |
|---|---|---|---|---|
| 1. (A) (B) (C) (D) (E) | 4. (J) (K) (L) (M) (N) | 7. (A) (B) (C) (D) (E) | 10. (J) (K) (L) (M) (N) | 13. (A) (B) (C) (D) (E) |
| 2. (J) (K) (L) (M) (N) | 5. (A) (B) (C) (D) (E) | 8. (J) (K) (L) (M) (N) | 11. (A) (B) (C) (D) (E) | 14. (J) (K) (L) (M) (N) |
| 3. (A) (B) (C) (D) (E) | 6. (J) (K) (L) (M) (N) | 9. (A) (B) (C) (D) (E) | 12. (J) (K) (L) (M) (N) | |

## Capitalization

| | | | | |
|---|---|---|---|---|
| 1. (A) (B) (C) (D) | 4. (J) (K) (L) (M) | 7. (A) (B) (C) (D) | 10. (J) (K) (L) (M) | 13. (A) (B) (C) (D) |
| 2. (J) (K) (L) (M) | 5. (A) (B) (C) (D) | 8. (J) (K) (L) (M) | 11. (A) (B) (C) (D) | |
| 3. (A) (B) (C) (D) | 6. (J) (K) (L) (M) | 9. (A) (B) (C) (D) | 12. (J) (K) (L) (M) | |

## Punctuation

| | | | |
|---|---|---|---|
| 1. (A) (B) (C) (D) | 4. (J) (K) (L) (M) | 7. (A) (B) (C) (D) | 10. (J) (K) (L) (M) |
| 2. (J) (K) (L) (M) | 5. (A) (B) (C) (D) | 8. (J) (K) (L) (M) | 11. (A) (B) (C) (D) |
| 3. (A) (B) (C) (D) | 6. (J) (K) (L) (M) | 9. (A) (B) (C) (D) | 12. (J) (K) (L) (M) |

## Usage and Expression

| | | | |
|---|---|---|---|
| 1. (A) (B) (C) (D) | 6. (J) (K) (L) (M) | 11. (A) (B) (C) (D) | 16. (J) (K) (L) (M) |
| 2. (J) (K) (L) (M) | 7. (A) (B) (C) (D) | 12. (J) (K) (L) (M) | 17. (A) (B) (C) (D) |
| 3. (A) (B) (C) (D) | 8. (J) (K) (L) (M) | 13. (A) (B) (C) (D) | 18. (J) (K) (L) (M) |
| 4. (J) (K) (L) (M) | 9. (A) (B) (C) (D) | 14. (J) (K) (L) (M) | 19. (A) (B) (C) (D) |
| 5. (A) (B) (C) (D) | 10. (J) (K) (L) (M) | 15. (A) (B) (C) (D) | |

Name _____ Date _____

# Answer Sheet for SAT 10

## Vocabulary

| | |
|---|---|
| 1. Ⓐ Ⓑ Ⓒ Ⓓ | 4. Ⓕ Ⓖ Ⓗ Ⓙ |
| 2. Ⓕ Ⓖ Ⓗ Ⓙ | 5. Ⓐ Ⓑ Ⓒ Ⓓ |
| 3. Ⓐ Ⓑ Ⓒ Ⓓ | 6. Ⓕ Ⓖ Ⓗ Ⓙ |

## Reading Comprehension

| | | |
|---|---|---|
| 1. Ⓐ Ⓑ Ⓒ Ⓓ | 6. Ⓕ Ⓖ Ⓗ Ⓙ | 11. Ⓐ Ⓑ Ⓒ Ⓓ |
| 2. Ⓕ Ⓖ Ⓗ Ⓙ | 7. Ⓐ Ⓑ Ⓒ Ⓓ | 12. Ⓕ Ⓖ Ⓗ Ⓙ |
| 3. Ⓐ Ⓑ Ⓒ Ⓓ | 8. Ⓕ Ⓖ Ⓗ Ⓙ | |
| 4. Ⓕ Ⓖ Ⓗ Ⓙ | 9. Ⓐ Ⓑ Ⓒ Ⓓ | |
| 5. Ⓐ Ⓑ Ⓒ Ⓓ | 10. Ⓕ Ⓖ Ⓗ Ⓙ | |

## Spelling

| | | | | |
|---|---|---|---|---|
| 1. Ⓐ Ⓑ Ⓒ Ⓓ | 6. Ⓕ Ⓖ Ⓗ Ⓙ | 11. Ⓐ Ⓑ Ⓒ Ⓓ | 16. Ⓕ Ⓖ Ⓗ Ⓙ | 21. Ⓐ Ⓑ Ⓒ Ⓓ |
| 2. Ⓕ Ⓖ Ⓗ Ⓙ | 7. Ⓐ Ⓑ Ⓒ Ⓓ | 12. Ⓕ Ⓖ Ⓗ Ⓙ | 17. Ⓐ Ⓑ Ⓒ Ⓓ | 22. Ⓕ Ⓖ Ⓗ Ⓙ |
| 3. Ⓐ Ⓑ Ⓒ Ⓓ | 8. Ⓕ Ⓖ Ⓗ Ⓙ | 13. Ⓐ Ⓑ Ⓒ Ⓓ | 18. Ⓕ Ⓖ Ⓗ Ⓙ | |
| 4. Ⓕ Ⓖ Ⓗ Ⓙ | 9. Ⓐ Ⓑ Ⓒ Ⓓ | 14. Ⓕ Ⓖ Ⓗ Ⓙ | 19. Ⓐ Ⓑ Ⓒ Ⓓ | |
| 5. Ⓐ Ⓑ Ⓒ Ⓓ | 10. Ⓕ Ⓖ Ⓗ Ⓙ | 15. Ⓐ Ⓑ Ⓒ Ⓓ | 20. Ⓕ Ⓖ Ⓗ Ⓙ | |

## Language

| | | | |
|---|---|---|---|
| 1. Ⓐ Ⓑ Ⓒ Ⓓ | 5. Ⓐ Ⓑ Ⓒ Ⓓ | 9. Ⓐ Ⓑ Ⓒ Ⓓ | 13. Ⓐ Ⓑ Ⓒ Ⓓ |
| 2. Ⓕ Ⓖ Ⓗ Ⓙ | 6. Ⓕ Ⓖ Ⓗ Ⓙ | 10. Ⓕ Ⓖ Ⓗ Ⓙ | |
| 3. Ⓐ Ⓑ Ⓒ Ⓓ | 7. Ⓐ Ⓑ Ⓒ Ⓓ | 11. Ⓐ Ⓑ Ⓒ Ⓓ | |
| 4. Ⓕ Ⓖ Ⓗ Ⓙ | 8. Ⓕ Ⓖ Ⓗ Ⓙ | 12. Ⓕ Ⓖ Ⓗ Ⓙ | |

## Language

| | | | | |
|---|---|---|---|---|
| 1. Ⓐ Ⓑ Ⓒ Ⓓ | 6. Ⓕ Ⓖ Ⓗ Ⓙ | 11. Ⓐ Ⓑ Ⓒ Ⓓ | 16. Ⓕ Ⓖ Ⓗ Ⓙ | 21. Ⓐ Ⓑ Ⓒ Ⓓ |
| 2. Ⓕ Ⓖ Ⓗ Ⓙ | 7. Ⓐ Ⓑ Ⓒ Ⓓ | 12. Ⓕ Ⓖ Ⓗ Ⓙ | 17. Ⓐ Ⓑ Ⓒ Ⓓ | |
| 3. Ⓐ Ⓑ Ⓒ Ⓓ | 8. Ⓕ Ⓖ Ⓗ Ⓙ | 13. Ⓐ Ⓑ Ⓒ Ⓓ | 18. Ⓕ Ⓖ Ⓗ Ⓙ | |
| 4. Ⓕ Ⓖ Ⓗ Ⓙ | 9. Ⓐ Ⓑ Ⓒ Ⓓ | 14. Ⓕ Ⓖ Ⓗ Ⓙ | 19. Ⓐ Ⓑ Ⓒ Ⓓ | |
| 5. Ⓐ Ⓑ Ⓒ Ⓓ | 10. Ⓕ Ⓖ Ⓗ Ⓙ | 15. Ⓐ Ⓑ Ⓒ Ⓓ | 20. Ⓕ Ⓖ Ⓗ Ⓙ | |

## Listening

| | |
|---|---|
| 1. Ⓐ Ⓑ Ⓒ Ⓓ | 4. Ⓕ Ⓖ Ⓗ Ⓙ |
| 2. Ⓕ Ⓖ Ⓗ Ⓙ | 5. Ⓐ Ⓑ Ⓒ Ⓓ |
| 3. Ⓐ Ⓑ Ⓒ Ⓓ | |

**Standardized Test Preparation Workbook**

# Answer Sheet

**Short Answer/Essay**

_____

_____

_____

_____

_____

_____

_____

_____

_____

_____

_____

_____

_____

_____

_____

_____

_____

_____

_____

_____

_____

_____

_____

_____

_____

_____

_____

_____